The Narreme in the Medieval Romance Epic

UNIVERSITY OF TORONTO PRESS

EUGENE DORFMAN

The Narreme in the Medieval Romance Epic

AN INTRODUCTION TO NARRATIVE STRUCTURES

UNIVERSITY OF TORONTO ROMANCE SERIES NO. 13

To Sylvia, Joseph, and Michael
in memory of David

Foreword

PIERRE GUIRAUD

Criticism has been traditionally dogmatic; its essential object has been to pass judgment on the value of works using aesthetic criteria defined by rhetoric. In more recent times emphasis has shifted to an external interpretation primarily concerned with establishing such factors as origin, biographical and historical sources, and influences. Today the trend is towards an internal critique based on analysis of the content in order to isolate, define, and classify the components, that is, the themes, of a literary work.

This new typology generally has a functional aim, and criticism thus returns to one of its most ancient purposes – that of classical rhetoric – in poetics, dramaturgy, the art of the novel, namely to reassess themes in terms of the purposes of the work.

It is clear that themes and their functions can be effectively defined only within the system of oppositions which they form within a total structure. This structuralist postulate, to which most humane studies lay claim today, could not fail to hold the attention of those concerned with criticism, especially since literature, a special form of verbal expression, is essentially a corpus of material which has meaning by virtue of its relation to some system of signs.

It is now recognized that we owe to linguists, and more particularly to phonologists, definitions and methods of structural analysis which have furnished new *models* and a new epistemological framework for the historian, the sociologist, and the anthropologist. Thus we must not be surprised if today literary criticism approaches this problem in the light of linguistics. And no man is better qualified or prepared than Eugene Dorfman, phonologist and grammarian, pupil of Martinet and direct heir of the great masters of functional phonology, to undertake a task so obviously ambitious and formidable as the present structural analysis of the medieval epic.

Calling them *narremes* (the word mythemes has also been used), just as one refers to phonemes in distinguishing them from sounds, the author defines and isolates the elementary themes of epic narrative. The distinction between substructure and superstructure puts the subject in a new light and shows us that the death of Roland is only a secondary theme, whereas the quarrel between Ganelon and his son-in-law constitutes one of the essential features of the work. This *narreme*, in fact, governs the whole chain of subsequent events, and is to be found in all the epics studied by the author, and especially in the *Pèlerinage de Charlemagne* where some apparently insignificant lines describe the quarrel between the emperor and his wife and thus unleash the whole expedition.

It is therefore evident in which sense the words "principal" and "secondary" are to be interpreted here. *Narremically*, the death of Roland is only an accident, and the hero might very well have survived without the narrative structure being otherwise modified. The episode thus appears as a stylistic variant of the narreme, but its secondary nature by no means detracts from its literary interest. (Similarly, the rolled *r*, a phonetic variant without significant importance phonologically, assumes great importance stylistically, for example, in the simulation of rustic pronunciation on stage.) Thus the ideas of narreme and of substructure on the one hand, and of superstructure and stylistic variants on the other, give us a new view of the themes of the epic and raise new questions.

Eugene Dorfman, as an orthodox structuralist, has focused strictly on the formal description of the works; but his analysis leads into the great traditional problems of literary history, and in particular poses anew the old problem of the origins of the epic.

UNIVERSITY OF GRONINGEN

Preface

This book has two principal aims: first, to present an experimental theory on the functional analysis of literary structures into constituent units, *narremes*, parallel with the phonemes and morphemes of linguistic analysis; second, to exemplify the theory in practice, mainly by the detailed analysis of two major Romance epics, the *Roland* and the *Cid*, supported by a less detailed examination of twelve additional Romance narratives. These consist of four French epics, *Gormont et Isembart*, *Pèlerinage de Charlemagne*, *Chanson de Guillaume*, and *Couronnement de Louis*; four Spanish epics, *Poema de Fernán González*, *Gesta de los Infantes de Lara*, *Gesta de Sancho II de Castilla*, and *La condesa traidora*; and four Arthurian romances of Chrétien de Troyes, *Erec et Enide*, *Cligés*, *Lancelot*, and *Yvain*.

The theoretical part has been presented first, in the interest of exposition. In actuality, however, the theory of the narreme evolved slowly and inductively, from the analysis of the texts. These were approached as far as possible without preconceptions, but with the intention of seeing whether the methods of functional and structural linguistics could be applied to the literary analysis of the medieval Romance epics. The initial findings, which were related to the French and Spanish epics enumerated, though not the romances, were presented in my Columbia dissertation, *The Roland and the Cid: A Comparative Structural Analysis*.

In the latter work, the narrative incidents were divided into two groups: either *external* (those incidents which could be omitted without thereby changing the story line), or *internal* (those incidents whose omission would break the continuity of the story). The major change in the theoretical formulation, which has been elaborated considerably, has been a shift to two new groups: the *superstructure*, containing the totality of incidents, both *marginal* (similar to *external*) and *central* or *core* (similar to *internal*); and the *substructure*, containing only the *central* or *core* incidents which are organically linked. As much as possible of the detailed analysis of the texts has been retained, but with extensive revisions throughout, particularly in the footnotes, to take recent criticism into account.

Linguists, in their ever increasing numbers (see Sebeok, "Structure and Content of Cheremis Charms"), no longer need, perhaps, to apologize for their invasion, as linguists, of the literary domain. Since the analytic method for determining central incidents as constituent units of literary structure is analogous to that used for isolating phonemes and morphemes (see chap. 3, n.14 and chap. 4, n.14), I coined the term *narreme* for the unit of narration. This hybrid neologism may not meet with universal favor; unfortunately, its nearest possible competitor, the *epeme*, is much less self-explanatory. A similar hybrid, the *motifeme*, has been introduced in literary analysis (see Dundes, "Structural Typology in North American Indian Folktales"). Augustine's remark in another context may serve us here: "Better that the grammarians censure us than that the people do not understand."

The term *narreme* (and the concept of narremic analysis) was presented in a number of papers for general discussion. It was first introduced at a panel discussion, "Linguistics and the Humanities," Fourth Annual Round Table Meeting on Linguistics and Language Teaching, Georgetown University, 1953. There were three papers in 1955: "The Structure of the Narrative: A Linguistic Approach," Eighth Annual Foreign Language Conference, University of Kentucky; "Speech, Literature and Language," joint meeting of the Linguistic Circle of New York and the Linguistic Circle of Columbia; and "Narrative Structure in the Medieval Epic," Romance Seminar, University of Washington. The romances were first considered in "Medieval Epics and Romances," Lecture-Discussion Series, University of Washington, 1958. The topic was elaborated in "The Narreme in the Medieval Epic and Romance," Fourteenth Annual Meeting of the Pacific Northwest Conference on Foreign Languages, Banff, Alberta, 1963; and in "La lingüística y el estudio de la literatura narrativa," Centro Lingüístico de Montevideo, Uruguay, 1964. For publications resulting from these papers, see *infra*, chap. 1, n.1.

This form of functional and structural literary analysis, applied here to French and Spanish medieval epics and Arthurian romances, has found some application in the French epic studies of Alain Renoir and Peter F. Dembowski. It has been extended by Paul V. Vehvilainen to the study of the Swedish folktale; and is being used by Glen W. Campbell, in a thesis now in progress at the University of Montpellier, to determine the constituent units in the picaresque novel of Lesage. I believe that it can be usefully employed in a rereading of other types of narrative as well.

An explanation may be required for a deliberate omission in this book: the problem of epic origins. This is a subject of enduring interest, masterfully reopened by Menéndez Pidal in *La Chanson de Roland y el neotradicionalismo: Orígenes de la épica románica*. There is, however, a twofold problem involved: a legitimate interest in historical origins; and an equally legitimate interest in the separate, and autonomous, description of the literary text as we have it. For the latter, historical information should be used sparingly, if at all, as a footnote and a sidelight. My concern has been with the literary work as it stands; as the last poet to shape its material, manipulating his sources and resources, left it; as the reader finds it. The problem of epic origins is connected with the techniques of the story-teller's craft; much descriptive work still lies ahead which may yet yield the information for advances in that field.

E.D.

DEPARTMENT OF ROMANCE LINGUISTICS
UNIVERSITY OF ALBERTA

Acknowledgment

My indebtedness to many who had a share in the development of my thought and in the preparation and publication of this book is greater than I can ever express. The chief debt is to André Martinet, teacher, colleague, friend, whose contributions to the theory of functional and structural linguistics will be recognized as the foundation of this approach to literary analysis; to Professor Lawton P. G. Peckham, who first suggested a comparison of the *Roland* and the *Cid*; and to Professors Mario Pei, Nathan Edelman, and the late Angel Del Rio, whose comments, criticisms, and kindly encouragement helped to bring that work to completion. I owe much to Professor Roman Jakobson for discussions in general linguistics, and to the late Henri François Muller for helpful suggestions in medieval Romance philology. I gladly take this opportunity, also, to express my deep gratitude to Abraham D. Zweibel, who first awakened a young mind to the humane values of language and literature, and whose special class in the *Cantar de Mio Cid* (at Barringer High School, Newark, N.J.) kindled a lifelong interest in this literary work of art.

For their patient attention over the years and for their useful comments as the theory of the narreme developed, I wish to thank my good friends, Professors Pierre C. Oustinoff, Victor E. Hanzeli, Howard S. Robertson, Peter F. Dembowski, Xavier Mignot, and José Pedro Rona. I am grateful to Professor Pierre Guiraud for his kindly Foreword, originally in French, and to my friends, Charles H. Moore and Paul Robberecht, who generously helped to edit the translation. Special thanks are due to Professor E. J. H. Greene for disinterested friendship and for constant encouragement in support of original approaches to old problems. I wish to thank Mrs. Joy Sullivan, formerly secretary, University of Washington, for her care in typing this manuscript; Mrs. June Panteluk, administrative officer, University of Alberta, and Mrs. Silvia Budde, secretary, for the arduous task of typing many of the revisions; George W. Patterson, graduate research assistant, University of Alberta, for his kindly assistance in compiling the index; and Miss Donna Gordon, student assistant, University of Alberta Library, for generous bibliographical aid. My sincere thanks are also due to the University of Toronto Press for including this book in the Romance Series; and to Mrs. Diana Swift Sewell, and the editorial department, as much for the cordial relationship as for the meticulous care devoted to preparing the manuscript for publication.

I am indebted to Dr. Trusten W. Russell and to the Fulbright authorities for various grants, including one enabling me to spend a year as visiting professor at the University of Montpellier, since this made it possible to visit relevant localities in France and Spain.

This work has been published with the help of a grant from the Humanities Research Council of Canada using funds provided by the Canada Council, and with the assistance of the Publications Fund of the University of Toronto Press.

E.D.

Contents

The Narreme in the Medieval Romance Epic

PART ONE

Methods of Functional Analysis

CHAPTER ONE

*Function and Structure in
the Literary Narrative*

1 Function and Structure in the Literary Narrative

1/1

UNITS OF NARRATIVE STRUCTURE AND THEIR FUNCTION

A narrative is a literary form: a story. It is an unfolding account of events or experiences, true or fictitious. Differing from such literary forms as the essay, an expository treatment of a particular subject, and the lyric, a concentrated outpouring of feeling, the narrative may be analyzed as a progressive chain or string of incidents, organized to tell a story. For stylistic reasons, the order of events may be straightforward or flashback. In a structural analysis, however, the connection between events is fundamental: each incident that occurs must have a place in a linear progression, following on the heels of a preceding incident and giving way to the next in line. The structure of a narrative depends on the arrangement of the incidents making up the story; each incident is a structural unit, with its own specific function to perform.

An event is by definition anything that happens, an incident of some kind, particularly if some importance is attached to its occurrence. In any given narrative, some incidents are more important than others; it would be difficult to imagine an artistic narrative in which every happening carried equal weight in the development of the story. For this reason, the incidents, as structural units, may be divided into two main classes: *central* or *core incidents*, whose function is to serve as the central focus or core of a larger episode, and *marginal incidents*, which cluster around the core, supporting it and filling out the episode. The structure of a narrative may thus be analyzed in two ways: as a larger chain, containing all the incidents, central and marginal, that form the complete story; and as a much smaller chain of functionally central incidents, linked to each other in an organic relationship. By reason of their special function as core incidents in the structure of the narrative, these central units will be called *narremes*.[1]

1. See Dorfman, Panel Discussion on "Linguistics and the Humanities," in Hill, *Report of the Fourth Annual Round Table Meeting on Linguistics*

1/2

NARREMES AND MARGINAL INCIDENTS

The division of structural units into two functional classes, central and marginal, permits the recognition of two different kinds of chain, that of the temporarily undifferentiated story incidents in absolute linear progression, and that of the selected narremes or core incidents, which leap over the marginal incidents to form a series of internally related units. The many individual events which may be isolated and enumerated in a given narrative are ordinarily far greater in number than the relatively few core incidents. Taken from the heterogeneous stock-pile available to an author, they are presumably selected for their potential effect: to heighten the mood, deepen the understanding, reveal insight into character, increase the entertainment value, and hopefully result in a memorable work of art. Including both central and marginal incidents in an undifferentiated series, the larger chain functions as an intricate network forming the *superstructure* of the story. The superstructure, defined here as the total inventory of incidents that occur from the beginning to the end of the story, is not to be considered a minor or inferior aspect of the narrative to be analyzed, but simply a functionally different kind of structure from that of the narremic core.

The inventory of all the incidents in the superstructure may be divided into episodes, in which marginal incidents are grouped around others of a more fundamental nature. The test of whether or not an incident is fundamental to the story must not be subjective; it must be strictly based on the criterion of function. In each case, there is a simple but decisive question: can the incident under consideration be omitted from the inventory without interrupting the continuity of the story? Except for the initial narreme, which serves as the necessary foundation for what is to follow, and the final narreme, which is the natural outcome of what has preceded, the test of a narreme is that it be the organic consequence of the preceding narreme and the effective cause of the

and Language Teaching, pp. 96–97; "Structure of the Narrative"; "Narreme in the Medieval Epic and Romance"; and in Spanish translation, "Narrema en la epopeya y el romance medievales."

For brief discussion or listing, see Hill, "Principles Governing Semantic Parallels," reprinted in Hill, *Essays in Literary Analysis*; Sebeok, "Structure and Content of Cheremis Charms"; Grimes, "Thread of Discourse"; Pei, *Glossary of Linguistic Terminology*; Pei and Gaynor, *Dictionary of Linguistics*.

For use of the narremic concept, see Renoir, "Roland's Lament"; Vehvilainen, *Swedish Folktale*; Dembowski, "Autour de Jourdain de Blaie."

following one. All incidents are marginal and belong solely to the superstructure if their omission would not affect the basic story line, however poetic, delightful, entertaining, artistic, and otherwise memorable they may be. The remaining incidents, proved functionally necessary to the continuity of the story as written, are narremes, forming the *substructure* or internal framework of the narrative.

1/3
THE DEATH OF ROLAND:
NARREME OR MARGINAL INCIDENT?

The application of functional analysis may be exemplified in the incident of Roland's death,[2] as recounted in the *Chanson de Roland*. The scene of the battle in which Roland is killed is one of unparalleled dramatic power and emotional intensity, and it is difficult to imagine the *Roland* without it. Its omission would undoubtedly diminish the impact of the poem. The only problem is whether it is important for the superstructure or for the substructure. In the organization of the poem, is it a narreme or a marginal incident? The criterion of function requires proof that the death of Roland occur as the consequence of a preceding incident and be the direct cause of one that follows.

The incidents relating to Roland's death, as they occur in the superstructure, may be briefly summarized. Roland's stepfather Ganelon, a high French official on an ambassadorial mission to the Saracens for the Emperor Charlemagne, conspires with Marsile, the Saracen chief, to trap and ambush Roland, who is in command of the French rearguard in Spain. Although facing overwhelming odds, Roland refuses, in his great pride, to sound the horn in time to bring Charlemagne and the main army back to protect the rearguard. Despite fierce resistance, Roland and his twenty thousand men are defeated and slain. For his act of treachery, Ganelon is tried, convicted, and executed. This portion of the story may be reduced to three apparently linked events in the superstructure: *Ganelon's act of treachery* leads to the *death of Roland* which is followed by the *trial and punishment of Ganelon*. Connected though these three incidents are in the larger chain of events, are all three equally essential to the continuity of the story, and thus part of the substructure?

2. For a stylistic, textual analysis of this incident, see Vinaver, "La Mort de Roland," pp. 138 ff.

In the tale as told by the poet, Roland dies as a consequence of the act of treachery; this fulfils the first requirement of the criterion for the narreme. Equally important is the second requirement, that Roland's death be the direct cause of Ganelon's trial. Is Ganelon being tried for the murder of his stepson? The trial itself leaves no doubt that Ganelon is actually charged with *treason,* for conspiring against Roland while the latter was on the king's service; Ganelon's punishment, being drawn and quartered by means of horses, is of the dread type administered to traitors. The trial is therefore the direct consequence of the act of treachery, rather than the result of Roland's death. On this basis, the death of the hero must be regarded functionally as a marginal incident, forming part of the episode which includes the more fundamental *act of treachery* as its central core. The incident of Roland's death is related to the act of treachery, as part of the superstructure; the act of treachery, however, now deserves consideration as a functional unit of the substructure.

1/4
THE ACT OF TREACHERY IN THE *ROLAND*

The place of the act of treachery in the structure of the *Roland* may be seen, somewhat obliquely, in some of the attempted outlines of the story. In none of these was the critic concerned with a functional analysis; applying this criterion, however, we may conclude that Bertoni[3] includes too much: part I, Preparation – the two (pagan and Christian) ambassadorial missions, Ganelon's treason, Charlemagne's departure for home, leaving Roland in charge of the rearguard; part II, The Central Nucleus – the battle of the rearguard, and the death of Roland; part III, Conclusion – vengeance for Roland's death, that is, the punishment of Marsile and Ganelon. Milá y Fontanals[4] does not say enough: the death of the hero is caused by the treachery of Ganelon and is followed by the punishment of the latter. Bédier's[5] summary, further reduced as follows, comes closest to completeness: moved by hatred of Roland, Ganelon treacherously conspires with the Saracens to ambush the Frankish rearguard; caught in the trap, Roland and his companions die; their death is avenged by Charlemagne. Each of the three outlines cited is accurate, reflecting subjectively outstanding events in the superstructure. Can they be

3. La "*Chanson de Roland,*" pp. 141–42.
4. *Tratados doctrinales de literatura,* pp. 215 f., n. 1.
5. *Les Légendes épiques,* III, 409.

utilized, however, to determine the functional nature of the act of treachery and its relation to other functional incidents of the substructure?

Bertoni's outline of the *Roland* cannot be used for a functional analysis since Ganelon's treason is not the *consequence* of either the pagan or the Christian ambassadorial missions, nor the *cause* of Charlemagne's departure for home; in the same way, the remaining incidents listed fail to show an organic and unbreakable continuity. The summary of Milá y Fontanals has two defects (for our special purpose): it implies that Ganelon is punished for the death of Roland rather than for the crime of treason, and it fails to provide a motive for the act of treachery. Bédier's version, from which the death of Roland must be extracted as superstructural, has the virtue of listing the reason for the act of treachery: Ganelon's hatred of Roland. It will be shown later that this hatred really involves two narremes: a quarrel between Ganelon and Roland and insults passed between the two, which lead to Ganelon's crime. In all three outlines cited, the central factor is the commission of a crime, an act of treachery, which will lead to punishment. In the poem, events are explicitly described which cause Ganelon, justifiably or not, to perpetrate his deed. The act of treachery is thus a fundamental narreme in the substructure of the *Roland*; the act of treachery occurs in numerous other epics as well, including the Spanish poem of the *Cid*.

1/5

THE *ROLAND* AND THE *CID*:

BASIS FOR COMPARISON

The *Cantar de Mio Cid* has often been compared[6] with the *Chanson de Roland*. They are both long narrative poems, each taking for its subject the epic exploits of a national hero. Composed in sister languages, they represent the highest aspirations of their peoples, joined by the ties of a somewhat common historical heritage.[7] Their undeniable poetic merit and apparent chronological priority as major literary works in their respective

6. See Dorfman, *The Roland and the Cid*, pp. 1–32, for a full discussion.
7. Menéndez Pidal, *La Chanson de Roland y el neotradicionalismo*, pp. 3–4: "... ningún estudio comparativo de dos literaturas puede dar resultados tan esclarecedores como éste, puesto que la épica francesa y la española vivieron bajo circunstancias históricas muy semejantes, pero con una desigualdad de tiempo y de carácter que hace en extremo reveladora la confrontación de ambas."

countries place them in an analogous central position in the early literatures of France and Spain. Ever since the relatively recent discovery of the *Cid*, toward the end of the eighteenth century, and the later discovery of the *Roland*, in the nineteenth, the controversy concerning the possible relationship between these two famous poems has flourished and promises to continue unabated. In a general and doubtless over-simplified manner, the controversy over the relationship can be divided into three main stages.

It was Sánchez who, in 1779, first published the *Cid* for modern readers in Spain, initiating the first stage[8] in the investigation. At a time when the *Roland* was all but unknown in Europe, except as a memory, Sánchez established positive, technical similarities in versification and pronunciation between the *Cid* and French epic poems in general (the Oxford text of the *Roland* did not appear in print until 1837). Additional evidence to support these views was later furnished by Bello, the Latin American humanist.

In the second stage,[9] introduced by Milá y Fontanals, later strongly supported by Menéndez y Pelayo and Menéndez Pidal, the voices of authority in Spanish literary criticism, efforts were directed toward moderating exaggerated claims of strong French influence on the *Cid*; the aim was nonetheless to seek out valid similarities, where they existed. Toward the end of the second stage, Bertoni[10] noted a number of correspondences: 1/ parallels in the portrayal of Charlemagne and the Cid, Turpin and Gerónimo (the warrior bishops), Ganelon and García Ordóñez ("a little Ganelon"); 2/ similarities in the virtues ascribed to the heroes' swords and horses; 3/ correspondences in the *acts of treachery*, the subsequent *public trials*, the *judicial duels* and the eventual *triumph of justice* (my italics). Despite the possibilities of structural comparison inherent in the acts of treachery and the ensuing incidents, Bertoni concluded that there was a basic difference in the "spirit" of the two poems. This emphasis leads to the third stage, currently in vogue, of emphasizing the differences between these two epics.

The differences between the *Roland* and the *Cid* are real, and should not be minimized. The two poems tell markedly different

8. Sánchez, *Colección de poesías castellanas*, I, pp. 50–55, 222–24. See also Bello, *Bello*, Prólogo del doctor Gabriel Méndez Plancarte, pp. 138–43.

9. *De la poesía heróico-popular castellana*, pp. xiv, 463–70; Menéndez y Pelayo, *Tratado de los romances viejos*, I, 80–81; Menéndez Pidal, *Poema de Mio Cid*, pp. 38–48, 63–64, and *La epopeya castellana*, pp. 19–20. See also Fitzmaurice-Kelly, *Chapters on Spanish Literature*, pp. 14–17.

10. "Il 'Cid' e la 'Chanson de Roland.' " See also Pellegrini, "Epica francese e *Cantare del Cid*."

stories. They were composed in different (though related) languages, in different (though neighboring) countries, by authors who were at least several generations[11] removed from each other. Among modern Spanish critics, Castro[12] describes the *Roland* as more "epic" in quality, filled with warlike deeds bordering on the fabulous; the *Cid* he declares rooted in Spanish "realism" and Spanish soil. Their essential difference, he believes, is manifest in the development of two fundamentally diverse streams of literature: the modern novel of the Cervantes type, and the adventurous tale of chivalry.

The current preoccupation[13] with the search for differences, important as that is for an understanding of the individuality of the two poems, is too restrictive, relying exclusively on the events of the superstructure. Narrowly pursued, it takes us little farther along the road to deeper understanding than the dictum of Ford, pronounced shortly after World War I, that the relationship between the *Roland* and the *Cid* is chiefly "formal."[14] There still

11. See Menéndez Pidal, "Sobre la fecha del Cantar de Medinaceli," in *En torno al Poema del Cid*, pp. 163–69. In "Dos poetas en el 'Cantar de Mio Cid,'" *ibid.*, pp. 106–62, Menéndez Pidal presents convincing evidence for two poets, an earlier poet of San Esteban de Gormaz, composing his work with greater faithfulness to the historical facts, shortly after the death of the Cid in 1099, and a second poet, of Medinaceli, several generations later, who "... se distingue por adiciones y reformas novelescas, libremente descuidadas de la exactitud histórica" (p. 154). Among the notable innovations ascribed to the second poet are the incident of the lion, which humiliates the Infantes, inducing their act of treachery; and the marriages of the Cid's daughters in response to the king's request, permitting the hero to hold the king responsible for the punishment of the traitors (p. 157). The inclusion of these two episodes changes the character of the narrative from a more or less realistic, historical account to an epic poem, structurally analogous to the other epics analyzed in this study. The difference in period between the *Roland* and the *Cid* is therefore based on acceptance of the dating of the Medinaceli version.

Strong as may be the arguments of Menéndez Pidal for an earlier version, it is well, in the present state of research, to bear in mind the caution recommended by Jules Horrent, "Tradition poétique du *Cantar de mio Cid* au XIIe siècle."

12. "Poesía y realidad," pp. 20–22.

13. Alonso, *Ensayos sobre poesía española*, pp. 70–91. See also Battaglia, *Poema de Mio Cid*, pp. 14–18; reviewed by Ruggieri, in *Cultura Neolatina*, 4–5 (1944/45), 171. Curtius, "Antike Rhetorik und vergleichende Literaturwissenschaft," p. 27. Del Río, *Historia de la literatura española*, I, 30–31. Pellegrini, pp. 233–38. Petriconi, "Das *Rolandslied* und das *Lied vom Cid*," p. 220.

14. *Main Currents of Spanish Literature*, p. 30: "The author [of the *Cid*] had some knowledge of the methods of the French epic poems ... for there are instances of imitation by him of situations. ... But when we cast up the sum total, we find that, after all, the French influence on the *Poema del Cid* does not go far. It is chiefly formal, and does not extend to important details of the poetic substance, which remains essentially of native tradition."

remains the problem of analyzing the functional elements of these two narrative structures as a new basis for comparison.

1/6
THE THEME OF THE *CID*

A functional analysis of the *Cid* into narremes is a more difficult operation than that of the *Roland*, since the Spanish poem is more loosely[15] organized, divided as it is into three *Cantares*: "The Song of the Exile," "the Song of the Wedding," and "The Song of the Affront at Corpes." What exactly is the theme or principal subject of the poem in its entirety? This is not easy to identify. Hatzfeld[16] believes it to be a feudal conflict, the "antithesis: king and revolting vassal," in which case the main point of climax might be the reconciliation scene between Alfonso and the Cid. Battaglia[17] also considers the poem primarily a historical document; but he views it as a tribute to a self-made man of destiny,

15. "The Song of the Exile" is loosely related to the other two, as introduction and build-up of the hero, inviting the attention of the Infantes to the Cid and his daughters. The poet himself considers the "Geste of the Cid" to begin with the first verse of the "Song of the Wedding" (v. 1085), significantly the section where the functional incidents first start to link up with each other; see *infra*, 9.1, chap. 12, n.21.

The Baligant episode in the *Roland* (vv. 2609–3674), similarly a section of over a thousand verses, has also been described as loosely related in organization; see Menéndez Pidal, *La Chanson de Roland y el neotradicionalismo*, pp. 114–22. Critical opinion ranges from rejection of the episode as outside the original plan of the poem (Rychner, *La Chanson de Geste*, pp. 39–42), to insistence that it is its very "razón de ser" (Riquer, *Los cantares de gesta franceses*, p. 87). If we accept the poem as we have it, the death of Baligant is structurally like the death of Roland: a consequence of the act of treachery, but *not* the cause of the punishment of the traitor. The episode, a part of the superstructure, supports the core incident, act of treachery, by continuing the battle, reversing the defeat, and giving Charlemagne total victory over the Saracens; equally, it supports the core incident, punishment, by foreshadowing the doom of Ganelon. The Baligant episode is therefore more closely integrated in the text as a series of marginal incidents attached to narremes within the core group, while the "Song of the Exile" is appended as a prologue in a long preliminary series of marginal incidents, leading eventually to the first narreme of the core system.

16. "Esthetic Criticism Applied to Medieval Literature," p. 312. See De Chasca, "King-Vassal Relationship in *El Poema de Mio Cid*," and *Estructura y forma*, p. 41: "La relación entre el rey y el Cid constituye el fundamento de la estructura."

17. Pp. 10, 24–25. See Entwistle, "Remarks Concerning the Order of the Spanish Cantares de Gesta," p. 114. De Chasca, *Estructura y forma*, pp. 28–29: "Tiene la obra como tema el restablecimiento de la perdida honra del héroe. ... todo lo que ocurre ... contribuye al engrandecimiento progresivo de Rodrigo: le enaltece la serie de victorias ... hasta Valencia. ..." Huerta, *Poética del Mio Cid*, p. 100: "El modelo de caballeros, el que vence a la alta nobleza y da lecciones de justicia al rey, está al mismo tiempo ganándose un puesto entre los príncipes de España, haciéndose señor de Valencia."

the warrior whose life was climaxed by the glorious conquest of Valencia. Petriconi,[18] on the other hand, asserts that the marriages of the Cid's daughters, rather than the victory at Valencia, furnishes the dramatic climax of the poem. This diversity of opinion may be traced to exclusive preoccupation with details mainly belonging to the superstructure.

1/7

THE RECONCILIATION SCENE

The incident of reconciliation between Alfonso and the Cid is an effective and highly dramatic detail in the story; a tribute to an unjustly exiled but loyal vassal, it represents the hard-earned reward of a brave warrior, and leads directly to the marriages of his daughters to royal princes. Sponsored by the king himself, the matrimonial alliances unite the Cid, who is less nobly born, with one of the reigning houses in Spain. In the story, however, the Cid's sons-in-law, the Infantes of Carrión, soon after their marriages inflict a terrible outrage on their wives, beating them viciously and leaving them for dead. If the quarrel were really between the Infantes and their wives, then the reconciliation scene between Alfonso and the Cid, which resulted in the marriages, might well show an organic link with the ensuing events. The effective cause of the Infantes' action, however, was something quite different, as we shall see later;[19] and therefore, the relationship between the king and his vassal, despite its importance in the superstructure, does not form part of an unbroken chain of narremes.

1/8

THE CONQUEST OF VALENCIA

As history, the *Cid* tells a double tale. The first part, "The Song of the Exile," is a biographical sketch of a successful military career; the remainder of the poem records the achievement of dynastic status. It is this double aspect, the description of the penniless exile reaching the pinnacle of power, and of the low-born marrying his daughters to princes, that makes identification of the theme so difficult. Historically, the conquest of Valencia represents the Cid's crowning achievement. Almost a king in fact, though of modest origin, and possessing a prize like Valencia, the

18. P. 224. See De Chasca, *Estructura y forma*, pp. 31–33; Horrent, p. 452.
19. See *infra*, chap. 10 and 11/1.

Cid symbolizes the tangible rewards of courage in adversity. Despite the importance of the conquest of Valencia in the delineation of the Cid as an epic character, however, it does nothing as an incident to move the internal plot along to its denouement.

Perhaps the conquest of Valencia and the Cid's growing wealth and fame arouse the envy of the Infantes de Carrión. If true, and it does not appear unequivocally so from the text itself, this must be balanced by the fact that it is precisely the wealth and reputation of the Cid which make him so attractive to them as a father-in-law in the first place. What makes the Cid undesirable in this respect is the persistent, undeniable, and unchangeable fact, which no victories and no prizes can alter, that he is of humbler birth than the Infantes.[20] It is this, and not the military exploits of the hero, which sets in motion the succeeding incidents of the poem.[21] For this reason, the conquest of Valencia cannot be considered part of the internal chain of development.

1/9

THE MARRIAGES OF THE CID'S DAUGHTERS

With the marriages of the Cid's daughters, which ally Ruy Diaz de Bivar and the house of Carrión, there is an apparent beginning to a linked chain of events. However, the marriages as such are not the direct cause of the outrage which the Infantes perpetrate on their wives in the woods at Corpes. Nor do the girls, by any act of theirs, provoke a cruel retaliation; and it is not indicated in the text that the Infantes hate women or the institution of marriage. In reality, the first incident which calls for consequences of a clearly defined sort is the brutal *act of treachery*, the affront to the Cid through the beating of his daughters, the aftermath of which will include the demand for punishment of the traitors. Tormented by circumstances to which their own failings of haste and avarice have contributed, shamed by these marriages beneath their station,[22] hating the service they owe the Cid as their father-in-law, the Infantes plan and carry out a tragic act of betrayal. Vengeance must follow.

20. See *infra*, 11/3. Historically, the Cid was of less noble descent on his father's side, as compared with the maternal line: "Tenía, por parte de madre, nobleza muy alta y muy valida en la corte; por parte de padre era de nobleza famosísima, pero no principal ...," Menéndez Pidal, *El Cid Campeador*, p. 23. See also *infra*, n.22; chap. 9, n.14.

21. See *infra*, chap. 12, n.21.

22. Menéndez Pidal, *Poema de Mio Cid*, pp. 91–92: "... en su presunción, creen [los infantes] que debían *casar con fijas de reyes o de emperadores* (vv. 3297, 2553). De aquí nace la tragedía del Poema."

It was Alfonso who sponsored these alliances. We must agree with Castro[23] that the Cid's appeal to the king, to avenge this royal affront, marks the high point of the action; the act of treachery, therefore, may be considered a central narreme in the *Cid*.

1/10

THE ACT OF TREACHERY IN THE *ROLAND* AND THE *CID*

It would appear from the foregoing that the *Roland* and the *Cid* have at least one indubitable element in common: an act of treachery as the central pivot of the action. We shall expect to find that in each case the larger chain of events in the superstructure will reveal itself in the form of a story fundamentally different in detail and incident. The smaller chain of narremes, however, will depend on the act of treachery which, serving as the mainspring of action, requires a plausible motivation and a satisfactory conclusion.

This makes it possible to set up, for both poems, a substructural pattern, based on a series of four questions:
1/ What is the setting which makes the act of treachery possible?
2/ What is the immediate and effective cause of the act?
3/ What form does it take?
4/ What conclusion does it evoke?

With this formula,[24] we will be able to determine whether or not there is a structural similarity between the *Roland* and the *Cid*. Two considerations may serve to minimize the value of such a similarity, even if revealed. A correspondence in the internal structure may be coincidental; or it may result from the use of a uniform and conventional pattern in the contemporary epic poems. The problem of accidental similarity can best be understood after the full analysis of the texts themselves, but a preliminary investigation of some contemporary French and Spanish epics can be useful, at this point, in disclosing some of the narrative techniques of the period.

23. Pp. 20–22. "... el Cid ... alcanza su cénit al responder como lo hace al acto irresponsable y cínico de los infantes de Carrión."
24. Knudson, "Etudes sur la composition de la *Chanson de Roland*," p. 49: "Il s'agit de trouver l'économie du plan, c'est-à-dire de distinguer entre les éléments qui sont déterminés par quelque chose d'autre dans le poème même, et ceux qui, au lieu de résulter de la construction, sont à la base." It is our premise that the literary economy is best revealed precisely by those elements in the poem which link to form an unbreakable chain.

CHAPTER TWO

The (Sub)Structural Pattern of the Contemporary French Epics

2 The (Sub)Structural Pattern of the Contemporary French Epics

2/1

CHANSONS DE GESTE AND CANTARES DE GESTA

In the period just before the beginning of the twelfth century to the middle decades, the *chansons de geste* or French epics made their appearance, came to be widely imitated, and found some of their most celebrated examples. Among the most famous of these epics are: *Gormont et Isembart*, the *Pèlerinage de Charlemagne*, the *Chanson de Guillaume*, and the *Couronnement de Louis*; it is difficult to date[1] them in strict chronological order, and the ranking is therefore arbitrary.

On the Spanish side, there are no *cantares de gesta* extant from that period (except for the *Cid, ca.* 1140). By utilizing reconstructions, however, we can draw a number of useful conclusions from a study of the following epic material which, in the original form, is possibly older[2] than the *Cid: Poema de Fernán González, Gesta de los Infantes de Lara, Gesta de Sancho II de Castilla,* and the *Condesa traidora.*

These eight French and Spanish epics, plus the *Roland* and the *Cid*, approximately 15 per cent of the medieval epics which could be studied, are probably too small a sample for a complete structural typology. The intention here is not to provide such a complete typological analysis, but to suggest and illustrate a method of functional analysis, which may make the larger scheme possible.

---

1. Holmes, *History of Old French Literature*, pp. 78, 91, 103–04. Zenker, *Das Epos von Isembard und Gormund*, pp. 2–3. Suchier, *La Chançun de Guillelme*, pp. xxix–xxx; McMillan, *La Chanson de Guillaume*, II, 115–31. Koschwitz, *Karls des Grossen Reise*, pp. xiii–xiv; also, Horrent, *Le Pèlerinage de Charlemagne*, "Bibliographie," pp. 151–54. Langlois, *Le Couronnement de Louis*, p. viii. Menéndez Pidal, *La Chanson de Roland y el neotradicionalismo, passim.*

2. Menéndez Pidal, *La epopeya castellana*, p. 19; *Historia y epopeya*, p. 15; "Dos poetas en el *Cantar de Mio Cid*." See also, Puyol y Alonso, *Cantar de gesta de Don Sancho* II, p. 10.

2/2

GORMONT ET ISEMBART: SUPERSTRUCTURE

No more than a slight fragment of the *Gormont et Isembart* text remains extant.[3] It is possible for us, however, to form a general idea of the poem through the reconstructions of the subject matters by Fluri and Zenker, arrived at almost simultaneously but independently of each other.

Isembart, a vassal of King Louis, the son of Charlemagne, has, like the Cid, an enemy faction opposed to him at court. The king, a brother of Isembart's mother, insults his nephew; the young man responds with arms in hand. Forced into exile, Isembart takes service with Gormont, the Saracen king, who converts him to the Moslem faith. The renegade then persuades his new master to make a sortie into France. In the ensuing battle, Louis himself kills Gormont, but receives a mortal wound. Isembart, in the melee, strikes his own father unwittingly; discovering what he has done, he flees the battlefield, and the Saracens are repulsed. Hated as a renegade by the Christians, he is now blamed for the defeat by his former friends, the Saracens, who reject him as a traitor. He dies, after returning to the Christian religion.

2/3

SUBSTRUCTURAL PATTERN

Although the fragmentary text precludes the use of the reconstructed material with full confidence, we may permit ourselves certain tentative conclusions. The central incident of the poem appears to be the entry of the Saracen troops into France under the leadership of Gormont and the renegade, Isembart. Since the latter is a French Christian turned Moslem, the war he has fomented must be considered an act of treachery against king, country, and religion.

Isembart's motive is revenge. Unlike the Cid, also exiled by his king, but bending every effort toward reconciliation, he believes he must wipe out his disgrace by physical force. It is a point of honor with him; the intensity of this feeling is revealed by the rapidity with which he took up the sword, the moment the king insulted him. If we consider further that Louis and Isembart are uncle and nephew and that, before insulting his nephew, the king

3. For the fragmentary text, see Bayot, *Gormont et Isembart*. For the reconstructions of subject matter, see Fluri, *Isembard et Gormund*; and Zenker. See also Bédier, *Les Légendes épiques*, IV, 35; Nichols, "Style and Structure in *Gormont et Isembart*."

had ranged himself on the side of the youth's enemies, we find that the origin of the trouble between them may well have been a family quarrel.

The hypothetical substructure of the poem would thus consist of the following narremes:

    1/ The family quarrel
    2/ The insult
    3/ The act of treachery
    4/ The punishment

It remains to be seen whether this substructural pattern, or variants of it, can be discovered in epics where the facts are more certain.

2/4

THE *PÈLERINAGE DE CHARLEMAGNE:*

SUPERSTRUCTURE

The structural form of the *Pèlerinage de Charlemagne* is the simplest and most transparent imaginable. At the very beginning of the poem, there is a *family quarrel* between Charlemagne and his wife, when the queen foolishly tells her husband that she knows of a handsomer prince, who wears the crown more regally than he (vv. 13–16; verse citations are from the Koschwitz edition). Smarting under the *insult*, Charlemagne threatens to cut off her head if he discovers that she has not been telling the truth (24–25).

Motivated by this challenge, Charlemagne sets off with the Twelve Peers on a voyage to the court of Hugo the Strong, emperor of Constantinople. Here as a result of injudicious boasts, the Franks are compelled by Hugo to accomplish *acts of prowess,* in the form of seemingly impossible deeds. Their unexpected success induces Hugo to become the vassal of Charlemagne. In the triumphal procession, for all to behold, Charlemagne is obviously the handsomer prince and wears the crown more regally than Hugo. In spite of his promise to behead his wife, if she were wrong, Charlemagne pardons (868–69) the queen, presumably as a *reward* for the great accomplishments set in motion by her insulting remark.

2/5

NARRATIVE TECHNIQUE

Few poems in Old French literature reveal as transparently the necessity for, and the technique of, the substructural pattern. In a scant fifty-seven verses, the poet sets up the family quarrel between Charlemagne and his wife. He devotes just two verses, at the very end, to the happy conclusion in which the queen is forgiven. Everything else, between these incidents, makes up the body of a story which could well be complete in itself. This tale within a tale is a recital of some highly amusing and very exciting adventures of Charlemagne and his knights. In addition, this interior section teaches an explicit moral, all by itself. The focal[4] point of the action is a series of vainglorious and impossible boasts or *gabs* made by the Franks; Hugo overhears them and demands their accomplishment. Charlemagne himself concedes that, under the influence of wine (664–66), things were said that should not have been. The lesson is further reinforced in the strongest possible manner by the sudden appearance of an angel, who promises the Franks the aid of God in their "great folly" but passes on to them the command of Christ to "gab" no more (674–76). There must then be a reason, having to do with possible rules of narrative composition, to account for the special incidents at either end of the poem.

2/6

SUBSTRUCTURE

The poet might conceivably have begun by declaring simply that Charlemagne and his followers were seeking renown or adventure. Arriving at the court of Hugo, the brave but boastful knights involved themselves in painfully amusing difficulties which were ultimately resolved to the satisfaction of all. As a result of their success, Charlemagne obtained a new and powerful vassal, additional desirable territories, and precious holy relics. This would be the whole story, with no need for the fifty-seven verses at the beginning and the two at the end, which surround the tale like a frame. But the poem shows a different choice.

Skilfully, the poet introduces the emperor and his wife, involving them in a family quarrel. We observe the nature of the insult and its effect upon the victim; with amusement, we watch the awkward manœuvres of the queen, too late to soften the blow to his pride. In his use of this method, the poet, apparently in all consciousness, indicates that clear and sufficient motivation is necessary to introduce the adventures that follow. And it is true that these adventures take on deeper meaning; the interest is

4. See Horrent, pp. 115–22; for the remarkable diversity of opinion on the nature and purpose of the poem, pp. 9–13.

significantly heightened because the deeds are not without purpose. We may reasonably assume that the poet has given careful scrutiny to the arrangement of his story details in a structurally unified pattern, which may be outlined as follows:

1/ The family quarrel
2/ The insult
3/ The acts of prowess
4/ The reward

2/7

THE *GORMONT* AND THE *PÈLERINAGE*: TWO TYPES OF SUBSTRUCTURE

The narremic patterns of the *Gormont et Isembart* and the *Pèlerinage de Charlemagne* show a striking similarity in the setting or initial force of the action: both begin with a family quarrel. In both, this quarrel produces an insult.[5] Here, the two patterns separate. Isembart's response to the insult is an act of treachery; Charlemagne's reaction is not to seek vengeance in some treacherous fashion, but to set out to prove that his wife is wrong, by performing worthy feats of prowess. Within the pattern, therefore, the acts of prowess are analogous to the act of treachery; they are the victim's personal response to the preceding incident, the insult. In both poems, the punishment (or reward) fits the crime. The devastation wrought by Isembart could allow no lesser punishment than death; the measure of success attending Charlemagne's exploits assures the queen the reward of a royal smile and complete forgiveness.

We may call the substructural pattern of the *Gormont* "Type I" and that of the *Pèlerinage* "Type II." The two narremic outlines might then be combined as follows:

TYPE I	TYPE II
1/ The family quarrel	
2/ The insult	
3/ The act of treachery	3/ The acts of prowess
4/ The punishment	4/ The reward

5. In practice, it may appear that the insult is the first, and possibly the only, indication that a family quarrel exists. Since the family relationship precedes the insult, and since an insult is a sign of trouble making itself manifest, the incident of the conflict between Charlemagne and his wife may be designated as a *portmanteau narreme*, The family quarrel/insult (cf. the English portmanteau word "brunch," blending breakfast and lunch). This would not materially affect the substructural outline of the *Pèlerinage*, since the four narremes would all be present, and in the same order.

2/8

THE *CHANSON DE GUILLAUME*: SUPERSTRUCTURE

The *Chanson de Guillaume* presents a very complex structure, considerably more so than the other epics described. This has no connection with the possibility[6] that it consists of two poems rather than one, since most of the complexity is included in the first half.

There are several occasions where *family quarrels* and *insults* seem to be in the making. Guibourc, Guillaume's wife, more than once uses highly dubious[7] language to her husband. When he appears to be lagging at a time of danger, she encourages him to go off to battle by offering to send along her own nephew; but she also threatens to refrain from her conjugal duties if her nephew is not brought back (vv. 1034–37; Suchier edition). When the defeated Guillaume returns, berating himself as a coward, she insults him by declaring that he were better dead than a living stain to his lineage (dynastic status!) and a disgrace to his heirs (1326–28). Urged once more into battle, he again reappears, defeated and alone; this time she absolutely refuses him entry into his stronghold of Orange, stating that she does not know him: a hero like Guillaume would obviously have his army with him, and she will have no dealings with an imposter (2242–50).

Another type of family quarrel is manifested by the insult which Guillaume directs at his nephew Gui, when the youth boldly offers to take his uncle's place, should the latter die in battle (1453–58). The most serious quarrel in the superstructure occurs when the queen, Guillaume's own sister, accuses her sister-in-law of planning to poison the king and herself (2592–98).

2/9

THE ACTS OF PROWESS

The outstanding feature about the quarrels in the *Guillaume* is that, no matter how grave the insults may be, they never give rise to any act of vengeance or treachery. When Blanchefleur makes her charge of assassination through poison against Gui-

6. Cf. Suchier (two poems); Tyler, *La Chançun de Willame* (one); McMillan (a non-homogeneous composition, divided into parts), II, 127–31. For the descriptive view, see Robertson, *La Chanson de Willame*, p. 16: "... the *Chanson de Willame* looks like the union of two separate legends, but the real point is that it does not matter. What matters is whether or not the poem is a thematic whole. ..."

7. Robertson, p. 28.

bourc, Guillaume responds with a string of the choicest epithets (2600–26). The net result of the episode, however, is that the hero succeeds in obtaining from his brother-in-law Louis the aid he has been seeking.

The effect of the insults is in general to induce warlike sentiments and *acts of prowess*. The remarks addressed by Guillaume to his nephew, which might easily be construed as deadly insults, serve only to spur the youth on to deeds of glory. Most significant of all, perhaps, Guibourc's dynastic anxiety, expressed in insults and sharp prodding, sends Guillaume again and again into battle, until he finally justifies her faith in him by the final victory.

2/10

SUBSTRUCTURE

Since the central incident of the poem is the attempt of the hero to repel the Saracen invaders, primary consideration should be given to the efforts of Guibourc to prod him into this activity. Well-intentioned and necessary as these efforts are, they are couched in terms which can only be described as insulting. No other interpretation is possible for her angry remark to Guillaume that, as things stand, he is a disgrace to his family and that unless he drives out the Saracens, he would be better off dead. It is true that her remarks are made in more indirect fashion, but their import is perfectly clear. How else could Guillaume respond but with a display of prowess? The *reward* for this is a happy ending.

Thus the *Guillaume*, like the other epics under discussion, reveals a pattern of general structural unity, disclosing itself as Type II: the family quarrel, the insult(s), the acts of prowess, and the reward.

2/11

THE *COURONNEMENT DE LOUIS*:

SUPERSTRUCTURE

Despite the fact that the *Couronnement de Louis* has been said[8] to consist of five independent poems, called branches, a theory

8. Langlois, pp. iv–v: "... il est généralement admis que les 'branches' n'ont pas toujours été réunies, soit qu'elles aient formé originairement autant de poèmes distincts, soit qu'elles aient été successivement composées en vue de leur annexion au poème primitif. Cette hypothèse est parfaitement défendable, mais l'opinion contraire, celle qui considère toutes les parties comme étant du même auteur, peut être aussi soutenue." See also Bédier, I, 235–83.

disputed by Bédier, its substructural pattern is essentially similar to that of the *Pèlerinage* and the *Guillaume*. The superstructure, however, shows certain noteworthy variations and complexities.

The poem opens with a *family quarrel*. Charlemagne wants to crown his young son Louis, but is enraged when the youth timidly hesitates to accept the symbol of royal authority. The emperor *insults* his son, calling him a coward, questioning the legitimacy of his birth, and offering to send him to a monastery (vv. 90–98; Langlois edition). Thereupon Anseïs of Orléans, a traitor, attempts by flattery to have himself appointed the youth's regent for a period of three years. Guillaume comes upon the scene just in time; knowing Anseïs for his treacherous character, he kills him. Throughout the rest of the poem Guillaume performs many *acts of prowess*, whose principal purpose is the defense of Louis' rights. Although Louis betrays cowardice on many occasions, Guillaume remains ever loyal to his king and his duties. The hero receives his just *reward*, when he marries off his sister to the king and acquires a royal brother-in-law.

2/12

SUBSTRUCTURE

The analysis of the *Couronnement* discloses an apparent variation from the structural patterns of the two different types, the *Gormont* and the *Pèlerinage,* according to which the aggrieved parties, Isembart and Charlemagne, smarting under insult, themselves undertake the adventures which form the core of their stories. The *Couronnement,* however, describes Louis as a coward; hence the adventures, which take place after the family quarrel and the insult, are the work of a proxy, who serves as his sovereign's champion and the real hero of the poem.

Since the insult acts only indirectly on Guillaume, being actually directed against Louis, there is an apparent break in the internal chain of continuity. This is not a real objection to the theory of substructural unity, however; in the Middle Ages, a champion *completely* represented the man whose place he was taking, as we know from the example of Ganelon and Pinabel, in the judicial duel of the *Roland.* On this basis, the *Couronnement* belongs structurally to Type II: the family quarrel, the insult, the acts of prowess (by proxy), and the reward. There is still, however, a question concerning the structural relationship of the Anseïs episode to the poem as a whole.

2/13

CORE AND MARGIN

The first part of the *Couronnement*, the so-called first branch, presents in miniature a structural pattern of the kind we have called Type I. It will be recalled that Anseïs was the first to react when Charlemagne *insulted* Louis; he had formulated a plan to commit an *act of treachery* against the royal authority. This was followed by swift *punishment*, when Guillaume killed him.

Did the poet vary these patterns, using a Type I structure within a Type II substructure, for strictly ornamental reasons? This would no doubt be a legitimate purpose; the artistic introduction of novel arrangements would help to differentiate his work from that of contemporary productions. We will never know the poet's reasoning, but one thing is certain: there is a conscious selection and arrangement in the organization of the structural pattern; sufficiently so to justify the assumption that the Anseïs episode has its own function to perform.

We have said that there is an apparent break in the internal continuity, when Louis receives the insult, and Guillaume performs the acts of prowess. The function of the Anseïs episode is to establish the foundation for Guillaume's role as proxy. Guillaume's acts of prowess are thereby artistically brought within the *core narremes*; the miniature chain of events relating to Anseïs belong to a margin, however, not being unbreakably connected to the core. Thus the *Couronnement*, like the other French epics under discussion, gives evidence of a structurally unified pattern, and invites an over-all comparison with the others, from this point of view.

2/14

THE CONTEMPORARY FRENCH EPIC PATTERN:
SUMMARY

The functional analysis of the four poems discloses the following structural patterns:

1 The Family Quarrel
  a/ Gormont: Louis and his nephew Isembart.
  b/ Pèlerinage: Charlemagne and his wife.
  c/ Guillaume: Guillaume and his wife Guibourc.
  d/ Couronnement: Charlemagne and his son Louis.

2 The Insult
   a/ Louis joins Isembart's enemies, affronts and exiles him.
   b/ The queen disparages Charlemagne's person and bearing.
   c/ Guibourc calls her husband a disgrace to his family.
   d/ Charlemagne calls his son coward, fit for a monastery.
3 The Act of Treachery; or the Acts of Prowess
   a/ Type I: Isembart turns renegade and leads the enemy to France.
   b/ Type II: Charlemagne and the Twelve Peers perform the *gabs*.
   c/ Type II: Guillaume ultimately repels the invaders.
   d/ Type II: Guillaume successfully defends Louis' royal rights.
4 The Punishment; or the Reward
   a/ Isembart is punished; reconverted, he dies.
   b/ The queen is forgiven and the royal couple reconciled.
   c/ Guillaume recovers his lands, his honor and his wife.
   d/ Guillaume weds his sister Blanchefleur to Louis.

The starting-point for the French epic, if these samples are conclusive, is the family quarrel. Our poems show central disputes between uncle and nephew, husband and wife, father and son, and marginal ones between brother and sister and between brothers-in-law, as in the *Guillaume*; other family relationships can be expected perhaps to occur in other epics. The distinctive factor here is not the variant forms of family relationship, but the central fact of dynastic conflict. The narreme subsumes that least common denominator; all else is marginal.

The family quarrels take the form of an insult; usually, though not always, with no real harm intended. Except in the case of Isembart, to restrict ourselves to the samples, they do not arouse as a rule any desire for active vengeance, but serve instead as a spur to heroic action, in person or by proxy. The insult may vary from very mild to overpowering, but in all the cases discussed, it is utilized by the poet as a device to supply a reasonable motivation for the activity to follow.

Suitably motivated by the insult, the act of treachery and the acts of prowess foreshadow the ending. In the three poems where the central core does not hinge upon some form of treachery, the endings are all happy. One might suppose that an insult strong enough to arouse a threat of decapitation should result in some kind of punishment. Instead, Charlemagne rewards his wife with a smile; the insult, as poet and public are aware, is just an excuse to get him off on the road to glory.

In much the same way, had Guillaume wanted to take his wife's insults seriously, he would have had just cause for resentment.

But he (or the poet engaged in describing the situation) knew that the insults were a device to generate action for the achievement of necessary ends. Once these ends, good in themselves, were attained, the prime mover deserved and received a just reward. The Guillaume of the *Couronnement*, through his able defense of Louis' rights, proved that, even if through proxy, Louis could be a good king, and thus nullified the need for a negative reaction to Charlemagne's insult, opening the way to a reward instead. In form, the rewards vary, just like the acts they bring to a close; but it is their least common denominator which reveals their function in the chain of narremes.

The "reward" may take the form of a punishment. This is the only possible conclusion to the actions of Isembart. Death to a renegade and traitor!

Enough has been shown to indicate that, in the most general kind of way, a "pattern" exists, though it varies in type; and the features that seem most stable, the family quarrel and the insult, vary in intensity and in kind. It is difficult to resist the conviction, even without an elaborate functional analysis of the mass of French epic production, that this is a representative *structural frame* for the genre, even though additional variant types may be found. This pattern may now be compared with its possible counterpart in the Spanish epic.

CHAPTER THREE

The (Sub)Structural Pattern of the Contemporary Spanish Epics

3 The (Sub)Structural Pattern of the Contemporary Spanish Epics

3/1
POEMA DE FERNÁN GONZÁLEZ

The theory affirming the existence of a flourishing body of native epic literature prior to the *Cid* (in the Medinaceli version), of which only remnants remain, has met with increasing favor.[1] It has even been suggested that the Spanish epic may, in fact, have given the initial impetus to the French. This makes it necessary to analyze some of the Spanish epics which, in their original form, may have chronologically preceded or coincided with the appearance of the *Cid*.

One of the most important of these early productions is the *Poema de Fernán González*, which has been referred to as the possible model[2] for all later epics of its kind. The possibly revised[3] form of the poem as we know it today, composed *circa* 1250, really belongs to the category of the *mester de clerecía*, erudite rhymed narratives, although it has many characteristics in common with the *cantares de gesta*.

3/2
SUPERSTRUCTURE

The hero, Fernán González, previously unaware of his origin, discovers that he is count of Castile. After victorious battles to deliver his land of its oppressors, he slays King Sancho of Navarre.

1. Menéndez Pidal, *Poesía juglaresca y juglares*, p. 88, and *Historia y epopeya*, p. 5. See also Entwistle, "Remarks Concerning the Order of the Spanish Cantares de Gesta," p. 114. It now seems to be established that the *Cid* itself, in a prior version, goes back to this earlier period; Menéndez Pidal, "Dos poetas en el *Cantar de Mio Cid*," and Huerta, *Poética del Mio Cid*, p. 34.

2. Menéndez Pidal, *Historia y epopeya*, p. 5: "... G. Cirot, que antes se inclinaba a buscar un origen extranjero al episodio principal de la vida poética de Fernán González, sugiere ahora que la leyenda de este conde castellano debió servir de modelo a todas las demás europeas a fines a ella."

3. Marden, *Poema de Fernán González*. See also Menéndez Pidal, *Poesía juglaresca y juglares*, p. 192. Hurtado y Palencia, *Historia de la literatura*

Sancho Ordóñez, King of Leon, then convokes a *cortes* to which Fernán is invited. The king purchases a goshawk and a steed from Fernán, offering to pay an amount doubling in price for each day that the debt remains in force. Since he forgets to pay, the debt soon surpasses the limits of his financial resources.

At this point, a complicated family situation develops. The queen of Leon, whose brother, Sancho of Navarre, Fernán Gonzáles had killed, decides to avenge herself for his death by an act of treachery. She proposes that Fernán marry her niece Doña Sancha, her late brother's daughter and the sister of the reigning king, Don García. When Fernán unsuspectingly appears to claim his bride, García takes him prisoner. Doña Sancha learns of the incident; on Fernán's promise to marry her, she helps him to escape and flees with him to Castile. The king of Navarre thereupon attacks Castile, but is himself taken prisoner, after a personal duel with Fernán. Doña Sancha requests and obtains her brother's release, but not until he has served a term of imprisonment.

Soon afterward, the king of Leon calls upon Fernán for aid against the Caliph of Cordova. Angered by Fernán's success and arrogance, Sancho Ordóñez convokes another *cortes*. Unintimidated, Fernán demands payment for his steed and goshawk. He is thrown into prison, but again Doña Sancha helps him escape. In response to Fernán's second request for payment, since the price is impossible, the king of Leon grants Castile its independence.

3/3

SUBSTRUCTURE

In this poem, it is neither a *family quarrel* nor an *insult* which inspires the *act of treachery*. On the contrary, though her brother was slain in fair combat, the queen of Leon is motivated solely by a desire for blood vengeance. This thirst for private vengeance brings about the preparation of an act of treachery whose success depends upon a false offer of marriage.

The setting for the death of Sancho of Navarre, which will motivate the rest of the action, is a *dynastic quarrel*: the attempt of Fernán González to secure his hereditary rights and restore the independence of Castile; it will develop into a *family quarrel* only as a result of his marriage to Doña Sancha, a later development in

española, p. 79: "Tiene este poema muchos rasgos característicos de los cantares de gesta, y parece ser una versión erudita. ..." Huerta, p. 34: "Así, aun cuando la gesta de *Fernán González* haya sobrevivido en una obra de clerecía, nadie duda hoy que existió un primitivo texto juglaresco sobre el tema."

the poem. The consequence of the dynastic quarrel is a *killing in combat* which will lead directly to the *act of treachery*. The *punishment*, an ironic twist, consists in the fact that the marriage, planned as a trap, eventually takes place through the efforts of the supposed bait, Doña Sancha, who twice saves Fernán from the harm intended by his enemies, permitting the full accomplishment of Fernán's dynastic goal.

The substructural pattern of the *Fernán González* thus varies from the French epics examined, by complicating the initial narreme and introducing a new motive:

         1 / The dynastic quarrel –
               eventually a family quarrel
         2 / The killing in action
         3 / The act of treachery
         4 / The punishment

3 / 4

GESTA DE LOS INFANTES DE LARA:

SUPERSTRUCTURE

The somber *Infantes de Lara*, known to us through the scholarly reconstruction of Menéndez Pidal, based on thirteenth- and fourteenth-century chronicles, was apparently composed during the twelfth century.[4] The story concerns the seven sons of Gonzalo Gustioz, the Infantes de Salas,[5] who accompany their mother, Doña Sancha, to the wedding at Burgos of her brother, Ruy Velásquez, and Doña Lambra de Bureba, a cousin of the count of Castile. In a dispute during the festivities,[6] Gonzalo González, the youngest of the Infantes, kills Alvar Sánchez, Doña Lambra's cousin.

The new bride incites her husband, Ruy Velásquez, to take vengeance on his young nephew. A general fight breaks out, but peace is eventually restored. The Infantes then accompany Doña Lambra, their new aunt, to her estate at Barbadillo. Here, she arranges for one of her servants to insult the young men by spilling blood over them. Pursued and overtaken by the Infantes, the servant seeks refuge beneath Doña Lambra's mantle; despite this protection, the enraged Infantes slay him on the spot.

4. *La leyenda de los Infantes de Lara*. See also Hurtado y Palencia, pp. 68–70.

5. Paris, *La Légende des Infants de Lara*, p. 2, n. 2: "Salas ... était dans le district de Lara, d'où le changement du nom donné aux enfants. ..."

6. *Ibid.*, pp. 3–4; Paris suggests that this incident may have been borrowed from *Girart de Roussillon*.

Persuaded by his wife, Ruy Velásquez conceives an act of treachery against his nephews. After sending their father, his own brother-in-law, to Almanzor, with a message in Arabic requesting that the bearer be decapitated, he arranges a Moorish ambush in which the young men are trapped; they know they have been betrayed by their uncle. Though they fight desperately, the youths are captured and beheaded.

The seven heads are sent to Cordova where they are shown by Almanzor to the father, whom instead of murdering he has kept prisoner. During his incarceration, Gustioz has been attended by a Moorish servant-girl, who now declares herself to be with child. Freed by Almanzor, Gustioz tells the girl that if the infant is a male, he is to be sent to his father after he has grown up. In due time, the youth, Mudarra, reaches his father, and is recognized. It is Mudarra who defies and kills Ruy Velásquez, to avenge the crimes against his father and brothers. Doña Lambra escapes temporarily, as long as her protector, the count of Castile, is able to defend her; the moment he dies, however, she is taken prisoner and burnt alive.

3/5

SUBSTRUCTURE

Although the extreme cruelty of Doña Lambra is a late element in the poem, probably due to the influence of the French[7] epic, the central incident in the action is unquestionably the act of treachery. What makes this act of treachery possible is the conventional *family quarrel*. The killing of Doña Lambra's cousin by her nephews sets off an initial conflict, which is, however, temporarily smoothed over.

A second quarrel begins when Doña Lambra, still thirsting for vengeance, *insults* her nephews through the offensive action of her servant. The Infantes take vengeance immediately; their manner of killing the servant, however, in itself constitutes a deadly *counter-insult*.[8] Doña Lambra does not seek open vengeance at this point; instead, she inspires her husband to plan and commit an *act of treachery*. Following the twofold plan of *double family*

7. Menéndez Pidal, *Historia y epopeya*, p. 94: "... según la forma primera de éste, hasta el siglo xiii, la mujer agraviada no se venga por sus manos, y sólo en ulteriores desarrollos de la leyenda ... se introducen los rasgos de ferocidad femenina. ..." See also *ibid.*, p. 94, n.1; and *La leyenda de los Infantes de Lara*, pp. 33–34.

8. Menéndez Pidal, *ibid.*, p. 6, n. 4: "La deshonra de Doña Lambra era grandísima, no tanto por haberse matado a aquel hombre en su presencia, como por haberlo muerto bajo su manto."

quarrel and *double insult*, there is a *double act of treachery*, against Gonzalo Gustioz and against the Infantes, and a *double punishment*, first for Ruy Velásquez and later for Doña Lambra. The avenger Mudarra, a son of the family, acts as surrogate for the victims of treachery; this hiatus, which awaits the birth of a child and his growth to manhood in order to effect the private vengeance required by the act of treachery, is described by Menéndez Pidal as a break in the unity[9] of the plot. The break, however, is more apparent than real, since the narremes show an unbroken substructural pattern identical with Type 1, although artistically arranged in a double set of interacting functional incidents.

The core narremes of the *Infantes de Lara* fall into the following structural arrangement:

1 The (Double) Family Quarrel
   a/ Doña Lambra's recently acquired nephew, Gonzalo Gustioz, kills her cousin, Alvar Sánchez, during the wedding festivities.
   b/ Doña Lambra and her husband, Ruy Velásquez, come into conflict with their nephews, the Infantes, because of the killing.
2 The (Double) Insult
   a/ Doña Lambra insults the Infantes by causing her servant to spill blood over them.
   b/ The Infantes insult Doña Lambra by killing her servant while he is under the protection of her mantle.
3 The (Double) Act of Treachery
   a/ Persuaded by Doña Lambra, Ruy Velásquez sends Gustioz on a false mission to Almanzor, who makes him a prisoner.
   b/ Ruy Velásquez arranges a Moorish ambush in which his nephews are trapped and beheaded.
4 The (Double) Punishment
   a/ Mudarra, the avenger by proxy, takes private vengeance by killing Ruy Velásquez, the traitor, in a personal duel.
   b/ Doña Lambra, temporarily protected by the count of Castile, is captured and burnt alive, after he dies.

3/6

GESTA DE SANCHO II DE CASTILLA:
SUPERSTRUCTURE

Reconstructed through the efforts of Puyol y Alonso, the *Gesta de Sancho II de Castilla*[10] appears to have been composed in its primi-

9. *Poema de Mio Cid*, p. 74.
10. *Cantar de gesta de Sancho II de Castilla*, pp. 10, 22, 52, *passim*.

tive form before the beginning of the twelfth century. Its main theme is the revolt of the heirs of Don Fernando el Magno against the paternal mandate, which specified the division of his lands among them. In this *family quarrel* of sibling rivals, *fighting over the allocation of dynastic spoils*, Don Sancho is at first the victor; his brother Don García is taken prisoner, while his brother Don Alfonso (later the Sixth) is exiled to Moorish lands; his sister Doña Urraca is besieged at her fortress of Zamora.

Arias Gonzalo, who had advised the father, Fernando, not to divide up his territories among his children, now tries to warn the victorious son, Don Sancho, to beware of his councillor, Vellido Dolfos. Heedless of this excellent advice, Don Sancho continues to trust Vellido; the latter, encouraged by Doña Urraca, seizes the occasion to run a spear[11] through the unsuspecting monarch. Since there is some uncertainty about placing the guilt for this *act of treachery*, Diego Ordóñez, acting as surrogate for Don Sancho, challenges Doña Urraca's people, the Zamoranos, to a collective duel. Unfortunately, this duel is interrupted, so that the judges are unable to determine who has been the victor.

3/7
SUBSTRUCTURE

The functional incidents which make up the structural pattern of this poem appear to start with the *family quarrel*, aroused by the greed of heirs, disputing the provisions of their father's will. This quarrel leads to the *fight for the inheritance*, in which the victorious brother mistreats his two brothers and his sister. In revenge, the sister commits an *act of treachery*, through the murder of her brother by his trusted councillor. The *punishment*, sought by Diego Ordóñez as proxy, through the judicial duel, is inconclusive, since the fight is interrupted. In outline, the core narremes form the following structural pattern:

1/ The family quarrel
2/ The fight for the inheritance
3/ The act of treachery
4/ The (interrupted) punishment

3/8

LA CONDESA TRAIDORA: SUPERSTRUCTURE

The *Condesa traidora*, a narrative dated by Menéndez Pidal *circa* 1160, but presumably based on a much older epic, was for a long

11. Richthofen, p. 81, notes the resemblance of this incident to Siegfried's death in the *Nibelungenlied*.

time considered an imaginary tale devoid of poetic worth. Utilizing the *Crónica Najerense*, however, Menéndez Pidal has been able to eliminate some of the later deformations, revealing a legend of epic dimensions,[12] with a unified plot and an historical background.

The countess Aba, wife of Garci Fernández of Castile, has received a secret message of love from Almanzor, cunningly intimating that she can become his queen. In order to rid herself of the husband who stands in the way of her rise to royalty, Aba plans an *act of treachery*. After weakening her husband's war steed by depriving it of food, she asks her husband, the count, to send his knights back to their homes, to celebrate the feast of the Nativity; she then informs Almanzor of what she has done. On the day of the festival, Almanzor sends his picked troops to attack the weakened Garci Fernández and his few remaining knights. When his horse collapses in battle, the count is wounded, captured, and carried off to Cordova, where he dies shortly.

Almanzor devastates Castile, forcing the new count, Sancho García, son of Garci Fernández, to take refuge with his mother at the castle of Lantarón. Convinced that only by killing her son will she be able to marry Almanzor, the countess plans to poison the boy. Warned by a Moorish servant-girl, Sancho García calls for a drink which is handed to him by his mother. He compels her to drink it and she dies. The youth then kills Almanzor, destroys Cordova, and returns home, bearing his father's corpse.

3/9

SUBSTRUCTURE

The narremes in the structural pattern show clearly. There is a *family quarrel*, in which an unscrupulous wife seeks the destruction of her husband. The motive is akin to passion; fired by a love message, and urged on by pride and cupidity, the wife wishes to make room for a new husband. In consequence of the setting, and the motive, the wife commits an *act of treachery*, resulting in the death of her husband, and the attempted poisoning of her son. Saved in time, the son manages to administer *punishment* to his mother, by forcing her to drink the poison prepared for him.

Several important variations are introduced in this poem. For the first time, we see a family quarrel in which the victim appears to be unaware that he is *persona non grata*. This is no doubt due to the second variation, the love triangle,[13] which by its nature

12. *Historia y epopeya*, pp. 14–15, 6, and prefatory note.
13. Richthofen, pp. 44–54, illuminates the parallel with Beuve de Hantone and names the *Condesa traidora* as the source of the French poem.

requires secrecy. There is a superficial resemblance here to the love romance, which requires comparison with the epic; for the present, it may suffice to point out that the quarrel is not between lovers, Aba and Almanzor, but between husband and wife, as members of a family. The passion motive is also introduced here for the first time, among the epics being analyzed. The structural outline, in spite of these variations, shows a strong kinship with the other Spanish epics:

> 1/ The family quarrel
> 2/ The disruption of the marriage
> 3/ The act of treachery
> 4/ The punishment

3/10

THE CONTEMPORARY SPANISH EPIC PATTERN: SUMMARY

The functional analysis of the four poems gives the following narremic patterns:

1 The Family Quarrel
  a/ *Fernán González*: Fernán and his eventual aunt, queen of Leon.
  b/ *Infantes de Lara*: (Double Quarrel)
    i/ Doña Lambra's nephew and her cousin.
    ii/ Doña Lambra and her nephews.
  c/ *Sancho II*: The three brothers and their sister.
  d/ *Condesa*: The wife, the husband, and the son.
2 The Motive
  a/ The Killing in Action: Fernán kills Sancho, the queen's brother.
  b/ The (Double) Insult:
    i/ Doña Lambra's servant insults the Infantes.
    ii/ The Infantes insult Doña Lambra.
  c/ The Fight for the Inheritance: Sancho wars against his siblings.
  d/ The Disruption of the Marriage: Aba turns against her husband.
3 The Act of Treachery
  a/ Fernán is lured into a trap by a false offer of marriage.
  b/ (Double):
    i/ The father is sent on a false mission and imprisoned.
    ii/ The Infantes are ambushed and beheaded.
  c/ Doña Urraca encourages the murder of her brother, Sancho.
  d/ The countess gets her husband killed and almost kills her son.
4 The Punishment
  a/ The marriage proposed as a lure becomes a reality, and the queen's

own niece thwarts the revenge by twice rescuing her husband-to-be; Fernán gains his rights and an independent Castile.

b/ (Double):

i/ Ruy Velásquez is slain in a duel with Mudarra, the avenger.

ii/ Doña Lambra is burnt alive.

c/ An interrupted judicial duel precludes the final judgment.

d/ The countess is compelled to drink the poison she has prepared for her son.

As in the French epic, there are four narremes. The first, third, and fourth narremes fall easily into the French system: the family quarrel, the act of treachery, and the punishment. These vary, much as the French do, in external detail; yet they all share a least common denominator, permitting them to be grouped as a single class. The second narreme, however, presents a special problem. It would be difficult to find a least common denominator for the four different ways in which the quarrel manifests itself in the narremic chain, motivating the activity to follow. For want of a better term, perhaps, this functional incident will be generalized under the heading "Motive." The specific variations of the four narremes can now be considered, in relation to their French counterparts.

3/11

THE FAMILY QUARREL IN THE FRENCH
AND SPANISH EPIC

The family quarrel is the only narreme universally present in the French and Spanish epics analyzed. In all but one it is the initial gambit, the exception being the *Fernán González*. Even in this poem, however, the starting-point, a dynastic quarrel, eventually develops into a family quarrel, when the protagonists become allied through marriage. The union of Fernán and Doña Sancha makes it ultimately a complicated quarrel between: 1/ Fernán and his aunt, the queen of Leon; 2/ Fernán and his uncle, Sancho Ordóñez of Leon, the queen's husband; 3/ Fernán and his brother-in-law, García of Navarre, brother of Doña Sancha.

In the *Infantes de Lara*, it is again a wicked aunt by marriage who forces the family quarrel. The initial dispute between Doña Lambra and her nephew, Gonzalo González, youngest of the Infantes, results in a quarrel between: 1/ Doña Lambra and all the nephews; 2/ Ruy Velásquez and the same nephews; 3/ Ruy Velásquez and his brother-in-law, Gustioz, father of the Infantes.

The veiled nature of the family quarrel in the *Condesa traidora* may raise some question about its reality, since the husband is presumably unaware of any difficulty. The readiness, however, of a wife and mother to eliminate her husband and her son must be considered sufficient evidence that trouble exists.

In addition to all but one of the types of family quarrel found in the French epic (between uncle and nephew, husband and wife, father and son, brother and sister, and brothers-in-law), the Spanish epics also include conflict between aunt and nephew, brother-in-law and sister-in-law, and mother and son. The Spanish pattern seems to lack only the quarrel between father and son, but even this is indirectly present in Sancho's and his brother's rejection of their father's legally expressed wishes in his bequests.

The kind of family disputes added by the Spanish epics illustrate the striking fact that, in the four poems, it is the woman who is responsible for provoking the family quarrel, planning the act of treachery, or both. The *Gesta de Sancho II*, a family quarrel without a quibble, points more than a finger of suspicion at Doña Urraca. It is important to note also that, except for the poem just mentioned, the Spanish epics are much more concerned than were the French with the problems of marriage and in-law trouble. Charlemagne's wife and Guibourc may have provoked and insulted their husbands, but the Spanish ladies seem to have been capable of a great deal more.

3/12

THE MOTIVE

The narreme of motive in the four French epics was without exception the insult; though this always acted as the spur to further action, it did not always result in a retaliatory act of treachery. Among the Spanish epics, only the *Infantes de Lara* made use of the insult, and even here the offense included killing, adding the incentive of blood vengeance.

The heterogeneous nature of this second narreme in the internal chain of functional incidents in the Spanish epic makes it difficult to classify the structural patterns according to type, except under the generic rubric of "The Motive." The *Fernán González* utilized the killing in action. For the *Gesta de Sancho II*, we may speak of the fight for the inheritance. In the *Condesa traidora*, it was a disruption of the marriage. Since these are all followed by the act of treachery and the punishment, there seems some justification for associating them with Type 1 (cf. 2/7). Perhaps this is a sufficient classification for the *Infantes de Lara* (cf. 3/5), but because of the

different motives in the others, it may be best to classify them provisionally as: *Fernán González*, Type 1a; *Sancho II*, Type 1b; *Condesa traidora*, Type 1c.

3/13

TREACHERY AND PROWESS

In the French epic, the insult can be followed either by the act of
treachery or the acts of prowess; but whatever the motive in the
Spanish epics considered here, the third narreme is always the act
of treachery. Among the French epics discussed, the *Gormont et
Isembart* is the only one to make use of this incident; and here it
involves large issues of church and state: the invasion of his
native land by a renegade, allied with the Saracen enemy.

By comparison, the Spanish epics describe relatively small,
private affairs. Though heads of state and princes are involved,
the acts do not affect the state power as such; they reflect the quarrels of individual men and women as a rule. Fernán González is
fighting for his dynastic status and the independence of Castile;
but the act of treachery is a trap, baited by a woman. The Infantes
de Lara are caught in a small ambush, their death and that of their
father, the result of a fight at a wedding. Countess Aba destroys
her family, in the hope of making a better marriage alliance. The
Sancho II comes closest, perhaps, to dealing with affairs of state,
but essentially it is an intra-family dispute over a larger share in
the estate. The protagonists in all these events seem more earth-
bound, closer to the realities, good and bad, of life in a difficult
society.

3/14

PUNISHMENT AND REWARD

Since all the Spanish epics involve an act of treachery, there always follows some degree of punishment, a narreme not present
in the French epics where the insult is succeeded by great acts of
prowess; in the latter case, the result is a reward of some kind. In
the *Gormont*, the traitor finds death as the consequence of his
treachery.

In the Spanish epics, a remarkable picture is presented: *Fernán
González* appears to have lost sight of the necessity to punish the
queen of Leon in any vindictive fashion for her treachery; all
attention is concentrated on the hero, happy with his loving wife
and his independent Castile, a very different result from the one

planned by his enemy. *Sancho II de Castilla* moves in the direction of punishment for the murder of the king, but leaves the question exactly in mid-air, since no judgment is possible on the basis of the interrupted judicial duel. In the *Infantes de Lara* and the *Condesa traidora*, on the contrary, vengeance, privately administered, is complete and brutal.

3/15

CONCLUSION

The conclusion to be drawn from the comparison of the situation in France and Spain, according to the epics analyzed, is that the poets may draw on much traditional material taken from life, history, or legend, that they may vary this material in many ways, but that they are essentially bound to maintain a well-knit structural pattern of a very few[14] narremes. The types of narremic chain may vary somewhat, but the starting-point is usually a family quarrel, which leads to an insult or other motive, giving rise to an act of treachery or acts of prowess, and concluding in a suitable punishment or reward.

The analysis of additional epics may add other types to the list or suggest better headings for the narremes, particularly in the

14. If narremes do indeed form a parallel with phonemes and morphemes, the fact that they are few in number supports the analogy. The -*emic* unit is an abstraction, concentrating on the least common denominator and subsuming under one head any number of variable sounds or forms (or incidents).

In English phonology, the *t*-sounds of *ten, trip, turtle, net, eighth, mountain*, etc., different as they are from each other phonetically, are reckoned functionally as one phoneme /t/. The differences among them are marginal; the function, to indicate a distinction between *ten/den, trip/drip, bet/bed*, etc., is the same. The range of articulated English sounds is enormous; the actual number of phonemes very few (thirty-seven – in the author's analysis – plus a few additional prosodic features of pitch, stress, etc.).

Similarly, in English morphology, there are many ways to form the spoken plural of nouns: [z] *dogs*; [s] *cats*; [əz] *foxes*; [ən] *oxen*; [Ø] *deer*; [ə] *data*; [i] *alumnae*; [ay] *alumni*; with vowel modification, *men, women, children, geese, mice*; with consonant modification, *houses, knives*, etc. These varied forms compose *one morpheme* $\{Z^1\}$, symbolizing *plurality*. In this way, the entire inflectional system may be reduced to a few grammatical morphemes: $\{Z^1\}$; $\{Z^2\}$ *possession*; $\{Z^3\}$ the verb suffix for *third person singular*; $\{D^1\}$ the *past tense*; $\{D^2\}$ the *past participle*; {-ing} the *present participle*; {-er} *comparative*, and {-est} *superlative*. See Gleason, *Introduction to Descriptive Linguistics*, p. 96.

The search for structural constituent units, based on their abstracted least common denominator, need not, nor is it intended to, disguise or ignore their manifold, marginal differences; in narremic as in linguistic analysis, it is intended to reveal the functionally identical units, in order to clarify the relationship between central and marginal elements.

case of the motive, for the Spanish epics. It is felt, however, that a clearer insight into the structure of the epic as narrative may be gained by a comparison with a closely[15] related genre, the Arthurian romance.

15. That the epic and romance genres are related has long been evident; what came as a surprise was the closeness of the relationship, at least as revealed by the functional and structural analysis into narremes. Needless to say, the two genres do differ mightily in their superstructural details of subject-matter, picture of feudal society, treatment of women, use of history and imagination, relative realism and magical enchantment, etc. The close parallelism of their narremic structures is therefore all the more striking. See Auerbach, pp. 101–5; Dorfman, *Women in the Epic and Romance*; Horrent, "Chanson de geste et roman courtois."

CHAPTER FOUR

The (Sub)Structural Pattern of the Arthurian Romance

4 The (Sub) Structural Pattern of the Arthurian Romance

4/1

THE "GESTE" AND THE "ROMANZ"

"Geste," derived from Latin neuter plural *gesta*, "deeds, acts, exploits," and used to describe historical accounts, for example, the *Gesta Francorum*, developed in Old French as a feminine singular form, meaning "history." Epic poems, narrating heroic feats allegedly based on history, came to be known as *chansons de geste*, or *cantares de gesta*. In the course of time, "geste" began to signify the epic poem itself, a group of such poems featuring a principal hero (or heroes), or the family to which the heroes belonged. The great popularity of these epics or "songs" in the twelfth century, their rapid multiplication, and their diversity in subject matter led in time to attempts at classification. They were divided, somewhat artificially, into three gestes or cycles: the *geste du roi*, centering around the king or emperor, usually Charlemagne, though someone else may be the main hero; the *geste de Garin de Monglane*, or *Guillaume d'Orange*, devoted to the battles of Southern France against the Saracen invaders; and the *geste de Doön de Mayence*, dealing with the fierce conflicts among the feudal overlords themselves.

"Romanz," derived from Latin *romanice*, means "in the Roman tongue," as compared with *latine* "in Latin." The twelfth century, with new horizons opened by exposure to the Orient in the crusades, brought renascent interest in the Latin narrative poetry of Virgil, Ovid, Lucan, Statius, and in Latin versions of the Greek tales. The translation of these materials into the "Romance" vernacular (i.e., Old French), and their adaptation to feudal customs and traditions, led to the creation of new tales of wonder and enchantment, composed directly in the vernacular. Whether translated from Latin or not, these all came to be considered "romances" and were classified into three groups: The Matter of France (epics); the Matter of Rome (tales of antiquity); and the Matter of Britain (Arthurian romances).

4/2

THE ARTHURIAN ROMANCES OF
CHRÉTIEN DE TROYES

The creation[1] of the Arthurian romance has been attributed to Chrétien de Troyes, though Holmes deems this unlikely. Other poets have dealt with the Matter of Britain and with the closely related *romans d'aventure*: Raoul de Houdenc, Renaud de Beaujeu, Béroul, Thomas, Gautier d'Arras; but whether or not the first in chronology, Chrétien is generally recognized, in this genre, as "the outstanding representative whom all later writers of romances considered as their master and model."[2]

The romances of Chrétien which have come down to us include five, *Erec et Enide, Cligés, Lancelot, Yvain,* and *Perceval,* which are undoubtedly his work (though he seems[3] to have left the ending of the *Lancelot* to be completed by a certain Godefroi de Leigni, and to have died during the composition of the *Perceval*), and one rather pedestrian tale, *Guillaume d'Angleterre,* whose authorship is disputed.[4] In view of the doubt concerning the *Guillaume,* and the relatively fragmentary nature of the *Perceval,* it may be assumed that the remaining four romances should give an adequate insight into Chrétien's structural technique. There is considerable uncertainty about the dating[5] of the romances, but the period is the second half of the twelfth century.

4/3

EREC ET ENIDE: SUPERSTRUCTURE

The brave knight, Erec, is struck by a dwarf, while in the company of Queen Guenevere. Unarmed, he is unable to defend himself, but swears to follow the knight whose dwarf has insulted him, seek arms, and take revenge. Arriving unknown at a fortified town, he finds shelter with an old *vavasseur,* whose daughter Enide, though clothed in rags, is of matchless beauty. The father

1. Chrétien de Troyes, *Wörterbuch,* p. 18; also, *Erec,* pp. xi–xii. See also Holmes, p. 164.
2. Voretzsch, *Introduction to Old French Literature,* p. 323. See also Holmes, p. 164; Cohen, *Le Roman courtois,* p. 83; Frappier, *Chrétien de Troyes,* pp. 210–42; Lazar, *Amour courtois,* p. 199.
3. Nitze and Dargan, *History of French Literature,* pp. 46–47.
4. Holmes, p. 140; see also Voretzsch, p. 279.
5. Dorfman, "Women in the Epic and Romance" (Master's essay, Columbia University, 1947), pp. 12–14.

notes the confusion troubling Erec and Enide, and asks his shy, submissive daughter to care for the stranger's horse. At table, Erec inquires about Enide's appearance; the venerable *vavasseur* explains how the wars have wasted his resources, declaring nonetheless that he expects a brilliant marriage for his daughter who is endowed with spiritual qualities beyond beauty.

Though he has listened with rapt attention to his host's discussion of his daughter, Erec recalls the reason for his presence here and wishes to learn more about the great concourse of knights and ladies gathering in the town, for among them is the knight he is following. The *vavasseur* replies that each year the lord of the castle gives a fete, during which the prize goes to the lady whose beauty gives her the right to take it. This right, if contested, must be defended by her knight. For the past two years, the prize has gone to the *amie* of the *chevalier aux armes d'or et d'azur*, the knight responsible for the insult to Erec. Revealing himself now as the son of a king, Erec promises that, if he may borrow arms, he will defeat the knight, win the prize for Enide, and make her queen of three cities. Victorious in the combat with the Blue and Gold Knight, Erec determines to take Enide back to King Arthur's Court, dressed in her rags, to be royally clothed by Guenevere.

Arrayed in splendor by the queen, Enide is presented to the Court. The king and all the knights rise in tribute to her beauty. Once again, modest Enide feels the flame in her cheek. The king, having awaited the return of Erec before bestowing the kiss of the White Stag on the most beautiful girl in court, now prepares to kiss Enide. No one of the knights present cares to contest her right to the kiss. The adulation of the others toward her only sharpens Erec's hunger; he is like the hunted stag, seeking the fountain. After a splendid wedding, Erec cannot wait for the guests to be gone and the two at last to be alone. Strengthened by love, Erec accomplishes wonders in the final tournaments given by the king in his honor. Then, overwhelmed with gifts, Erec and Enide take their leave, to make their home in the kingdom of Erec's father, settling down to the life of a young couple in love.

All is not well, however. Erec is no longer the valiant hero, displaying his prowess, but only the loving husband, staying at home. The people of the court begin to murmur that he is recreant, neglecting his duties; they blame Enide also, since she is his *amie* and *drue*, his lover, as well as his wife, and therefore in duty bound to spur him on, not hold him back. Learning of this, and shocked by the revelation, Enide, who has known nothing but happiness in the arms of her husband, takes to weeping. One night, her tears waken him and he demands to know the reason for her sorrow. After some evasions, which anger him, she finally unburdens herself, describing the rumors and the blame attaching to her. Erec quietly assures her that she and the others are right and asks her to dress for a quick departure. The honeymoon is over.

Erec's new attitude toward his wife receives prompt demonstration. Having impatiently waited for her to dress, he sends a servant after her. Her delay, however, is not without significance. In her distraught frame of mind, she cannot choose a dress, for she is lamenting her folly. What mad urge, she wonders, caused her to disrupt a happy life of ease with a husband who loved her?

The question may, perhaps, be answered[6] for her. Blinded for a while by her great happiness, she had no notion that all was not right with the world. Awakening to the realization, as lovers eventually do, that she and Erec are a part of the fabric of society, with obligations beyond the domestic circle, she was filled with a sense of guilt, a feeling too strong to keep buried within her.

This then is the climax of the romance: Enide, hitherto content to "love, honor and obey," has suddenly begun to "question" the actions of the man she loves. This she does against her better judgment, perhaps, but inevitably, because a powerful code, the cult of prowess, urges her on. From this point of view, Erec's anger and growing coldness is understandable; Enide has shown "disrespect for his sovereignty."[7]

It is this involuntarily insulting attack on his authority which acts as the immediate spur, provoking Erec to renewed deeds of knightly heroism. As Sheldon[8] has shown, Erec clearly recognizes the justice of Enide's complaint. Criticism, however, carries the implication of power; Erec, while in fact submitting to the moral pressure exerted by his wife, is unwilling to admit that he is no longer the unquestioned master. He will take to the road, prove his courage in action; and she will be there to observe! To convince himself he is still master, he commands her to maintain silence.

The subsequent series of adventures, interesting as they must

6. Borodine, *La Femme et l'amour au XIIe siècle*, pp. 41–42, discusses the views of Paris and Foerster on this question. See also Lazar, pp. 200–7, for additional views of principal medievalists.

7. Guyer, *Influence of Ovid on Chrétien de Troyes*, p. 238. See also Adler, "Sovereignty as the Principal of Unity," pp. 917–36.

8. "Why Does Chrétien's Erec Treat Enide so Harshly?" See also Lazar, pp. 202–3.

have been to a twelfth-century audience, do not need detailed description, since they merely furnish accumulating proofs of the prowess of Erec and the constant love of Enide. By an ironic twist, this love is manifested in a way not calculated to soften his heart or assuage his pride. Whenever Enide becomes aware of danger bearing down upon her husband who is seemingly unaware of it, her great love and fear for him forces her to violate his injunction to silence by warning him. This must not be construed as fear for her own life, should she be left unprotected by his death, as Erec himself learns when he witnesses a scene in which she displays personal heroism and undying love for him.

Erec has been wounded, almost to the point of death. His body is brought to the castle of Limors, by the servants of the count who has defeated him. In the presence of her husband's body, Enide is ordered by the count to prepare for marriage with him. At her refusal, he threatens her and showers her with blows. Enide defies him to do his worst. Her proud words recall Erec back to life. Leaping from his bier, he seizes a sword and decapitates the brutal count. Anger has given him strength, but there is something else also, the love he has for his wife. Once again the two are lovers, but this time with a difference. Although they are both ready to return home now, Erec is aware that man's place is in the world of deeds and adventures.

This aroused sense of responsibility is soon put to a final test. On their way to the court of King Arthur, Erec and Enide arrive at the castle of Brandigan, known as the *Joie de la Cour*. They learn that no one who has ever entered it has been known to return. Erec sees his duty and takes temporary leave of Enide. He enters the castle, engages in combat with Mabonagrain, and emerges victorious.

The defeat of Mabonagrain uncovers the mystery of the enchanted *Joie de la Cour*. The knight who has been guarding this otherworldly garden, an excellent example of the *chevalier courtois*, completely in the service of his *amie* (a cousin of Enide's), has promised never to leave the place until he has been defeated in combat. Erec's victory has liberated Mabonagrain from the bonds of a selfish love,[9] isolated from the world.

The lesson is not lost on Erec. Henceforth, he will continue to love Enide; at the same time, he is prepared to accept his obligations in the world of men. At the death of his father, he and Enide are crowned by King Arthur, in a final joyous celebration.

9. Hopkins, *Influence of Wace on the Arthurian Romances*, p. 145.

4/4

THE WHITE STAG CONTEST

It may be expected that the romance, probing into the many facets of love, will concern itself with the incident of the lovers' first meeting. This is no haphazard scene in the *Erec* but one skilfully motivated. At the beginning of the poem, King Arthur announces the contest of the White Stag: the prize, a kiss to the most beautiful girl at court. All the knights will defend the right of their own lady to the title and the prize.

Erec, a young knight, has no lady, nor is he apparently seeking one. In the company of the queen one day, he is sent by her to inquire about the identity of a strange knight traveling with a dwarf. Erec, who is unarmed, is struck by the dwarf. Maintaining control in the face of extreme provocation, Erec accepts the insult as the challenge to start on a quest, the search for weapons with which to avenge the affront; he cannot go back to court for his own, since he must follow the knight immediately or risk losing him.

While on this quest, which has nothing ostensibly to do with meeting any possible winner of the White Stag contest, Erec is given shelter by a poor but noble *vavasseur*, who happens incidentally to be the father of a most beautiful girl. The host tells Erec of the Hawk contest: the most beautiful lady at the tournament is entitled to the prize of the hawk, if her knight defends this right. This is the test, which Erec must undergo, to prove worthy of the reward, the love of the lady. Erec's victory over Yder, the dwarf's knight, avenges his insult; it also wins the initial reward, the hand of Enide in marriage. Erec now has a lady worthy of the kiss of the White Stag; and he has a lover, with whom to look forward to a lovers' quarrel.

4/5

THE LOVERS' QUARREL

There is some resemblance between the Family Quarrel of the epic and the kind of conflict in which Erec and Enide are engaged; they are after all husband and wife, a family. Yet there is an unmistakable difference. In the epic, quarrels between husband and wife are about other matters, not the love relationship itself. Erec is deeply in love with Enide and she with him, but it is the very depth of this feeling which blinds both of them to the true meaning of love. As members of a larger family, society, Erec owes it to his very love for Enide to make her proud of him by winning and holding the respect of their court. And Enide owes it to her love for Erec to urge him on in his knightly obligations, not keep him chained in domesticity.

Enide's challenge to his authority, involuntary and regretted though it may have been, is in a true sense a lovers' quarrel. It questions the nature of that love which has subjected her to the ugly murmurings of the court. The course of love, smooth as it may have been in the beginning, will run a rough road until Erec re-establishes himself, through continued acts of valor, as a worthy lover. The difference between this type of conflict in the epic and the romance may be seen by a comparison with a similar challenge in the *Chanson de Guillaume*. Guibourc, we recall, had threatened her husband with a denial of his conjugal rights, unless he repelled the Saracens. This challenge to the man's authority was directed, not to his duties as a lover, but as a legal husband and war-chief.

4/6
FORM AND FUNCTION –
MAJOR AND MINOR NARREMES

The structure of the *Erec* may be formally divided into three linked but semi-independent, self-contained units:

1/ The Prologue: the White Stag contest, containing its own narremes, arranged to bring the lovers together.
2/ The Main Plot: the conflict of the lovers, containing the narremes which divide the lovers and bring them together again.
3/ The Epilogue: the *Joie de la Cour*, containing its own narremes, separating the lovers again briefly and bringing them together for good.

The prologue has already been discussed (cf. 4/4); as a unit, its function is to make the conflict of the lovers possible. The episode of the *Joie de la Cour* is an epilogue. After the slaying of the count of Limors, Erec and Enide are completely reconciled; they have earned the reward, the reunion after the quarrel. The happy pair are on their way to King Arthur's Court, when they accidentally encounter a new danger. This is a final test: will Erec once again, as in their early days of marriage, shun his obligations, preferring to stay by Enide's side, and will she hold him from his duty? The new Erec meets his test valiantly; the separation is brief, and the final reward, the coronation of Erec and Enide as king and queen.

The function of this epilogue, then, is to prove conclusively that the lesson Erec has learned has been truly assimilated.

The connection between the prologue, the main plot, and the epilogue makes a continuous chain of functional incidents, but the narremes fall into two functional classes: the *major narremes*, making up the *core system*, and the *minor narremes* which, linked to the major narremes, make up the *expanded core system*. In theory, the core system is able to stand alone as an independent structural frame; the main plot in the *Erec* could be a complete poem in itself.

The incidents in the prologue, however, may be considered an expansion of the lovers' quarrel, in the sense that the italicized words are an expansion of the grammatical subject in the sentence: "The *tall, dark, and handsome* man is a friend." Similarly, the incidents of the epilogue are expansions respectively of the acts of prowess and the reward.

The core system is autonomous or independent, in the same way that, in the illustration above, "The ... man is a friend" is independent of the rest. The minor narremes are dependent, like "... tall, dark, and handsome ...," since their function is simply to expand the frame.

4/7
SUBSTRUCTURE

The functional analysis of the *Erec* thus reveals a chain of four minor narremes, followed by four major ones, and these by two more minor ones. This might perhaps be schematically presented as:

I Expansion: The Prologue
    a/ The insult, the blow struck by the dwarf
    b/ The quest, the search for weapons and for revenge
    c/ The test, the victory over Yder, the Blue and Gold Knight
    d/ The initial reward, the love and hand of Enide in marriage
II Core System: The Main Plot
    1/ The lovers' quarrel, between Erec and Enide
    2/ The insult, the challenge to his sovereignty
    3/ The acts of prowess, the deeds of valor on the road
    4/ The reward, the reunion with the lover, Enide
III Expansion: The Epilogue
    e/ The final test, the victory over Mabonagrain
    f/ The final reward, the coronation of Erec and Enide

The more intricate nature of the substructural pattern, with its minor narremes, is only part of the differences from the epic. The core system seems very much like Type II in the epic patterns, except for the first narreme; but this exception is extremely important. In the romance, the center of attention is focused on the couple as a unit, two people attempting to become one. Is this what we shall find in the other romances of Chrétien?

4/8

CLIGÉS: PART I – SUPERSTRUCTURE

The narrator, Chrétien, announces at the beginning of *Cligés* that he will tell the story of a youth from Greece who joined King Arthur's Court; but first he will describe the father's life and the family from which he came. Following Chrétien, we will consider the description of the father, part I; that of the youth, part II.

A great emperor of Greece and Constantinople had two sons; Alexander, the elder, was a grown youth before Alis, the younger, was born. Unwilling to vegetate in a life of royal ease, and resisting his father's offer of knighthood at home, Alexander sets off with some companions to earn their knighthood at King Arthur's Court. Alexander, who has won the affection of all at the court in England, embarks with King Arthur and the royal household on a trip to Brittany; the king has left Count Angrés of Windsor in command in England.

In the royal ship, besides Arthur and Guenevere, there are only Alexander and Soredamors, the queen's companion. It is common knowledge that Soredamors, Gawain's sister, hates love. So deeply accepted is this fact that, when Guenevere notes Soredamors' obvious confusion, she can only attribute this to the turbulent sea. Soredamors, however, is torn between desire for Alexander and her accustomed scorn of Cupid; she dare not speak, and so she continues, loving him one moment and hating him the next. Alexander pines for her, too; but he also dares not speak, since he would be taken for a madman!

Word comes that Count Angrés has risen in rebellion against Arthur. Alexander and his Greek companions request knighthood, in order to punish Angrés. The queen offers Alexander a parting gift, a white silk shirt into which Soredamors has secretly sewn one of her golden hairs.

The traitor, Angrés, has sacked London, and is now defending Windsor against the king. Alexander and his companions perform feats of prodigious prowess. Making his way into the castle,

Alexander captures the count. But his shield, lying outside the walls among the dead, causes the others to think him slain. Great is everyone's joy when he announces from the walls the capture of the town. The king has offered a precious cup in reward for this achievement; he now presents it to Alexander, adding that he may have any request in his power to bestow, except for the crown and the queen.

Alexander hastens to accept the cup, presenting it immediately to Gawain. He hesitates to ask of Arthur, however, the one favor he really wants: the hand of Soredamors. She, for her part, has seen him wearing the silk shirt and wants to speak, but still she dares not. It is Guenevere who forces the issue, telling them that she has seen how their two hearts have become one; to their joy, she arranges the marriage. Alexander now has three joys and honors: fame for the town he has captured; a kingdom in Wales, bestowed by Arthur; and Soredamors, to be his queen. Shortly afterward, their union is blessed with a son, Cligés.

4/9
PART II – SUPERSTRUCTURE

After the birth of Cligés, Alexander learns that his father, the emperor, has died, and that his younger brother Alis has usurped the throne. Although he is prepared to make war on his brother, Alexander wishes only to assure the succession for his son; he is willing to make an accord with Alis, if the latter agrees never to marry, thus guaranteeing the crown to Cligés as heir.

Profiting by the death of Alexander and Soredamors, however, and urged on by the perfidious advice of his court, Alis seeks the hand of Fenice, daughter of the German emperor. Since she has already been promised to another, her father invites Alis to come in person to Germany to fetch her, bringing with him a sufficient force to protect her against possible ravishment by her former suitor. Alis sets out for Germany, with Cligés in his *entourage*.

At the imperial palace, the emperor introduces his daughter to her future husband and his subjects. Fenice, a miracle of nature, has not covered her head; despite the gloominess of the day, her beauty lights up the palace. Cligés, too stands uncovered before the emperor; and it is as though a single ray of light radiates from their combined grace.

Recalling the timidity of his father, Alexander, in similar circumstances, Cligés casts covert glances of admiration in her direction, trying to remain unobserved, since he does not want to be taken for a fool. For all his caution, however, he attracts the attention of Fenice, and what she sees pleases her greatly. As the two young people eye each other in secrecy, Fenice discovers that she can love none other than this handsome stranger.

Fenice, like all ladies in love, is impatient to hear reports of the prowess of her lover. He is engaged in combat with the Saxon knights, sent to abduct Fenice by the Duke of Saxony, her rejected suitor. Watching the battle from her window, she can think only of this glorious young hero, whose name she does not even know. The feats of Cligés are so outstanding, and so great his beauty, that all who witness the battle demand to know his identity. In this manner, Fenice hears the name of Cligés. She learns also of the oath sworn by Alis in favor of his nephew, and her heart is joyous that Love has not shamed her, but has brought to her the perfect knight.

The great happiness she feels through love of Cligés is dimmed, however, at the thought of marrying the perjuror, Alis. Her growing pallor, noticed with increasing concern by her nurse, Thessala, invites questions. It is difficult to unburden herself, however, especially since she may be criticized for her temerity, or perhaps worse, persuaded to forego her desires. Thessala promises to keep her secret, whatever it is, and to make no attempt to dissuade her from her plans. Fenice describes her "malady," but even as she speaks, it is apparent that she wants no cure that would remove her "sweet distress."

On reflection, Fenice clarifies the nature of her dilemma: she is in a love triangle; loving the nephew, she must marry the uncle. But she deliberately forbids herself the adultery of Tristan and Isolde. Thessala prepares a potion which will effectively prevent Alis from enjoying his marital rights, although he will have an illusion to the contrary; Cligés, knowing nothing of this, offers his trusting uncle the cup.

As Alis is returning to Greece with his bride, the forces of the Duke of Saxony attack again. During the battle, twelve Saxon knights abduct Fenice. By good fortune, Cligés encounters them and discovers the identity of their prisoner; fighting savagely, he defeats them. Watching the struggle, Fenice does not know it is Cligés, but wishes it were he. Thus, in the moment of great peril, they have no thoughts but of each other. Afterward, there is an opportunity to speak of their love, yet they do not. The silence of Fenice is easy to understand; she is a simple girl who dares not speak. But Cligés has just demonstrated the utmost bravery against great odds. Why should he act in such cowardly fashion before a modest maiden? There are two reasons: a man must fear his master, and Love is his master; besides, she is the wife of his uncle.

Meanwhile the Duke of Saxony, enraged by the escape of Fenice, challenges Cligés to single combat, with her as the prize. Begging his uncle for the privilege, he is granted it. Temporarily brought down by the duke, Cligés finds his strength restored on hearing Fenice's cry of anguish; he defeats his opponent, in a sense winning Fenice, who needs no winning. Unable to face her any longer under present conditions, Cligés demands leave of his uncle, to go to his mother's relatives in Britain, at the court of King Arthur. He will be fulfilling a promise to his father to seek glory in competition with the best. In taking leave of Fenice, weeping, he declares ambiguously that he is asking her permission to go "as from one to whom he belongs." During his absence, she debates endlessly this remark: flattery or love?

All the time that Cligés is with Arthur, his thoughts keep returning to Fenice. In a great tourney, Cligés keeps appearing on successive days as the Black Knight, the Green Knight, and the Vermillion Knight, defeating as an unknown the mighty Sagremor, Lancelot, Perceval, and all the others. Proving himself, in accordance with the promise to his father, and finding it impossible to stay away any longer, he returns to Greece.

Face to face, Cligés and Fenice change color; they can hardly refrain from kissing and hugging. Fenice asks questions about Britain; she wants to know if he has loved anyone there. He answers that he loved "from there"; his body was in Britain, but his heart was in Greece. She replies that her heart was in Britain, though her body remained in Greece. This time, they begin to speak clearly of their love. Fenice describes the potion and its effect on Alis; she has reserved herself for him. At the same time, she asserts that she cannot belong to him while she is the "wife" of another man. They must think of a plan.

She rejects his project of a flight to Britain, since this would recall to people the affair of Tristan and Isolde. Instead, she suggests another potion, this time for her. By its means, she will feign death. In a properly prepared coffin, she can be taken to a secret place, and there they can be happy. The ruse works, though Fenice is tortured by certain doctors who suspect the trick. For fourteen happy months, Cligés and Fenice live together in an isolated tower. Discovered eventually, they flee to Britain. The emperor pursues them, goes mad, and dies. Cligés is restored to his rightful throne, with Fenice, formerly his mistress and sweetheart, now his wife, sweetheart, and queen.

4/10

THE DOUBLE-CORE SYSTEM

As a narrative, the *Cligés* presents an extremely complex structure. There is first of all the division into two independent parts.
The story of Alexander and Soredamors is a complete entity, with
an autonomous core of four narremes, as we shall see. Structurally, it is a romance in itself. Its function, however, is to prepare
the setting for the romance of Cligés and Fenice. The "conjunc-
tion" binding the two into a compound unit is the birth of the
baby, Cligés.

The second part is also structurally very complex, in its own
right. Since its leit-motif is the love triangle, the functional incidents will concern the relations between three people: the wife,
the husband, and the lover. There is no question in the *Cligés* that
the major figures in the multiple love relationships are Cligés and
Fenice; the functional incidents underlying their adventures will
therefore be considered as making up an autonomous core of
major narremes. The minor narremes, linking the activities of Alis
to the rest, must be included in the expanded core system.

4/11

ALEXANDER AND SOREDAMORS – SUBSTRUCTURE

The encounter between Alexander and Soredamors, the first incident in the romance to precipitate a chain reaction, may be ac-
counted a lovers' quarrel. The two are in love, but timidity keeps
them apart. Since in their thoughts they are one, their overt relationship may be termed a separation, voluntarily induced. Soredamors cannot make up her mind whether she loves or hates
Alexander, but even when she is sure she loves him, she still
maintains silence. Her well-known attitude to Love is an insult to
a lover. Alexander's hesitation in speaking is based on the expectation that she will call him a madman for approaching someone
with her views.

The thought occurs to Alexander that, provided he proves himself worthy of her, her attitude might change. His exceptional
feats, the acts of prowess, do indeed win him the ultimate reward.

The four narremes: the lovers' quarrel, the insult, the acts of
prowess, and the reward, making up the core system, are identical
with the autonomous core system of the *Erec et Enide*. In order to
distinguish this from the structural patterns of the epic, we may
call it Type RI.

4/12

CLIGÉS AND FENICE – SUBSTRUCTURE

The intricate structural framework of the second part, after the birth of Cligés, begins with a family quarrel. The old emperor of Greece, at the point of death, sends for Alexander, his heir; a faithless servant, partisan of Alis, reports that Alexander has been shipwrecked and lost. Alis unknowingly usurps the throne. But when Alexander arrives in Greece with military forces to claim his rights, Alis is unwilling to yield to his brother.

On the advice of his council to effect a just and reasonable peace, Alis reaches an accord with Alexander: the elder brother may govern, if the younger may keep the crown as emperor in name; to ensure the inheritance of Cligés, he swears on oath, never to marry. This oath, which arises directly out of the family quarrel, leads in consequence to an Act of Treachery; by marrying Fenice, Alis violates his pledge.

Conventional reaction to an act of treachery is punishment. Alis has not only usurped the throne; by marrying, he is disinheriting Cligés; and by marrying Fenice, he is "usurping" the queen, who belongs to Cligés by right of love. The function of this first section is then that of a prologue, arranging the setting for the conflict of the lovers, Cligés and Fenice. The first three functional incidents: the family quarrel, the oath, and the act of treachery are minor narremes, an expansion of the lovers' quarrel between Cligés and Fenice. The punishment, as we shall see, is also a minor narreme, but used to expand one of the later core narremes.

There is a fundamental difference between the conflict separating Cligés and Fenice, as compared with the quarrel between Erec and Enide, and Alexander and Soredamors. In the latter instances, the protagonists were concerned with their love obligations only to each other. In the former, there is a partition of duties: the heart belongs to one and the body to another. Fenice has the duty of filial obedience to marry as her father orders, and the duty of marital fidelity once the marriage is performed; the duty of love for its own sake has strong competition, and Fenice, like Soredamors, remains silent in the face of her love. Cligés has no reason to suspect her true feelings; his duty to his uncle, and to his uncle's wife, keeps him silent also, like Alexander. Since the forces separating the lovers are voluntarily accepted obligations, resulting from a conflict in a love triangle, we shall call this narreme the lovers'-triangle quarrel.

This complicated quarrel, which includes in its expansion Alis' act of treachery, reflecting Fenice's relations with both Cligés and Alis, produces a pair of insults. In the major relationship, Fenice insults Love (like Soredamors) and thereby Cligés by her silence; like his father, Cligés is afraid that the woman he loves will call him a fool if he speaks. In the minor relationship, Fenice *punishes* Alis for his perjury, the act of treachery, by arranging for a potion that will keep him from consummating the marriage: this is an insult to his status as a husband. Since it is Cligés who, though unknowingly, is the one to offer the cup, the triangle is kept strictly in balance. The punishment-insult of Alis, a portmanteau narreme, is an expansion of the insult in the core system.

In order to prove himself in competition with the best available opposition, Cligés shows himself fully worthy of Fenice's love by performing prodigies of acts of prowess at the court of King Arthur. At his return to Greece, an emotional scene between the two lovers releases the flood-gates of confession and produces the reward: a declaration of love between the two, a plan to unite them through the second potion which will "release" Fenice from her marital duties, and their life together in the secret tower.

The resolution of the love conflict, while a reward for Cligés, is an extension of the punishment of Alis, the perjured traitor; it is indeed a second insult, since his wife is not only depriving him of his marital rights, but actually living with another man. This discovery enrages the emperor, who sets out to hunt the pair down. The pursuit of the lovers, and the need of Cligés to protect his mistress, now induces the hero to seek help at Arthur's court to reclaim his throne: this is the final test. The final reward will come with the death of the emperor, which is his ultimate punishment, and the marriage of the lovers, followed by their coronation. It can be seen that these are minor narremes, expansions of the reward.

4/13

THE SUBSTRUCTURE OF THE
DOUBLE-CORE SYSTEM

The formal division of the Cligés into two parts, the stories of Alexander and of Cligés, may be functionally analyzed into three: a fore-plot, the autonomous core narremes of Alexander-Soredamors; a main plot, the autonomous core narremes of Cligés-Fenice; and a subordinate plot, the dependent core narremes of Alis-Cligés-Fenice (cf. *a* to *f* below).

PART I. ALEXANDER–SOREDAMORS: FORE-PLOT

> 1/ Lovers' quarrel
> 2/ Insult
> 3/ Acts of prowess
> 4/ Reward (conjunction: birth of Cligés)

PART II. CLIGÉS–FENICE: MAIN PLOT, ALIS: SUBORDINATE PLOT

Cligés–Fenice	Cligés–Alis	Alis–Fenice
A *Prologue: Subordinate Plot*		
a/ Family quarrel		
b/ Oath		
c/ Act of treachery		
B *Main plot*:		
1/ Lovers'-triangle quarrel		
2/ Insult *d/* Punishment		i/ First insult
3/ Acts of prowess		
4/ Reward (union of the lovers)		ii/ Second insult
C *Epilogue*:		
e/ Final test		
f/ Final reward		iii/ Death of the traitor

The narremic core of the fore-plot, as we have seen (cf. 4/11), is identical with that of Erec and Enide, and has been labeled Type RI. The main plot of the *Cligés* differs from these by opening with a lovers'-triangle quarrel, rather than with a lovers' quarrel. We may call this provisionally Type RII.

The subordinate plot strikingly resembles the structural pattern of the epic, since it begins with a family quarrel, has an act of treachery, and ends with punishment; the second narreme, however, the oath, is novel, at least in our samples.

The attention in this romance, as in the *Erec*, is fully focused on the couple as a unit (cf. 4/7). When Cligés offers his uncle the magic potion, even though he is unaware of it, he is already acting as a part of Fenice; his hand is literally hers. Thus, though the plan belongs to Fenice, she and Cligés are acting as one. They are a couple, even while they are estranged, in their life together as lover and mistress, and in their ultimate marriage.

4/14
LANCELOT: SUPERSTRUCTURE

The *Lancelot*, or *Chevalier de la Charrette*, like the *Cligés*, also concerns a triangle: the love of Lancelot for Guenevere, wife of

King Arthur. One day, a knight appears at Arthur's court to claim that he has made captive many of Arthur's knights and ladies. He will free them only if a knight of the court escorts Guenevere out to him in the forest, and if they return safely. Sir Kay begs the boon, which is unwillingly granted; he is defeated and Guenevere disappears. Gawain, in pursuit of the queen, encounters a knight whose steed is in a sweat and, at his request, lends him a fresh horse; this one is soon dead from hard riding. The knight is Lancelot, and he also is pursuing Meleaganz, the queen's abductor.

Lancelot comes upon a dwarf driving a pillory cart, such as is used for traitors, murderers, thieves, and other criminals. Asked for information about the queen, the dwarf tells him that he must ride in the cart for a day first. Unaware that this is a first test of his love for Guenevere, Lancelot hesitates for a few steps, because of shame; the incentive is too great, however, and he quickly leaps into the cart. His hesitation, through fear of humiliation, will exact a penalty later on. On the other hand, Gawain soon overtakes them; given the same opportunity by the dwarf, he rejects the offer as foolishness. But together the two proceed, one on the horse, the other in the cart, mocked by all who pass.

The next day, Lancelot obtains a horse from a damsel who declares that there are several paths to the queen: one across a dangerous Water-bridge, the path chosen by Gawain, and the other across an even more difficult Sword-bridge, toward which Lancelot now directs his way. On this road, Lancelot encounters another damsel who offers food and lodging, if he will lie with her. Forced by necessity, he promises; but his thoughts are only of Guenevere, and thus the damsel is compelled to return to her own bed, a beautiful victim of Lancelot's passing his second test. The narrator is careful to describe the maiden's considerable charm and Lancelot's discomfort at the temptation; like Fenice, however, the hero cannot bear the thought of *partage*: he has only one heart, and it belongs to Guenevere.

In the morning, the damsel asks Lancelot if she may accompany him to the kingdom of Logres, the home of Meleaganz. During the trip, they discover a fountain, and near it, a comb with strands of golden hair. Learning that the comb is Guenevere's, he falls forward almost in a faint. Since the damsel requests the comb, he carefully removes the strands, to prevent their tearing, and kisses them "a hundred thousand times." Thus far, he has withstood without faltering the humiliation of the insults while in the cart, repressed the delights of the flesh with the willing damsel, and succumbed to grief at the sight of his love's own comb, a grief mixed with joy in the possession of her tresses. The ultimate test awaits: facing death fearlessly.

Lancelot now prepares to enter the kingdom of Logres, from which no one ever returns. Despite heavy obstacles, which he courageously overcomes, he crosses the Sword-bridge, wounded and bleeding. A last warning that death is certain fails to deter him; he prefers death to returning. In Logres, he begins the dangerous task of rescuing Guenevere. His courage impresses King Bademagu, father of Meleaganz. When the son refuses to restore Guenevere, at Bademagu's request, to the "finest knight in all the world," a tournament is arranged between Lancelot and Meleaganz. The former is victorious, but spares the life of the queen's abductor, since she wills it. When Bademagu presents Guenevere to Lancelot, she angrily refuses to speak to him.

In ignorance of any culpability, Lancelot cannot understand her attitude, but as a true lover, he humbly refrains from questioning any act of hers. Guenevere does not break her stubborn silence until the false report is heard that Lancelot has been treacherously slain by the knights of Meleaganz. Even then, to prevent those about her from learning her secret, she berates herself silently, vowing to refrain from food and drink if the report be true. She feels responsibility for her cruelty, pining and losing much of her beauty in her grief. Her supreme regret, however, is that she has never held him in her arms; he has never received the reward earned by his acts in her behalf. She is not ready to follow her lover in death, however; it is better "to live in sorrow than die in order to have peace."

Meanwhile, Lancelot has also received a false report of the death of the queen. So profound is his grief that he decides upon immediate self-destruction. Just as Guenevere, in her regrets, could think of nothing but her failure to award her lover the consummation of an embrace, so Lancelot, preparing to die for her sake, can think of nothing else but that he has in some manner failed to show proper submission to her desires. He suspects that her coldness has something to do with the cart, though he feels no reason for self-reproach in this, having forgotten his hesitancy.

Lancelot and Guenevere each discover that the other lives. The favor with which she receives him induces him now to inquire about her previous coldness. She explains that his entry into the cart was not instantaneous; that the two steps of hesitation were shameful. Avowing his guilt, and recognizing the justice of her position, Lancelot at last earns the final accolade, a private rendezvous. She is in her room, he outside, a barred window between them. With her consent, he bends apart the bars which were immovable. In this shrine, the couple become one.

In tearing the bars from the window, Lancelot has cut his finger. The next day, Meleaganz discovers drops of blood on Guenevere's sheets and likewise on those of Sir Kay, her guard, whose wounds were still open. As a response to his insulting charges, a judicial duel is arranged, Meleaganz against Lancelot, the queen's champion. Bademagu asks the queen to separate the combatants; she replies that she is agreeable to whatever he wishes. Hearing this, Lancelot immediately stops fighting, refusing to protect himself against Meleaganz, who is thereupon stopped by his father.

Next, Lancelot and the others decide to seek Gawain at the Water-bridge. On the way, a dwarf lures Lancelot into a trap, and he becomes a prisoner of Meleaganz. A forged letter arrives, informing the queen that he is safe at King Arthur's court, where all await her return. Gawain, who has been saved in the meantime from a watery grave, escorts her home, only to find that Lancelot is not there. In her absence, a great tournament has been arranged.

In Logres, Lancelot begs the lady of the house permission to attend the tournament, on his oath to return afterward. She agrees on condition that he give her his love, and laughingly accepts his promise to give her "all the love that he has." At the tournament, he is accomplishing great feats as an unknown knight when a damsel brings him word that the queen commands him to do his "worst." From a hero of a moment before, he becomes the laughing-stock of the spectators. The next day, he is again commanded to do his "worst" and willingly agrees, whereupon the queen countermands her order; since it is now her will that he do his "best," he is once again the greatest champion of the tourney. Then he returns to Logres, to be shut up once more, this time in an escape-proof tower. The daughter of Bademagu, however, for whom he has once done a favor, now secures his freedom.

(From this point on, the work is that of Godefroi de Leigni, completing the ending for Chrétien.) Lancelot returns to Arthur's court, completes the judicial duel interrupted at Logres, and cuts off the head of Meleaganz.

4/15

THE THEME OF COURTLY LOVE

The love triangle in the *Lancelot* differs in a remarkable way from that of the *Cligés*, where the opposite poles of the central conflict were love and marriage, entangling Cligés and Alis in a constant web of action. In the *Lancelot*, Arthur, the husband, sadly observes Guenevere ride off with Kay, knowing she might not return, but not stopping her; he receives her joyfully when she comes back from Logres; otherwise, he does not participate in the action, except for the fact that it is he who has made Guenevere a married woman.

The tenets of Courtly Love hold, among other things, that the husband cannot enter into a "love" conflict. Marie de Champagne, to whom Chrétien attributes the *sens* (treatment) and *matière* (theme) of the *Lancelot* in the third verse of the poem itself, cogently illuminates this view in a letter published as part of the seventh dialogue in *The Art of Courtly Love* of Andreas Capellanus:[10]

We declare and we hold as firmly established that love cannot exert its powers between two people who are married to each other. For lovers give each other everything freely under no compulsion of necessity, but married people are in duty bound to give in to each other's desires and deny themselves to each other in nothing. . . .

. . . a precept of love tells us that no woman, even if she is married, can be crowned with the reward of the King of Love unless she is seen to be enlisted in the services of Love himself outside the bonds of wedlock.

The elimination of Arthur as an active force in the love triangle poses a problem of structural arrangement. In progressing along the road to his ultimate goal, the love of Guenevere, Lancelot must overcome many obstacles; among them, the claims of his love rivals, not Arthur but Gawain and Meleaganz.

4/16

THE LOVE RIVALS

The essential conflict in Courtly Love is the one which confronts two polar opposites:[11] pure love, "the union of the hearts and

---

10. See also Cross and Nitze, *Lancelot and Guenevere*, p. 69; Frappier, *Chrétien de Troyes*, pp. 124–27; Guyer, *Main Stream of French Literature*, p. 10; Holmes, pp. 170–74; Nitze, "Sans et matière dans les œuvres de Chrétien de Troyes," pp. 14 ff; Voretzsch, pp. 291–92; Lazar, pp. 60–64, 233–37.

11. Denomy, *Heresy of Courtly Love*, p. 23: "[Pure love] ... is a love wherein desire is a means towards an end: progress and growth in virtue, merit, and worth. Desire is an integral part, an essential part, but what is of the very essence of Courtly Love is its ennobling force, the elevation of the lover effected by a ceaseless desire and yearning for union with a worthy lady. ... Pure love consists in the union of the hearts and minds of the lovers." See also p. 26: "At the opposite pole according to the courtly code is false love, evil and impure, founded on sensuality for its own sake, faithless,

minds of the lovers," and false love, "faithless, promiscuous and mercenary." Gawain is Lancelot's rival in pure love, at least as a possibility; a brave and virtuous knight, second only to Lancelot, he is prepared to accomplish the most valiant deeds in her behalf. But his refusal to endure the mockery of the cart effectually proves the superiority of Lancelot's love and eliminates him as a true rival. The Gawain incidents, then, are marginal, functioning to throw Lancelot's submission as a lover into greater relief.

Meleaganz represents false love. Guenevere must be protected from him by guards delegated to do just that on orders of Bademagu. This false love is not entirely without power; one might expect Guenevere to resent her abduction sufficiently to allow Lancelot full retaliation against the defeated Meleaganz, yet it is she who orders Lancelot to spare his life. In this, as in all things, Lancelot shuns any manifestation of jealousy, content to obey her will. The other end of the triangle is thus Meleaganz, interacting in the web of the action; the Meleaganz incidents are therefore minor narremes, expanding the core narremes relating to the main conflict between the lovers, Lancelot and Guenevere.

4/17
THE COURTLY LOVERS'-TRIANGLE QUARREL

The theme of the *Lancelot*, which counterposes two main rivals, outside of wedlock, for the love of a married woman, must be taken into account in any scheme of classification. The difference between the structural patterns of the *Erec* and the *Cligés* is obvious: there are no rivals in the love affairs of Erec-Enide and Alexander-Soredamors; there is a rivalry in the Cligés-Fenice-Alis relationship. There is justification for classifying these as two different types of narreme: the lovers' quarrel and the lovers'-triangle quarrel.

In the *Lancelot*, however, the replacement of the husband by a second rival does not alter the basic situation of the love triangle. This is still a lovers'-triangle quarrel. We may say that in the two examples above, we have two different narremes. The courtly-lovers'-triangle quarrel does not add a third narreme to our inventory in this category, but simply a variant of the second narreme. We will therefore call this pattern Type RIIa, provided the autonomous core system otherwise agrees with the previous models.

promiscuous and mercenary. Such a love is but a counterfeit of true love, the source of evil, practiced by the wanton, the criminal and the debauched."

4/18

SUBSTRUCTURE

The opening scene of the *Lancelot* is an abduction of the queen. Meleaganz announces to the court that he holds knights and ladies in captivity, and then craftily stops, pretending that he has finished. After reaching the door of the hall, on his way out, he suddenly introduces the bait: the queen can free the captives, if she comes to the forest to him, escorted by her champion, and then safely return. This act of treachery of Meleaganz against Guenevere, forcing her to accompany him against her will (mildly against her will), is the brief prologue, which sets Gawain (mentioned first) and Lancelot (left unnamed) in rival pursuit of her.

The courtly lovers'-triangle quarrel then begins. The principal lover, Lancelot, proceeds to a number of tests, commencing with an insult. Guenevere's is the will that subjects him to ridicule, in this and later incidents as well, but it is only a goad to spur him on to the acts of prowess rendering him worthy of love. The tests are on an ascending scale: humiliation (the cart), desire (the willing damsel), anguish (the comb), joy (the strands of hair), torture (the Sword-bridge), and at last, the face of death. At the end of all this, the (almost) perfect lover (he did hesitate two steps at the cart!) is entitled to his reward: union with his mistress.

At this point, Meleaganz re-enters the expanded core system in an epilogue. He offers the queen an insult, charging her with adultery. Her champion, Lancelot, defends her in an (interrupted) judicial duel. To prevent Lancelot from resuming the duel, Meleaganz commits an act of treachery, luring him into a trap. Lancelot leaves on parole, is champion at the tournament, and returns to prison. This time, he escapes and kills Meleaganz.

The major and minor narremes fall into a main plot, Lancelot-Guenevere, and a subordinate plot, Meleaganz-Guenevere, linked by the status of Lancelot as Guenevere's champion:

LANCELOT-GUENEVERE	MELEAGANZ-GUENEVERE
I *Prologue*	*Subordinate Plot*
	a/ Act of treachery (abduction)
II *Main Plot*	
1/ Courtly lovers'-triangle quarrel	
2/ Insult	
3/ Acts of prowess	
4/ Reward	

III *Epilogue*

        b/ Insult (charge of adultery)
        c/ Inconclusive punishment (duel)
        d/ Second act of treachery (trap)
        e/ Punishment
        f/ Final test
           i/ Victory of Lancelot in tourney
        g/ Final reward
           ii/ Death of the traitor

Lancelot's final test, doing his "worst," is both an expansion of the acts of prowess, and a link with Meleaganz, since it is a part of the punishment of the traitor who wishes to prevent just that. The final reward for Lancelot, though it is conclusive in its total victory over Meleaganz and the firm establishment of Lancelot's fame, carefully omits any mention of Guenevere, now safely home with her husband. Chrétien undoubtedly had good reason to leave this insoluble problem to Godefroi de Leigni.

4/19

YVAIN: SUPERSTRUCTURE

The *Yvain,* or *Chevalier au Lion,* is the story of a shadow triangle; Yvain, the hero, falls in love with the inconsolable widow of a knight he has killed. In a preliminary episode, Yvain's cousin Calogrenant relates a humiliating adventure in the Forest of Broceliande; at the prodding of an ugly giant, he has poured water on a stone at a magic spring, calling forth a thunderous storm, and evoking an angry knight, who insultingly laid him low in combat.

Pledging his cousin vengeance for this insult, Yvain hurries to the spring, pours the water on the stone in the proper ritual, and fights his battle with the knight, whom he wounds mortally. Pursuing his fleeing opponent, Yvain is trapped in a narrow passage at the palace gate; a fair maiden of the castle, whom he had once befriended, gives him a ring to make him invisible, and gives him food and shelter. Because of the ring, the search for the knight's killer is fruitless; unseen, Yvain hears the knight's lady insult him for a craven and a coward. Exhausted by the fury of her despair and grief, she is yet so lovely that Yvain feels doomed to be her slave.

The damsel, Yvain's friend, now intercedes with the desolate widow, Laudine, pleading his case as a suitor. With her husband gone, who is there to defend the spring? And what stouter defender than Yvain, who has already proved himself superior in combat to her late husband? After a night of soul-searching, and at the advice of her liegemen, Laudine summons Yvain to an audience. When Yvain offers to do her will in all things, she falls in love with him, and agrees to marriage.

King Arthur and his knights arrive at the magic spring, to find Yvain settled as lord of the castle. After feasts and rejoicing, Gawain, who has fallen in love with Lunete, the damsel, now counsels Yvain on the dangers of degeneration after marriage, urging him to seek further adventures. Convinced, Yvain asks Laudine for permission to escort Arthur back to his realm and to participate in the coming tourneys. She grants him a year's leave, insisting that he return by St. John's day, on pain of losing her love. With a tearful farewell, Yvain pledges his word; but as new tournaments succeed old ones, the year passes before he remembers his promise to his wife. Laudine, having counted each day, sends word to Arthur's court that Yvain has betrayed her and need never return.

In a frenzy of despair, Yvain goes mad, living a savage, lonely life in the woods. He is found by two damsels and their mistress; with magic ointment they cure him, and he protects them from the fierce onslaughts of their enemy Count Alier. The lady offers him marriage and her possessions, or other reward, but he departs alone and pensive. Proceeding through the woods, Yvain encounters a lion in great danger from a serpent; set free, the lion accompanies him from here on, serving him as master. Soon Yvain comes upon Lunete, wandering in despair, since she has been accused of treachery to her mistress in favor of Yvain; she has furnished bail that in forty days she will present a knight to defend her or forfeit her life at the stake. He swears to reward her devotion to him by protecting her at the proper time.

On the way to the judicial duel for Lunete, Yvain slays a giant who has killed two nephews of Gawain and is now threatening their four brothers and a sister. He arrives as Lunete is at the pyre, defeats her enemies, and substitutes them for her at the stake. In his next adventure, Yvain is forced to fight two devils for the hand of a lovely maiden; the lord of the manor, whose daughter is the prize, holds three hundred damsels in thrall at the loom. With the aid of the lion, Yvain defeats the monsters and frees the bondwomen, refusing the daughter and the rich marriage offered him. Next, protecting a daughter of the lord of Noire Espine, who has been cheated of her rights by her sister, Yvain finds himself in combat with a knight he cannot defeat, even after long and agonizing struggle; it is Gawain. When they learn each other's identity, each concedes that the other is victor; Arthur is required to terminate the dispute, and he does, in favor of the wronged damsel. At long last, Yvain finds himself at the magic spring again.

Once more, Lunete reminds Laudine that she is defenceless. She tells her mistress that the famous Knight of the Lion is at odds with his lady; were Laudine to promise every aid in effecting a reconciliation between them, his services would be available. Laudine swears to do everything in her power. When Yvain is brought to her, she realizes that she has been neatly trapped. But her husband declares that he has dearly paid for his guilt and sin in staying away from his wife (the exact opposite of Erec's problem). The two lovers are now reconciled for good.

4/20

THE LOVERS' QUARREL

The relationship between Yvain and Laudine differs to a certain degree from that of the others previously described, since Laudine is a widow. There is a temptation, perhaps, to consider this a "shadow" love triangle, since the dead husband is a potent force, at least briefly, in keeping the couple estranged. For a time, Laudine appears to be inconsolable, and her grief too deep-seated to permit love to grow.

Esclados the Red, Laudine's husband, does not enter into the action, however, except for the insult to Calogrenant, which begins the romance, and the fight with Yvain, bringing the two lovers together for their first meeting. Thereafter, the conflict of the lovers concerns the two of them alone; there is no rival for the love of Laudine. In the true sense, she has no obligations to anyone else, and only her voluntary actions, in response to Yvain's behavior, keep the two apart. This must be considered a lovers' quarrel of the Type RI pattern, assuming that the other narremes of the core system are also identical in the substructure.

4/21

SUBSTRUCTURE

The *Yvain* opens with an account by Calogrenant, telling of an insult inflicted upon him by Esclados the Red. Yvain constitutes himself his cousin's champion, setting off on a quest for revenge. The battle with Esclados the Red is a test of his prowess, and results in the initial reward, love and marriage with Laudine. This then is the prologue, leading to the main plot.

The lovers, husband and wife, are separated by Yvain's conflicting desires, to stay with his new bride and to go off in search of adventure. The lovers' quarrel results from the wife's admonition to return by a certain date. This is an incipient insult, expressing doubt in the strength of his love, possibly furnishing the motivation for his "forgetfulness." In overstaying his leave, Yvain offered his wife a more serious insult; she in turn compounded the first by driving him away altogether. The depth of his love, however, is shown first by his giving himself over to madness, and after his cure in performing the notable acts of prowess which lead to the reward, the final reconciliation of the lovers.

The functional analysis thus results in an expanded core system, in which four minor narremes form a prologue to a main plot, containing four major narremes:

i Expansion: Prologue
  a/ Insult, the remarks and blows against Calogrenant.
  b/ Quest, Yvain, Calogrenant's champion, seeks revenge.
  c/ Test, the victory over Esclados the Red.
  d/ Initial Reward, the love and hand of Laudine in marriage.
ii Autonomous Core System: Main Plot
  1/ Lovers' quarrel, between Yvain and Laudine.
  2/ Insult, the doubt of one, and the forgetfulness of the other.
  3/ Acts of Prowess, the deeds in defence of the helpless.
  4/ Reward, the reunion with the lover, Laudine.

This scheme, very much like that of *Erec*, except for the lack of the expansion at the end (final test and final reward, see 4/7), shows remarkable unanimity with that romance, in the autonomous core system. All the romances show a strong family resemblance in the substructure, the chief functional difference relating to the nature of the lovers' quarrel.

4/22

THE ARTHURIAN ROMANCES OF CHRÉTIEN DE
TROYES: SUMMARY

The narremic patterns of the autonomous core systems in the four romances, like those of the eight epics, consist of four major narremes each:

1 The Conflict of the Lovers
  a/ *Erec*, Type RI, the lovers' quarrel, Erec and Enide.
  b/ *Cligés*, Types RI and RII.
    i/ *Cligés* I, the lovers' quarrel, Alexander and Soredamors.
    ii/ *Cligés* II, the lovers'-triangle quarrel, Cligés, Fenice, and Alis.
  c/ *Lancelot*, Type RIIa, the courtly lovers'-triangle quarrel, Lancelot, Guenevere, and Meleaganz (Arthur excluded).
  d/ *Yvain*, Type RI, the lovers' quarrel, Yvain and Laudine (Esclados the Red excluded).
2 The Insult
  a/ Enide challenges Erec's sovereignty.
  b/ i/ Soredamors makes Alexander feel like a fool.
    ii/ Cligés feels that he would look like a fool if he spoke.
  c/ Guenevere subjects Lancelot to abject humiliation.
  d/ Laudine exacts a promise which throws doubt on Yvain's love.
3 The Acts of Prowess
  a/ Erec proves his worthiness by deeds of valor in the presence of Enide.
  b/ i/ Alexander defeats the traitor, Count Angrés.
    ii/ Cligés defeats the Duke of Saxony, abductor of Fenice.
  c/ Lancelot passes every test of fitness in an ascending scale of difficulty.
  d/ Yvain successfully defends the interests of the helpless.
4 The Reward
  a/ Erec and Enide are reconciled, and crowned by King Arthur.
  b/ i/ Alexander and Soredamors are united at last, through the intercession of Guenevere.
    ii/ Cligés and Fenice, after punishing the traitor, regularize their union in marriage.
  c/ Lancelot and Guenevere find the solace of courtly love.
  d/ Yvain and Laudine are reconciled, through the intercession of Lunete.

4/23

NARREMIC VARIANTS

The second, third, and fourth narremes of the romances: the insult, the acts of prowess and the reward (very much like Type II of the French epic; see 2/14) show variations in the superstructural details, but these need no special discussion, since they are merely variants of the same narreme in each case. The first narreme, however, concerns the conflict of the lovers, and falls into two main classes: the lovers' quarrel and the lovers'-triangle quarrel. The love of husband and wife (Erec and Enide), of the timid lovers (Alexander and Soredamors), and of the suitor and widow (Yvain and Laudine) are variants of the former narreme. For the latter, the variants are: the good and the bad rival for the love of a married woman (Lancelot and Meleaganz for Guenevere); and the worthy lover and the wicked husband vying for the wife (Cligés, Alis, and Fenice). In the choice of the first narreme as the place for variants, the romances differ from both the French and the Spanish epics.

4/24

THE EPICS AND THE ROMANCES:

NARREMIC OPPOSITIONS

The epics and the romances analyzed all agree in beginning the main action with a quarrel among selected protagonists. The three narremes of quarrel arising most frequently are: the family quarrel, the lovers' quarrel and the lovers'-triangle quarrel; the single occurrence of the dynastic quarrel (*Fernán González*) suggests the possibility that still other kinds of relationship-conflicts may be found in the mass of medieval narrative production, for example, a heroes' quarrel between otherwise unrelated but evenly matched opponents, a rebellious-vassal quarrel, and the like.

The narreme of motive likewise occurs in a number of guises: the insult, the killing in action, the fight for the inheritance, and the disruption of the marriage. Among these, the insult is by far the most common. Although there is a wide range in the kinds of insult offered, to be discussed later, a possible division may be made between the covert insult, silent but definitely implied, and the overt insult; provisionally, however, these will be taken as variants of the same narreme. It may be expected that other narremes of motive will be added to the inventory, from other works.

The third and fourth narremes, respectively the act of treachery and the punishment, or the acts of prowess and the reward, appear to form a *cluster*;[12] in each case, the result is the natural one. If the

12. A cluster, in linguistic terminology, is a sequence of two or more items of the same class, for example consonants within a word. Eng. *bring* begins with a two-member consonant cluster /br/, *spring* with a three-member cluster /spr/; see Hockett, *Course in Modern Linguistics*, pp. 86–87. Among our narremes, the act of treachery regularly forms a two-member cluster, with the punishment as the second member; the narreme acts of prowess is regularly followed by the reward. Similarly, the family quarrel and the insult regularly form a cluster in the French epics analyzed, but only sporadically in the Spanish group.

samples are adequate basis for judgment, the medieval narrators did not indulge in the paradox of good rewarded by evil and evil rewarded by good; there is no telling, however, what thorough search will reveal.

The narremic oppositions are formed by the different choices possible in each of the four categories indicated:

QUARREL	MOTIVE	ACT	RESULT
Family	Insult	Treachery	Punishment
Dynastic	Killing	Prowess	Reward
Lovers'	Inheritance		
Lovers'-triangle	Marital break		

The four categories above constitute the frame of the narrative; and each one is a slot[13] to be filled in that frame. The narremes which may fill the same slot are said to be in opposition[14] to each

13. In the tagmemic approach to the analysis of syntax, a slot "is any position in an utterance where morphemes or morpheme sequences may occur, and which has some kind of grammatical function"; Elson and Pickett, *Beginning Morphology-Syntax*, p. 9. In the utterance *Boy meets girl*, there are three grammatical slots, or positions: subject, predicate, object. Each slot is filled with a member of a class of forms: *boy*, noun; *meets*, verb; *girl*, noun. The abstracted frame for this utterance is: subject-slot: noun; predicate-slot: verb; object-slot: noun. It accounts for numerous other utterances, structurally similar, but with different meanings, e.g. *Man needs food*, *Time heals wounds*, etc. The narremic frame (or core), as presented in this work, contains four slots: quarrel, motive, act(s), result. The classes that fill these slots are the subdivisions that appear under these four categories in section 4/24.

14. An opposition refers to a "... relationship which we conceive as existing between units which may figure in a given context and which, at least in this context, are mutually exclusive"; see Martinet, *Elements of General Linguistics*, pp. 36, 100. Eng. *pin* has three phonemes: /p i n/; the phoneme /p/ appears in the first position, in the context of /-in/; all the other phonemes of English which may figure in this same position, e.g. /b/ *bin*, /f/ *fin*, /t/ *tin*, /d/ *din*, /k/ *kin*, /l/ *Lynn*, etc., are in opposition to it, and all are mutually exclusive in that only one of them at a time can occupy the first position in the context of /-in/ to form a meaningful English word. The same holds true for the oppositions in the context of /p-n/, *pan, pun, pen, pone*, etc., and for /pi-/, *pip, pym, pick, pig, pill, pit*, etc.

In each slot of the narremic frame, there is an opposition, i.e. a forced choice among the various classes which may fill that position in the context of the rest of the slots. In the epic, for the first position, family quarrel and dynastic quarrel are opposed to each other (the *Fernán González* uses both in a striking variation, beginning with a dynastic quarrel, but using the family quarrel later, principally as a superstructural addition to fill out the act of treachery). In the romance, for the same slot, the oppositions are: lovers' quarrel and lovers'-triangle quarrel; the distinctive feature is the presence or absence of a love rival, and therefore the courtly lovers'-triangle quarrel is not in opposition to, but a variant of, the lovers'-triangle quarrel. See also Guiraud, "L'expression du virtuel dans le *Roland* d'Oxford"; Vinay and Darbelnet, *Stylistique Comparée*, p. 12; Marouzeau, *Lexique de la terminologie linguistique*, p. 161; Pei, *Glossary of Linguistic Terminology*, p. 188.

other; normally, only one narreme goes into a slot, though it may occasionally occur as a compound form, for example, the dynastic-family quarrel (*Fernán González*). In the frame, the narreme is a minimal structural unit filling a slot in the sequence of functional incidents constituting the narrative. Although segmentally a unit, the narreme is capable of subdivision into minimal characteristic features, permitting the classification of narremic variants.

4/25

MINIMAL NARREMIC FEATURES

The narremes which occur in each slot of the frame take on concrete form as variants, with their own characteristic minimal features. In the quarrel slot, the least common denominator is the tie that binds the antagonists; the differentiating factor is the nature of the conflict. The family quarrel, the lovers' quarrel and the lovers'-triangle quarrel all hinge on the problems of kinship. Kinship relations are either inherent, by blood, or acquired, by marriage, courtship, or adoption. The family quarrel may therefore be subdivided by internal type: husband and wife, uncle and nephew, father and son, and the like (see 3/11). These minimal features, however, may also characterize the lovers' quarrel (Erec and Enide, husband and wife), and the lovers'-triangle quarrel (Cligés and Alis, uncle and nephew), among such other variants as the suitor courting the maiden, the wife, or the widow. An additional, distinctive feature is involved, the presence or absence of love as a central focus of the quarrel and the presence or absence of rivalry in the love conflict.

In the motive slot, a distinctive feature is the presence or absence of disparagement, that is, the insult narreme, as opposed to such other narremes as the killing in action, the fight for the inheritance and the marital break. Variants of the insult fall into the overt and the covert types. The former may be verbal: disparagement of courage (Louis' father, Charlemagne), of appearance (Charlemagne's wife), or knightly diligence (Guibourc and Enide), of the lover's promise to return (Laudine); or it may be physical, for example, the killing of the servant under the protection of the lady's mantle (Doña Lambra). The covert insult may be oblique, attacking the lover through an acknowledged repulsion against love and lovers in general (Soredamors), or it may be direct, either inhibiting the lover from expressing his feelings (Fenice) or subjecting him to intense humiliation (Guenevere). All the narremes in this category involve an injury, an attack on the pride, the property, the marital status, or the life of the injured party, individually or in combination; it is the nature of this specific attack which is the minimal distinctive feature differentiating these narremes.

The third slot, the act of treachery and the acts of prowess, likewise shows a wide range of variants. Treachery may take the form of military invasion (Isembart), false offer of marriage (Fernán), ambush (Infantes de Lara), false mission (Gustioz), attempt on the brother (Doña Urraca), poisoning of the husband (Countess Aba). The acts of prowess may involve success in war (Guillaume and the Saracens, Alexander and Angrés at Windsor, Cligés), success against intrigue (Guillaume and Louis' rights), the performance of impossible deeds (The Twelve Peers and their *gabs*), the tests of personal valor in individual combat (Erec, Lancelot), the protection of the helpless (Yvain). The least common denominator in all these variants is violent activity, called up in response to the challenge proposed; the distinctive feature differentiating the two narremes is the goal of the activity: treachery is evil and prowess good.

The variants in the fourth slot are tied to those in the third. The more evil the treachery, the more serious is the punishment. Isembart, Ruy Velásquez, Doña Lambra and the Countess Aba merit death by their acts; Doña Urraca is suspected of an unsuccessful plot, but not convicted, and so escapes punishment; Fernán González is not badly harmed, indeed the contrary, and the queen of Leon is not molested. The punishment may be effected by the injured party, or as a variant, by a surrogate (Mudarra). The reward variants are: reconciliation of husband and wife (Charlemagne and the queen, Guillaume and Guibourc, Erec and Enide, Yvain and Laudine), reconciliation of the lovers (Alexander and Soredamors, Cligés and Fenice, Lancelot and Guenevere), royal alliance (Guillaume with Louis through Blanchefleur).

4/26

CONCLUSION

There is a striking parallelism in the narremic sequences or patterns of the autonomous core systems in the French and Spanish epics and in the romances. Noteworthy is the underlying uniformity of a structural framework consisting of four major narremes in each one analyzed. Equally remarkable is the overlapping, in epic and romance, of identical narremes: the insult, acts of prowess, and reward, serving as conclusive evidence of the intimate structural relationship between the two genres. The most striking aspect of the comparison, however, centers not around the similarities, but the special differences in the slot sequences of the core system.

The French epics differ from the other two groups in selecting the third slot as the center of typological difference; uniformly spurred on by the insult, the protagonists respond either with an act of treachery or acts of prowess. The Spanish epics also differ from the other two groups; but the typological division, centering on the second slot, is based on a variety of motives, though the response is uniformly the act of treachery. The typological division in Chrétien's romances falls into the first slot, where the basic issue is the nature of the quarrel in the love relationship.

These results, though preliminary and tentative, show the need for a new approach, through functional analysis, of the complete epic output in medieval France, Spain, Germany, and neighboring regions, including the Scandinavian[15] saga, and related narrative productions such as the romances; a gigantic task, outside the scope of this work. They make possible an objective reappraisal of literary strictures such as those of Comfort:[16]

... for [Chrétien's] lack of sense of proportion, and for his carelessness in the proper motivation of many episodes, no apology can be made. He is not always guilty; some episodes betoken poetic mastery. But a poet acquainted, as he was, with some first-class Latin poetry, and who had made a business of his art, ought to have handled his material more intelligently, even in the twelfth century. The emphasis is not always laid with discrimination, nor is his yarn always kept free of tangles in the spinning.

Regardless of the changes which new knowledge may bring, helping in the revision of these concepts, one conclusion seems definitive: the medieval narrative poets consciously ordered their material in a specific structural sequence, analyzable into nar-

---

15. Outside the medieval field, narremic analysis was the method used in Vehvilainen, *Swedish Folktale*; it is being applied by Glen W. Campbell to the picaresque novel of Lesage, in a thesis nearing completion at the University of Montpellier.

16. Chrétien de Troyes, *Arthurian Romances*, p. xi. This kind of criticism is reminiscent of scholars' complaints that the "lapses" of Vulgar Latin were due to the "carelessness" of the scribes, violating the standards of Classical Latin. We prefer to see in the "errors" the evolution of new standards. Similarly, the medieval poets were "acquainted ... with some first-class Latin poetry," but were under no obligation to follow the structural norms of another age. It is their own norms, revealed by analysis of their own productions, with which we are concerned.

remes. As a consequence, no matter how widely stories may differ in their superstructure, or in the intricacies of formal arrangement into main plot, subordinate plot, prologue, and epilogue, a common basis is provided for structural comparison by the narremes of the autonomous core system, the heart and center of the narrative. It is this method that will be applied to such outwardly different stories see (1/3–1/10) as the two great epics, the *Roland* and the *Cid*.

A Functional Analysis of the Roland and the Cid

CHAPTER FIVE

Chanson de Roland: The Family Quarrel

5 Chanson de Roland:
The Family Quarrel

5/1

THE FAMILY QUARREL:
NARREME OR MARGINAL INCIDENT?

In all the epics previously analyzed, the main action has developed from a family quarrel; and everywhere, except in the *Poema de Fernán González*, this quarrel has been the initial impetus giving shape and dimension to the elaboration of the plot. This is true also of the *Roland* where the dispute between Roland and his stepfather Ganelon is unquestionably a family quarrel.[1] Although Ker recognizes[2] the connection between this quarrel and the catastrophe which follows it, he inclines to the view that it is a subordinate element in the poem: "In *Roland*, for example, though the main action is between the French and the Moors, it is jealousy and rivalry that brings about the catastrophe. ... This sort of jealousy, which is subordinate in *Roland*, forms the chief motive of some of the other epics. These depend for their chief interest on the vicissitudes of family quarrels. ..." It is the criterion of function which must determine whether the conflict between Roland and Ganelon is subordinate, that is, a marginal incident; or rather narremic, one of the essential links in the structural sequence of events.

5/2

THE CONFLICT BETWEEN ROLAND AND GANELON

The first key to the understanding of the further action of the poem is supplied by the dispute between Roland and Ganelon. It is this dispute which leads directly to Ganelon's act of treachery, the central core of the poem (see 1/4). Although there has been considerable discussion, as we shall see, concerning the basic causes for the conflict between the two men, the poet himself

---

1. The quarrel between stepfather and stepson adds another type to the list (see 3/11).
2. *Epic and Romance*, p. 298.

provides the evidence that not least to blame is the family relationship which binds them together.

Although, as Knudson[3] maintains, the poet does not explicitly state that Roland and Ganelon have had family difficulties in the past, he clearly never lets us forget they are related through marriage. Roland's mother has taken a second husband, a rich, proud, and powerful noble, respected and admired by all; his only fault, if it can be called that, is the fact that he is a "stepfather."[4] The attempt by Jenkins to relegate the stepfather motive and the dangerous-mission motive to secondary status and to consider as "the real spring of the action" Ganelon's envy of Roland's greater wealth is not clearly supported by the text itself; on the contrary, in the text, the reference to the family relationship is sharp and unmistakable.

5/3

THE "STEPFATHER" AS EPITHET

In his edition of the poem, Jenkins[5] himself points to the most likely center of the gathering storm which will envelop the older and the younger man, namely, the use or misuse of the word "stepfather." It is Roland who first interjects the word in a deceptively casual fashion. At the council held by Charlemagne to discuss Marsile's peace offer, the emperor requests the nomination of an envoy to send to the Saracens with the French reply.

277 Ço dist Rollant: "Ço ert Guenes, mis parastre."[6]

Roland's suggestion that Ganelon be sent as the envoy may in itself be sufficient to account for the towering rage with which

3. "Etudes sur la composition de la *Chanson de Roland*," p. 55: "... si le poète avait été clair on n'aurait eu ni à poser cette question ni à y répondre par des conjectures hasardées."

4. Monge, *Etudes morales et littéraires*, p. 88: "Ce Ganelon a épousé la mère de Roland; depuis longtemps il est jaloux de son beau-fils, de sa gloire et de sa puissance." See also Jenkins, "Why Did Ganelon Hate Roland?" p. 120: "... the step-father motive, and the dangerous mission motive, were both secondary in the poet's mind, not primary; ... for the poet the primary motive, the real spring of the action, was that Ganelon, being a covetous man and envious of Roland's greater wealth, had hated him on that account before ever Charles had reached the seventh year of the Spanish war."

5. *La Chanson de Roland*, p. 28, note: "*Parrastre* may mean not only 'stepfather,' but also 'a poor imitation of a father'; it may well be that Roland ... was at the moment not averse to risking the ambiguous word in the presence of the same barons who had heard Ganelon accuse him of *orgueil* and *folage*."

6. Mortier, *La Version d'Oxford*. (*Roland* quotations are from this paleographic ed.).

Ganelon greets the proposal, but the evidence strongly supports Jenkins' opinion that the word he uses implies a gratuitous insult, serving in effect as an epithet. This would help to explain the fury of Ganelon's immediate response, in which the repetition of the word clearly marks it as the source of his anger:

> 286 Dist a Rollant: "Tut fol, pur quei t'esrages?
> Ço set hom ben que jo sui tis parastres ..."

Ganelon plainly considers the family relationship to be at the bottom of their mutual antipathy; he explicitly gives this as the basic reason for Roland's selection of him for a mission of almost certain death:

> 288 Si as juget qu'a Marsilium en alge!

Roland may not be seeking initially here to provoke his stepfather, but careless words may have serious consequences.

5/4
ROLAND'S DEFENSE OF GANELON

Feeling the need for some deep-seated reason, beyond the text, to account for Ganelon's violence, Bédier[7] postulates an obscure, ancient grudge against Roland; this is plausible, but the accusation made directly, that Roland is trying to get rid of an unwanted stepfather, is serious enough to explain, if not to justify, the immediate outburst of rage and its tragic consequences later. This interpretation is supported by the fact that throughout the poem both men are continually aware, in a negative as well as a positive sense, of their kinship. On the positive side, Roland will not permit his companion Oliver to malign his stepfather. Suspecting treachery, just prior to the ambush, Oliver calls Ganelon a "felon" and "traitor" (1024). Roland is deeply disturbed at this reflection on his family:

> 1026 — "Tais, Oliver," li quens Rollant respunt,
> "Mis parrastre est, ne voeill que mot en suns."

Obviously, Roland cannot believe that a member of his family would stoop to such an act of treason; even this late, he is ready to defend his stepfather, to the point of telling Oliver to keep quiet! When he later comes to accept Ganelon's guilt as fact, he

---

7. *Les Légendes épiques*, III, 413: "... il croit que Roland veut sa mort, et sa méprise vient de ce qu'une haine obscure, ancienne, dont lui-même ne sait pas encore toute l'intensité, l'anime contre son fillâtre ..."

mentions his stepfather by name, but this time in a negative spirit, since he refrains, undoubtedly by design, from any allusion to their relationship.

> 1456 Ço dist Rollant: "Oliver, compaign, frere,
> Guenes li fels ad nostre mort juree;
> La traïsun ne poet estre celee ..."

Only with the uncovering of the treachery is Roland prepared to disown his stepfather.

5/5
THE "STEPSON" AS EPITHET

There is an artistic parallel, noted by Bédier,[8] in Ganelon's reciprocal treatment of the problem of kinship. After Ganelon returns safely from his mission to Marsile, Charlemagne calls another council, and requests another nomination, this time for the leader of the rearguard which will protect the main army on its way back to France. In perfect correspondence to the scene in which Roland has named his stepfather to be sent on the dangerous mission as envoy, Ganelon now designates his stepson for the present arduous task.

> 743 Guenes respunt: "Rollant, cist miens fillastre ..."

The connotation of contempt[9] is clearer here than in Roland's use of "parastre," since Ganelon adds with ill-concealed sarcasm:

> 744 "N'avez baron de si grant vasselage."

It is not difficult to imagine the tone in which this "praise" was uttered, since Charlemagne publicly excoriates him for it.

> 746 Si li ad dit: "Vos estes vifs diables.
> El cors vos est entree mortel rage ..."

Thus the term "fillastre" parodies Roland's usage in form and content. Even more important, perhaps, it stresses the fact of their family relationship.

8. III, 421.
9. Jenkins, p. 62, note: "... *fillastre* may mean 'poor imitation of a son;' for this contemptuous or derogative force, see the exx. collected by Cooper *Word Formation in the Roman Sermo Plebeius* (1895), p. 192 ff. and cf. Dante, *Inf.* xii, 112."

5/6

GANELON'S REJECTION OF ROLAND

In contrast to Roland's defense of Ganelon's character against Oliver's charges, we know that very early in the poem Ganelon has already set the trap which will destroy his stepson, thus indicating a crude rejection of Roland as a member of his family. In order to succeed, this plan must remain secret. Later, however, when Ganelon faces a charge of treason involving the murder of Roland, he denies that his act is treason, but readily admits causing Roland's death. Since there is no longer any need to conceal his rejection of the younger man, he refers to him not as his stepson, but as Charlemagne's nephew:

> 3769 "Seignors, jo fui en l'ost avoec l'empereür,
> Serveie le par feid e par amur.
> Rollant sis nies me coillit en haür,
> Si me jugat a mort e a dulur."

According to this evidence, Roland and Ganelon are always conscious of their kinship, even to the point of deliberately denying it when circumstances call for an open break between them. We must try then to find the basis for the ill-feeling which, given the nature of their characters, divides them.

5/7

THE ANTIPATHY OF ROLAND AND GANELON

Roland's dislike of his stepfather, which comes through in his quarrel with him in council, is nevertheless moderate. This is proved by the fact that, in spite of the violence of their dispute, and even after being formally defied in public and later designated for the rearguard by Ganelon, Roland refuses at first to believe Oliver's charge of treason. Ganelon, on the contrary, hates his stepson so bitterly that he is capable of entering into a plot with the Saracen enemy to encompass his death.

It might be inferred that Ganelon is a person characteristically given to hate. The poet, however, precludes this supposition instantly by showing another phase of his private family life, his devotion to his wife and son, Roland's mother and half-brother. Afraid that he may not return from his mission, Ganelon carefully entrusts these loved ones to Charlemagne's care (310–16), leaving his properties and honors to his son, whom he expects never to see again. The apparent mawkishness of his tone elicits a curt criticism from the emperor, his brother-in-law.

> 317   Carles respunt: "Tro avez tendre coer ..."

In spite of Charlemagne's obvious sarcasm, Ganelon's attachment to his family seems real enough. It may be that this is the ultimate source of his hatred for a son thrust upon him.

5/8

THE SIGNIFICANCE OF THE FAMILY QUARREL

Before his departure for the Saracen camp, Ganelon sends a last, tender farewell greeting to his wife and child:

> 361   "De meie part ma muiller saluez,
>
> . . .
>
> 363   E Baldewin, mun filz que vos savez,
>   E lui aidez e pur seignur le tenez."

Ganelon's insistence that Baudouin is his heir, and should receive the homage due him, may provide a clue to his hatred of Roland. The popularity, power, and *desmesure* (excess of character) of the latter may well have aroused in the older man the suspicion that Roland might attempt to deprive his half-brother of his birthright. On at least one occasion, when Roland offers to undertake the mission to Marsile in Ganelon's place, the stepfather declares very plainly that, whatever the bond of kinship between them, there is no relationship of a property nature.

> 297   "Tu n'ies mes hom ne jo ne sui tis sire."

Far from being a subordinate element, this family quarrel between stepfather and stepson[10] is the foundation for the incident of the insult, giving it a new meaning in the frame of the events which follow.

10. Pellegrini, "Intorno al vassalaggio d'amore," "... la macchina degli avvenimenti della *Canzone* riceve il moto iniziale da un odio famigliare (quello tra Rolando e Gano). ..."

CHAPTER SIX

Chanson de Roland: The Insult

6 Chanson de Roland: The Insult

THE NARREME OF MOTIVE

The poet has so cleverly concealed the inner springs of the developing conflict that critics have been led to doubt the existence of a recognizable motive for it. Plath[1] sees no motive at all given in the text and therefore posits, as did Bédier (see 5/4), differences of long standing, occurring even before the poem begins. In an effort to solve this problem, while remaining close to the lines of the poem, Jenkins[2] tried the method of emending certain passages. The quarrel can nevertheless be fully understood on the basis of the text itself.

Concretely, the conflict between Ganelon and Roland begins to take form at the first council of Charlemagne, meeting to discuss the Saracen offer of peace, after seven years of war. It is in character for Roland to suspect a trick and to hold out for a conclusive decision; Ganelon, on the contrary, has had enough and is willing to settle for a bird in the hand. This spark of difference, fanned into flame by the heady winds of debaters' eloquence, is ignited by the clash in temperament and character of the two men.

6/2

THE CHARACTERS OF ROLAND AND GANELON

From the very beginning, Roland and Ganelon are presented as diametrically opposite[3] in character. They are both warriors, and good ones, but differ in their attitude toward war. Roland loves combat: in a good cause, for God, sovereign, friends, honor; but chiefly for its own sake as knightly competition, and for the glory that goes with victory.

> 1110   Quant Rollant veit que la bataille serat,
>   Plus se fait fiers que leon ne leupart.

1. P. 8: "... der Dichter gibt kein Motiv an und lässt auch so ohne weiteres keines erkennen, da schon zu Beginn des Rolandliedes die Differenz zwischen Ganelon und Roland besteht."
2. "Why Did Ganelon Hate Roland?" Also Waltz, *Rolandslied*, pp. 29–33.
3. Sternberg, p. 4.

Nothing is more characteristic than his rash refusal to sound the horn summoning Charlemagne to his aid and that of his beleaguered rearguard; not only is he ready to meet the challenge of battle unafraid, he looks forward to it with eager anticipation.

Ganelon can also give a good account of himself in dangerous situations. At no point is his courage a matter of doubt. But the basic difference between the two men is very clearly shown in the scene at the council where one urges war and the other peace. Not unexpectedly the first to speak, Roland boldly counsels the emperor to continue the fight, if need be, forever.[4]

> 210   "Faites la guer(re) cum vos l'avez emprise:
> En Sarraguce menez vostre ost banie,
> Metez le sege a tute vostre vie. ..."

While the other Franks maintain silence, Ganelon begins to attack Roland fiercely ("mult fierement," 219). "What matters it to this man," he cries, "how we die?"

> 226   "Ki ço vos lodet que cest plait degetuns,
> Ne li chalt, sire, de quel mort nus muriuns."

Unlike Roland, Ganelon is not interested in the fight for its own sake, nor does he wish to court death unnecessarily.

6/3

THE VERBAL DUEL

The peace offered by the Saracen Marsile includes his conversion to Christianity, submission as vassal to Charlemagne, and surrender of Spain to the conquerors. Since the full purpose of the war would thereby be achieved, Ganelon in council sees the issue as a simple choice between folly and wisdom; nor does he hesitate to point out which side he represents, and which side Roland.

> 228   "Cunseill d'orguill n'est dreiz que a plus munt.
> Laissun les fols, as sages nus tenuns."

It takes a brave man to call Roland, Charlemagne's "strong right arm," a fool, in public and to his face; Ganelon is beyond all doubt courageous. Uttered with a smile, in jest, these words might perhaps have been passed over easily, but the indications are that Ganelon did not smile as he spoke them. Knowing Roland as we

---

4. Bédier, *La Chanson de Roland*, p. 198. "Roland conseille à Charles la guerre à outrance. ..." (Bédier here rejects Jenkins' emendation of *vie* to *vide* "shrewdness, ability." See Jenkins, *La Chanson de Roland*, p. 22).

do, we may rightly suspect that they will burn, linger, and return. ... The opportunity for Roland to reply in kind to his stepfather presents itself almost immediately.

Charlemagne needs an envoy to deliver the Frankish reply to Marsile; a man powerful enough to convince the Saracens of Frankish resolution. Naimon, Roland, Oliver, and Turpin each volunteer in turn, but are rejected as being too valuable[5] to risk being lost in this enterprise. When the emperor calls for the nomination of a baron of his marches for this purpose, a brilliant idea occurs to Roland. Since it is Ganelon's advice to continue the peace negotiations that has carried, let Ganelon bear the message.[6]

Roland's immediate motive in thus selecting his stepfather for the admittedly risky enterprise has been subject to considerable speculation. According to Bédier[7] and Bertoni, it was his intention to confer honor in this way upon Ganelon. Pellegrini and Ruggieri convincingly refute[8] this idea, at least as Roland's main motive. Jenkins argues, on the other hand, that Roland has sincerely chosen the best[9] man available. Let us consider the circumstances: an envoy is needed for a delicate affair of state. Nominating an incompetent, untrustworthy, or cowardly delegate would be an act of disloyalty to the emperor and his interests. Roland has no reason to doubt Ganelon's qualifications or ability; on the contrary, who is better fitted to implement the peace plan than the man most convinced of its wisdom? It is along this line of subtle, brilliant reasoning that the underlying basis of the insult must be examined.

Ganelon responds to the nomination with intense displeasure. Since he is obviously not motivated by fear or lack of courage, the source of his irritation must be sought in Roland's attitude. The latter has been smarting under a verbal attack as a counselor of foolishness; this a man of his pride cannot overlook. He notes that the others, himself included, have volunteered for the task, but not Ganelon. Those who do offer themselves are quickly refused because the emperor has too great need of them. Nothing could

5. Plath, p. 6.
6. Monge, *Etudes morales et littéraires*, p. 88: "Ganelon lui a répliqué d'une façon très acerbe. Puisqu'il trouve si bon et si sage de faire la paix avec Marsile, qu'il s'en charge!"
7. *Les Légendes épiques*, III, 413; see also *La "Chanson de Roland,"* p. 113.
8. "L'Ira di Gano," pp. 161–62. See also "A proposito dell'ira di Gano," p. 163; and Waltz, p. 30.
9. *La Chanson de Roland*, p. 28: "Roland's motive ... is, in all probability, sincere: Ganelon is the best man for the difficult task; the Francs (*sic*) think so (v. 279) and Roland says so (v. 294). Roland even offers to go in Ganelon's stead." See also Le Gentil, *La Chanson de Roland*, pp. 94–95.

be more satisfying and psychologically rewarding in the circumstances than to name the "wise man" whose very acceptability to the emperor would prove how much less he was needed than the others. Ganelon understands the situation very well; he knows that Roland is paying back a score.

Jenkins assumes correctly that in accepting and confirming Ganelon's nomination the Franks show they respect his abilities;[10] in the present context, however, their action also implies that they consider him more expendable than the others. A perceptive individual, Ganelon responds to the implication rather than to the comparatively less important compliment. Thoroughly enraged, he hurls his rich furs to the ground and does not hesitate to utter open threats of vengeance against his stepson.

> 289 "Se Deus ço dunet que jo de la repaire,
> Jo t'en muvra(i) un si grant contr(a)ire
> Ki durerat a trestut tun edage."

If God permits him to return, declares Ganelon, he will engage in so great a feud with Roland that it will last his whole lifetime! How will Roland react to this?

Roland's proud response to Ganelon's public defiance is deeply significant for an understanding of the developing dispute.

> 292 Respunt Rollant: "Orgoill ói e folage. ..."

These words of Roland's are an exact duplication[11] of Ganelon's own expressions; they are perfectly apt to the new occasion, and they are sweet revenge. If further proof is needed that these same words have rankled, and that Roland has now seized an opportunity to repay his former humiliation, the evidence is at hand; Roland gives an explicit reason for nominating Ganelon.

> 294 "Mai(s) saives hom, il deit faire message. ..."

Is this a simple statement of sincere belief on the part of Roland that Ganelon is actually the best man for the task, or is it rather an echo of the older man's advice to the emperor:

> 229 "... as sages nus tenuns ...,"

words with which Ganelon has characterized his own wisdom in comparison with Roland's folly? The inherent logic is as perfect

---

.. 10. *La Chanson de Roland*, p. 28. See also Le Gentil, p. 95; and Haase, *Über die Gesandten in den altfranzösischen Chansons*, p. 9.
11. Jenkins, p. 30. See also Le Gentil, pp. 95–96.

as the parallel in language. The messenger chosen must be a wise man, if success is to be achieved; therefore, the best man is the one who has virtually nominated himself by vaunting this quality in himself. Roland is now ready to press home his advantage.

In the face of Ganelon's resistance to his nomination, Roland delivers the *coup de grâce*, offering directly to go in his place:

> 295 "Si li reis voelt, prez sui por vus le face. ..."

Is this to be regarded literally as no more than a simple offer to substitute for Ganelon? The words themselves may be taken initially at their face value; Roland would have gone without a murmur had he been permitted to do so, just as he would gladly have undertaken the dangerous mission when he first volunteered for it. In the present context, however, Roland's offer carries overtones of meaning. It was originally Ganelon's idea to classify the two men in separate categories, one wise, the other foolish. Roland has now made it clear that a wise man is needed for the difficult undertaking. It has thus become completely impossible for a man of Ganelon's pride and position to concede that Roland is after all the wiser of the two, the implication of his acceptance of his stepson's proposal. There is absolutely nothing left for him to do but to reject the offer, as Roland very well knows.

6/4
INSULT AND DEFIANCE

Were Ganelon the insensitive person that Bertoni[12] describes, his anger at being nominated should have been mollified by Roland's apparently generous proposal. It is precisely because of his acute sensitivity, however, that his emotional balance is so disturbed at this juncture. Thoroughly worsted in a battle of wits which he himself has started, caught in a trap[13] devised by his own cleverness, he must consider his dilemma: accept Roland's offer to replace him, branding himself a fool and a coward; or reject it and be forced into a dangerous mission, exactly as planned by his enemy. Either way, he loses and Roland wins.

Cornered in this manner, Ganelon knows he must accept the

12. P. 113: "Gano non è uomo da comprendere il sentimento eroico, che anima Orlando. ..." See Waltz, p. 31.

13. Plath, p. 6: "Nun hat sich Ganelon in seiner eigenen Falle gefangen, und er gerät in eine ungeheure Wut, denn er glaubt, Roland habe den Rat in schlimmer Absicht gegeben."

mission; he knows also that he must give vent to his lacerated feelings:

299 "En Sarraguce en irai a Marsilie;
Einz i f(e)rai un poi de (le)gerie,
Que jo n'esclair ceste meie grant ire."

With this admission of Ganelon's, Roland has achieved the fullest possible measure of success in retaliation for verbal injuries received, and he now bursts into a roar of laughter.

302 Quant l'ot Rollant, si cumençat a rire.

Revenge is sweet, and hurt pride, in a hero, must be assuaged; but he has perhaps carried the matter just a little too far.[14] His laughter, though understandable, causes Ganelon's cup to overflow.

The impact of Roland's laughter is immediate, sweeping, and far-reaching; Ganelon is so thoroughly incensed that he becomes almost insane.

303 Quant ço veit Guenes que ore s'en rit Rollant,
Dunc ad tel doel pur poi d'ire ne fent,
A ben petit que il ne pert le sens. ...

Whatever Ganelon's previous sentiments toward Roland may have been, they are now[15] nothing but frank and undisguised hate. Turning to his stepson, he declares, in a tone not too difficult to reconstruct:

306 ... "Jo ne vus aim nient. ..."[16]

Taking the emperor to witness, Ganelon publicly proclaims his hatred of Roland, and issues a formal defiance not only to his stepson, but to his boon companions, the Twelve Peers, as well.

14. Ruggieri, p. 165: "Il nipote di Carlomagno intuisce tutto ciò, e ne ride apprezzantemente; male a proposito, perchè aumenta così nel padrigno il desiderio di vendetta. ..."
15. Plath, pp. 7–8: "... sicher ist, dass Roland Ganelon schwer gereizt und nichts getan hat, um ihn zu versöhnen." Plath himself, however, considers this insufficient motivation for the terrible act of treachery: "... denn noch nichts ist geschehen, was solch ein furchtbares Verbrechen wie den späteren Verrat Ganelons begründen könnte." (Plath is of course correct; Ganelon's failure to realize this weakness in his position will bring him public humiliation and tortured death.)
16. Jenkins, p. 31: "This may seem an anti-climax, but it is not so: the phrase is a legal one, still in use with diplomats who speak of 'friendship' and 'unfriendly' acts."

322 – "Sire," dist Guenes, "ço ad tut fait Rollant!
Ne l'amerai a trestut mun vivant,
Ne Oliver, por ço qu'il est si cumpainz;
Li duze per, por (ço) qu'il l'aiment tant,
Desfi les ci, sire, vostre veiant."

Ganelon is here deliberately setting the stage for a wholesale act of private vengeance. There is no indication of the form this vengeance will take, but one thing is certain: violence will occur. The urge which drives Ganelon forward is a most powerful incentive: the need for a proud man to avenge a public insult. It is therefore evident that this insult is essential to the internal sequence of incidents leading to the next development in the action.

CHAPTER SEVEN

Chanson de Roland: The Act of Treachery

7 Chanson de Roland: The Act of Treachery

THE ALTERNATIVES FOR VENGEANCE

The humiliating position in which Ganelon finds himself as a result of Roland's clever and insulting provocation has forced him into public expression of direct threats against his stepson and a formal defiance addressed to Roland and the Twelve Peers. Since the emperor and the assembled barons of the realm are witness to all this, he stands committed. There is nothing left for him but to select the manner of vengeance. Theoretically, according to Fundenburg,[1] he has three alternatives: "When *desfiance* has been regularly made, the results, as a general rule, might be of three kinds: (1) private warfare; (2) individual execution of vengeance; (3) the duel."

As Ganelon leaves on his mission, he is still a "noble vassal" (352) to the Franks. There is no evidence that he has, as yet,[2] formulated his plan of vengeance, not to speak of an act of treachery. The first hints, however, of a scheme involving treason begin to appear during conversations with Blancandrin, Marsile's envoy to Charlemagne, as they journey together to the Saracen camp. The ground is being carefully prepared for an act of treachery.

Blancandrin, described by the poet earlier as "des plus saives paiens" (24), proceeds now to give proof of his pagan wisdom in his rich and suggestive conversation with Ganelon. The opening phrase is the one best suited to bridge the gap of enmity and gain Ganelon's accord.

> 370   Dist Blancandrins: "Merveilus hom est Charles. ..."

Preoccupied as Ganelon must have been with his own tumultuous thoughts concerning death, humiliation, and vengeance, he is nonetheless impelled to listen and agree.

> 376   "Jamais n'ert hume ki encuntre lui vaille."

1. *Feudal France in the French Epic*, p. 92.
2. Faral, *La Chanson de Roland*, pp. 208–09.

A common ground between them thus established, Blancandrin presses his advantage by praising the other Franks as great also, subtly suggesting, at the same time, the presence of evil counselors among them who are the cause of all the trouble. Rising eagerly to the bait,[3] Ganelon can think of only one such trouble-maker, Roland.

> 381 Guenes respunt: "Jo ne sai veirs nul hume,
> Ne mes Rollant, ki uncore en avrat hunte. ..."

In his cunning, Blancandrin has focused Ganelon's attention on the need to separate in his mind the evil counselor Roland from the good but misguided Franks. The way is now open for a plan of revenge to begin taking shape.

7/2

THE IDEA OF ROLAND'S DEATH

Thinking through his problem while conversing with Blancandrin, Ganelon announces that peace between the two camps can only be established by the death of Roland. It is at this point, no doubt, that the possibility of murder enters his calculations.

> 391 "Seit ki l'ociet, tute pais puis avriûmes."

Although still without specific plan, Ganelon indicates that he may have found his step-son's Achilles' heel.

> 389 "Li soens orgoilz le devrait ben cunfundre.
> Kar chascun jur de mort (il) s'abandunet."

Roland's well-known stubborn pride can be used as the key to his destruction. Since all this is exactly what the cunning Saracen has been so adroitly working toward, there can be no doubt of his sincerity as he hastens to agree.

> 392 Dist Blancandrins: "Mult est pesmes Rollant. ..."

Fired by a common purpose, the two supposed enemies, Ganelon and Blancandrin, ride along, watching each other carefully, but essentially in agreement, pleasantly anticipating the death of a mutual enemy.

> 402 Tant chevalcherent Guenes e Blancandrins,
> Que l'un a l'altre la sue feit plevit,
> Que il querraient que Rollant fust ocis.

3. Jenkins, La Chanson de Roland, p. 38: "Ganelon does not care to discuss the Franks: he still thinks of himself as loyal to them and to Charles ... but he welcomes the opportunity to denounce Roland. ..."

As they approach Marsile's camp, they are still thinking in general terms of a mutual pledge to seek Roland's destruction. Ganelon[4] has, however, come to two fundamental conclusions: that Roland's desire for conquest is insatiable and that only his death can assure the peace and the success of this mission. Blancandrin's eager assent suggests to him a vague but developing plan whereby the Saracens, whose stake in the peace and thus in Roland's death is as great as his own, can serve as the instrument of his vengeance.

7/3

GANELON'S PLOT

Ganelon is aware that the Saracens have themselves initiated the negotiations for peace. With all of Spain, except Saragossa, conquered by the Franks, Ganelon knows that they are at the end of their resources. In order to attain his goal, which requires a renewal of the fighting spirit on their part, he must now arouse them to a pitch of fury.[5] This he proceeds to do by first making Marsile thoroughly angry with the burden of his message. In a hostile tone, he conveys Charlemagne's order that Marsile become a convert to Christianity in return for the right to keep half of Spain, or be prepared for the alternative, a shameful death.

The importance of this speech in the working out of the plot is clearly indicated by the narrator's specific reference to the oratorical skill[6] demonstrated by Ganelon at this point.

> 426 Par grant saver cumencet a parler
> Cume celui ki ben faire le set. ...

The poet is obviously not referring to skill in the art of the diplomat, an ability which Ganelon probably possessed in great measure, but to the skill of the artful schemer whose every word is a weapon. Every word, every phrase, every intonation forces the blood pressure of his listener a notch higher.

> 430 "Iço vus mandet Carlomagnes, li ber,
> Que recevez seinte chrestientet;
> Demi Espaigne vos voelt en fiu duner."

---

4. Faral, p. 209.
5. Bédier, *Les Légendes épiques*, III, 417: "Lui qui sait Marsile découragé, désemparé, prêt à s'humilier très bas pourvu que Charles s'éloigne, il s'acharne à réveiller sa colère, et ... il l'injurie, gratuitement, à plaisir, il le fouaille de son message, comme à coups de fouet." See also Knudson, "Etudes sur la composition de la *Chanson de Roland*," p. 53: "Cette colère et cette révolte, c'est le traître qui doit lui-même les provoquer. ..."
6. Bédier, III, 416–20; Jenkins, p. 41.

Step by step, the punishment is outlined, should Marsile be unwilling to accept the terms:

> 433   "Se cest acorde ne vulez otrier,
> Pris e liez serez par poested;
> Al siege ad Ais en serez amenet,
> Par jugement serez iloec finet;
> La murrez vus a hunte e a viltet."

There is great courage here, as well as cunning, but the stakes are high.

Ganelon, while speaking to Marsile as boldly as he does, has by no means forgotten Basan and Basile, his predecessors as envoys of Charlemagne, who were beheaded by the Saracens for their pains. In calling this a risky game for Ganelon, Bédier is correct, although his explanation of its motivation[7] is perhaps overly ingenious; if Ganelon's own words bring him within a hair's breadth of death, Roland can hardly be blamed. There is, however, subtle irony in these very words of Ganelon's (435–37), which, so efficacious of his immediate ends, at the same time clearly, if unwittingly, foreshadow his own death before Charlemagne "al siege ad Ais." Perhaps he has a momentary inkling of the punishment in store for him should his plans go awry.

Faral's analysis (p. 210) of Ganelon's conduct and motivation is more plausible: the traitor is arousing the Saracens to a frenzy in order to concentrate their hatred on Roland. In addition, as Le Gentil[8] has shown, the bolder Ganelon's challenge, the stronger is his self-justification of complete loyalty to Charlemagne's interests, with which his own private rancor against Roland has nothing to do. His success in this ambiguous project fully justifies the poet's praise of his forensic skill.[9] Repeating Charlemagne's offer that Marsile may keep half of Spain, Ganelon now adds gratuitously that the other half will go to Roland who will prove a difficult partner indeed!

7. III, 418: "Au jeu qu'il joue, Ganelon risque sa vie. ... Il veut que Roland l'ait réellement mis à deux doigts de la mort pour que demain ... il puisse se dire qu'il ne fait que réclamer son dû." See Pellegrini, "L'Ira di Gano"; Ruggieri, "A proposito dell'ira di Gano," p. 163.

8. *La Chanson de Roland*, pp. 98–99.

9. Knudson, p. 52: "Il est intéressant de voir comment le traître entreprend sa tâche à la fois délicate et ardue. Il ne sait pas d'abord, que la soumission des Sarrasins n'est pas sincère. Il n'a aucune raison de soupçonner qu'ils ne demandent pas mieux que de trouver un autre moyen de salut. C'est donc avec beaucoup de précautions qu'il procède." Also, p. 53: "D'abord il prend un ton altier, insolent, méprisant, et ensuite il invente un mensonge propre à décevoir les espérances des Sarrasins et à les irriter profondément."

472 "Demi Espaigne vus durat il en fiet.
L'altre meitet avrat Rollant, sis nies:
Mulz orguillos parçuner i avrez!"

Ganelon's blunt statement about the division of Spain, half to Marsile and half to the "orguillos parçuner" Roland, is not the speech of a skilful diplomat solely intent upon the king's business. On the contrary, his deliberately irritating references to Roland and his reiterated threats of ignoble death unless Marsile capitulates, as well as the manner of delivery, prove that his main purpose is to anger Marsile. In response to this provocation, Marsile twice threatens his life; each time, Ganelon bravely takes sword in hand to defend himself. Then comes the moment for which Ganelon has been waiting; Blancandrin informs his master that the Frankish envoy has indicated a disposition to be helpful to them.

506 Dist Blancandrins: "Apelez le Franceis:
De nostre prod m'ad plevie sa feid."

Assuming a friendlier attitude, Marsile asks Ganelon when Charlemagne will tire of making war.

528 "Quant ert il mais recreanz d'osteier?"

This is Ganelon's opportunity; he responds that the war is not Charlemagne's fault at all.

529 Guenes respunt: "Carles n'est mie tels. ..."

In answer to Marsile's repetition of the question, Ganelon makes his point: the war will never end during Roland's lifetime.[10]

544 – "Ço n'iert," dist Guenes, "tant cum vivet sis niés. ..."

A third time, Marsile repeats his question and Ganelon again unhesitatingly replies:

557 – "Ço n'iert," dist Guenes, "tant cum vivet Rollant. ..."

The intricate pattern of repetition in the *Roland* has been described in detail;[11] in this instance, the purpose of the poetic device is clear. It brings into sharpest possible relief the goal toward which Ganelon is striving: the death of Roland. At the same time, it forcibly directs the attention of Marsile, who has his

10. Jenkins, p. 49: "Ganelon is here engaged in shifting the talk away from Charles and in concentrating attention upon Roland."
11. Gräf, *Der Parallelismus im Rolandslied*. See also Le Gentil, pp. 118–20.

own problems, toward that same goal. Even despite this repetition, Marsile still wonders if it might not be possible and preferable to defeat the Franks in open battle (564–66). Ganelon hereupon advises Marsile with the same wisdom he has displayed toward Charlemagne, employing in fact the same words.

> 569   "Lessez (la) folie, tenez vos al saveir."

Ganelon has a touching confidence in his own dark wisdom and in the stormy path down which it takes him on the road to treachery.

The time is now ripe for Ganelon to advance adroitly his treasonable proposal.

> 573   "En dulce France s'en repairerat li reis;
>   Sa rereguarde lerrat derere sei:
>   Iert i sis nies, li quens Rollant, [...] ço crei,
>   E Oliver, li proz e li curteis.
>   Mort sunt li cunte, se est ki mei en creit."

There is still, perhaps, a lingering spark of suspicion in Marsile's mind for, even yet, he does not see how this will bring about the certain destruction of Roland.

> 580   – "Bel sire Guenes, ...
>   "Cum faitement purrai Rollant ocire?"

The plot is now made explicitly clear: against the twenty thousand of the rearguard, Marsile must send five times that many.

> 587   ".xx. milie Francs unt en lur cumpagnie.
>   De voz paiens lur enviez .c. milie. ..."

Since Ganelon's private objective is revenge against Roland, he again displays his skill by underlining the certain results to be gained by the death of the young man: cessation of the war and lasting peace in Spain, that is, the accomplishment of Marsile's objective as well.

> 596   – "Chi purreit faire que Rollant i fust mort,
>   Dunc perdreit Carles le destre braz del cors,
>   Si remeindreient les merveilluses oz;
>   N'a semblereit jamais Carles si grant esforz;
>   Tere Major remeindreit en repos."

No prospect could be more pleasing to Marsile. Since the plan itself seems feasible, he embraces Ganelon in good fellowship. For the sake of form, however, he requires that his companion in conspiracy swear loyalty on his sword, Murgleis. He himself swears on a book devoted to the laws of Mohammed and Ter-vagant. They are now in this affair together; and they are aware of the implications of their undertaking.

7/4

THE IDEA OF TREASON

In coming to terms with each other, it is noteworthy that neither Marsile nor Ganelon balks at the word "traïsun." It is the Saracen who utters it first[12] in his request that the Frank swear an oath of loyalty.

> 605   "La traïsun me jurrez de Rollant si illi est."

Far from objecting to this, Ganelon gives assurance that he is prepared to do as Marsile wishes.

> 606   Ço respunt Guenes: "Issi seit cum vos plaist."

The poet concludes the scene with the very explicit statement:

> 608   La traïsun jurat, e si s'en est forsfait.

Apparently Ganelon squarely faces the fact that he is commit-ting an act of treason. It is therefore necessary to determine the meaning that the word has for him. The idea or concept of treason during the period in question has been defined by Riedel in *Crime and Punishment in the Old French Romances* (p. 25): "... we find actually listed as treason only about five offenses: theft from an overlord, truce-breaking, bearing false testimony with criminal intent, wounding without warning, and murder. ... To sum up: the fundamental concept of treason was ... the act of secret attack and injury. ..."

Ganelon and Marsile are thus equally guilty in a partnership devoted to treason; the former, since he is planning a murder in secret, the latter, because he is deliberately planning to make false promises with intent to break a truce. As usual, the poet adds his touch of saving irony: just before Ganelon's departure, to re-turn to Charlemagne with the traitorous message promising the submission of Marsile, the latter reminds him to be sure that Roland is actually designated for the rearguard.

> 656   "Pois me jugez Rollant a rereguarde."

12. The first mention of "treason" occurs earlier in the poem: 178 "Guenes i vint, ki la traïsun fist." This is not one of the personnages speaking but the poet himself, preparing his audience for future events.

Ganelon's reply to this is classic in its simplicity: he thinks he is wasting time.

> 659   Guenes respunt: "Mei est vis que trop targe!"

No doubt he sees the aptness rather than the irony of Marsile's remark; the crime is, after all, as yet only half committed. The next decisive step is to make certain that Roland is placed in harm's way; and it is Ganelon's task to arrange it. This surely accounts for his taking his life in his hands and, in fact, being impatient to do so, as he journeys swiftly to meet again the men he is betraying.

Back again in council, Ganelon reports the successful accomplishment of his mission, adding one lie upon another (680–91). Charlemagne, well pleased with the results, calls for the nomination of a leader to command the rearguard (see 5/5). This is the supreme moment for which Ganelon has risked and is risking so much; he hastens to name his stepson.

> 743   Guenes respunt: "Rollant, cist miens fillastre:
> N'avez baron de si grant vasselage."

Bédier[13] has skilfully analyzed the expertness with which the poet uses this scene to cast the first shadow of suspicion on the traitor. In spite of any fears or foreboding aroused, however, as the poet himself announces, there is a law of chivalry involved; like Ganelon in a similar position, Roland can make but one answer.

> 751   Li quens Rollant, quant il s'oït juger,
> Dunc ad parled a lei de chevalier:
> "Sire parastre, mult vos dei aveir cher:
> La reraguarde avez sur mei jugiet. ..."

It is indeed an honor for a worthy knight to be assigned a dangerous task and Roland is properly thankful to his stepfather. He boasts, as he is expected to, that Charlemagne will not suffer the slightest loss on his account. Ganelon concedes[14] this gracefully.

> 760   Guenes respunt: "Veir dites, jol sai bien."

With this temperate and courteous reply, Ganelon appears to be holding a door open which could lead to either friendship or enmity.

---

13. III, 421: "Qui donc dénoncera Ganelon? Il se dénoncera lui-même. ..."
14. Jenkins, p. 63: "... the traitor can afford to be polite. ..."

7/5

ROLAND'S DILEMMA

Ganelon's smooth response to Roland's boast was obviously not the kind that the latter was expecting. It seems a fair assumption that Roland has been baiting his stepfather. Perhaps Ganelon has already gone too far to turn back; it is certainly unlikely that he would confess his treasonable agreement with Marsile. He can nevertheless still prevent what he knows to be treason by simply telling Charlemagne that he fears treachery on the part of the Saracens and by warning him to guard against possible ambush. Even if Ganelon were prepared to take this improbable step, Roland himself, with his prideful character,[15] would prevent it.

It is perhaps an even fairer assumption that Roland was fully aware that his stepfather's courtesy was part of his hypocrisy. In any case, it is at this point that he sets the seal, as he will do once again in the affair of the horn, on his own death warrant. Since he has failed with his ironic thanks[16] to arouse anything but an apparently reasonable remark from Ganelon, Roland mockingly reminds the older man about his maladroit dropping of the glove and the baton, which had been part of his earlier humiliation. Neither the tone of his voice, which may easily be imagined, nor the violence of his language can lead to any but the most violent results.

> 763 "Ahi! culvert, malvais hom de put aire,
> Qui(d)ás le guant me caïst en la place,
> Cume fist a tei le bastun devant Carle?"

7/6

THE NARREME OF INSULT AND THE DEATH
OF ROLAND

Roland's mockery, in taunting Ganelon about his nervousness prior to his mission, simply reinforces the insult. It is not strange, however, that Ganelon feels no need to reply; the tables have now

---

15. Sternberg, *Das Tragische in den Chansons de geste*, p. 6.

16. Bédier, III, 426: "C'est Roland, qui dit tour à tour à son parâtre son remerciement ironique, puis son mépris. C'est Ganelon qui savoure pareillement l'ironie de Roland et son mépris. ... Et là est en effet le ressort de toute l'action. Ganelon a spéculé sur la fierté de Roland et de ses compagnons. ..."

been completely turned. This time it is Ganelon who places Roland in a position with just one move open.[17]

On the advice of Naimon, Charlemagne offers Roland one-half of the main army to strengthen the rearguard (785), but the latter's pride[18] does not permit him to accept; this would have been a display of the same kind of fear shown by Ganelon when the latter declared he was being marked for death. Just as the traitor foresees, Roland insists that he wants no more than the normal assignment of twenty thousand men. All along the way, Ganelon's plans are working out perfectly; the lamb[19] is being led, under his own power and by his own character, to the slaughter.

The insult has led directly to an act of treason. As part of that treason, the ambush takes place; the heroes, including Roland, are outnumbered and slain. The description of these events, though moving and effective, belongs to the superstructure of the story. Whatever the outcome of the battle, the next step in the substructure is inevitable: the punishment of the traitor for his real crime, the act of treachery.

17. *Ibid.*, III, 422: "Roland refusera donc de rester à l'arrière-garde? Il est bien tenu d'accepter, au contraire: il faut bien que quelqu'un reste, quel qu'il soit, comme naguère il a bien fallu que quelqu'un se chargeât de l'ambassade, quel qu'il fût. Le péril était-il alors moins évident qu'aujourd'hui? Ganelon s'y est-il dérobé? Ganelon a-t-il accepté qu'un autre le courût à sa place? ... le souci de son honneur suffit à retenir Roland au Port de Cize. ..."

18. Jenkins, p. 65: "This is a hint ... of Roland's recklessness, his *desmesure*; in blunt soldier fashion, he refuses reinforcements."

19. Bédier, III, 421: "Tout se passe en effet comme Ganelon l'avait prévu: ... Le traître bien à l'abri dans la coulisse, sûr de l'impunité, ses victimes menées confiantes au coupe-gorge, comme des moutons à l'abattoir. ..." See also Le Gentil, pp. 101–2.

CHAPTER EIGHT

Chanson de Roland: The Punishment and Epilogue

8 Chanson de Roland:
The Punishment and Epilogue

THE DEATH OF GANELON

The death of Ganelon, legally executed in the course of organized justice, is a spectacular climax toward which the poet has directed the activities of the story; in a sense, it gives the story its true meaning. But since, with the exception of Charlemagne,[1] nearly all the chief characters die, it is necessary to analyze the difference in the poet's attitude toward the deaths of the main characters (see 1/3–1/4).

Death is for some the reward of glory, to be enjoyed in the flowered fields of Paradise. The best example of this is Roland who meets death through the exaggerated virtue[2] of *desmesure*, a knightly fusion of reckless pride and overconfidence; in his own words:

> 1854   "Seignors barons, de vos ait Deus mercit!
> Tutes vos anmes otreit il pareïs!
> En seintes flurs il les facet gesir!"

It may well be that the death of Roland was the original kernel[3] around which the poem developed, for the poet was at least

---

1. Knudson, "Etudes sur la composition de la *Chanson de Roland*," 50: "On a prêté beaucoup d'intentions à l'auteur de la *Chanson de Roland*, mais la seule qui me paraît claire et indiscutable, c'est le dessin de servir à la gloire de Charlemagne." The *Roland* does serve the glory of Charlemagne by endowing him with a threefold victory: the triumph of arms, against the Saracens, of religion, through the conversion of Bramimunde, and of justice, exemplified by the execution of Ganelon. At the apex of this glory stands the triumph of organized justice.

2. Le Gentil, *La Chanson de Roland*, pp. 102–3: "Le drame de Roncevaux ... est par ses origines un drame humain. C'est la démesure de Roland qui l'explique. ... Roland, emporté par sa folle bravoure et son héroïsme plus qu'humain, fidèle jusqu'au bout à lui-même, vole vers la mort qu'on lui apprête et que lui-même se prépare. ... Roland aime la guerre pour la guerre. Il savoure l'âpre joie des combats. Il rêve de conquêtes. Le sentiment de l'honneur dicte toutes ses paroles et inspire tous ses actes. Nobles passions que les siennes, mais passions très terriennes, dont on ne sait encore s'il faut les condamner ou les absoudre, les admirer ou les blâmer." In Le Gentil's apt description, Roland's outstanding characteristic is "la splendide folie de l'héroïsme."

3. Pei, *French Precursors of the Chanson de Roland*, p. 103.

aware[4] that his hero had died at Roncevaux. This incident may indeed have been the immediate inspiration for the poem, rather than the conflict[5] between Roland and Oliver, as Bédier believes.

The killing of the Saracens[6] brings out another facet of the poet's attitude to death. Marsile, who dies as an infidel and breaker of his pledged word, is borne off by devils – and not to Paradise.

> 3646 Morz est de doel. Si cum pecchet l'encumbret,
> L'anme de lui as vifs diables dunet.

It is the death of Ganelon, however, the culmination of just punishment for a terrible crime, that serves as the explicit moral and *leitmotif* of the poem.

> 3974 Hom ki traïst altre, nen est dreiz qu'il s'en vant.

According to the poet himself, it is not right for one man to be able to boast of betraying another. For an act of treachery the culprit must be punished, and so serious is this crime in the eyes of the narrator that its punishment can only be death.

> 3959 Ki hume traïst sei ocit e altroi.

The responsibility of a traitor is great indeed, since it involves not only himself but others ("altroi") as well.

8/2

GANELON'S FAMILY

The criminal is not alone in his crime; not only the guilty individual, but the other members of his family as well must be rooted out, to extirpate the seed of treachery. This idea is so prominent and so persistent in the poet's mind that he gives a preview of it quite early in the poem. In the very midst of the battle of Roncevaux where the outnumbered Franks under Roland are losing heavily, he calls attention to the forthcoming trial of the traitor at Aix.

> 1406 Malvais servis(e) le jur li rendit Guenes
> Qu'en Sarraguce sa maisnee alat vendre;

4. Bédier, *Légendes Epiques*, III, 193: "Dans ce combat furent tués Egginhard, prévôt de la table du roi, Anselme, comte du palais, et Hrodland, comte de la marche de Bretagne. ..." Also, p. 194: "... la trame du récit d'Einhard ... est aussi la trame de la *Chanson de Roland*. ..."
5. *Ibid.*, p. 448.
6. See *supra*, chap. 1, n.15 for discussion of the death of Baligant, and the Baligant episode, as part of the superstructure.

So poorly did Ganelon perform his feudal duty to his household that he "sold" them at Saragossa; he will pay for this at Aix with his life and the lives of thirty of his household.

> 1408 Puis en perdit e sa vie e ses membres;
> El plait ad Ais en fut juget a pendre,
> De ses parenz ensembl'od lui tels trente
> Ki de murir nen ourent esperance.

Although the thirty members of Ganelon's family, held as hostages, do ultimately die by hanging, it is curious that the poet seems to be planning here the same punishment for the traitor (see 8/7). The suggestion of dismemberment ("ses membres") in this passage and the actual quartering by four horses, however, indicate that the poet leans more and more to a spectacular climax, in order to drive home his lesson. At all events, the poem moves inexorably toward the punishment of Ganelon; and the prime mover is the emperor himself.

8/3

THE DREAMS OF CHARLEMAGNE

Even prior to his departure on his mission to the Saracen camp, Ganelon had already stirred Charlemagne to personal criticism.

> 327 Ço dist li reis: "Trop avez maltalent. ..."

The emperor will remember Ganelon's quickness to anger. When the latter returns from his mission, Charlemagne must presumably thank him for a job well done. Noted for his wisdom, however, and recalling the malevolence of Ganelon, displayed in the incident of the *desfiance,* he is troubled. This shows up in the form of a first dream.[7]

> 718 Carles se dort, li empereres riches.
> Sunjat qu'il eret al greignurs porz de Sizer,
> Entre ses poinz teneit sa hanste fraisnine,
> Guenes li quens l'ad sur lui saisie. ...

Prophetically, Charlemagne directly envisions Ganelon seizing and breaking his ashen staff. This is followed by an even more terrifying, allegorical animal dream.

> 727 El destre braz li morst uns uers si mals.
> Devers Ardene vit venir uns leuparz,
> Sun cors demenie mult fierement asalt.

7. See Krappe, "The Dreams of Charlemagne."

Rushing to protect Charlemagne from the fierce bear (or boar)[8] and the leopard, a hunting-dog ("uns veltres") attacks the foe, but the outcome of the great battle is uncertain.

> 734   Dient Franceis que grant bataille i ad:
> Il ne sevent liquels d'els la veintrat.

Although these omens make Charlemagne reluctant to accept Ganelon's nomination of Roland for the rearguard, the requirements of *chevalerie* nevertheless compel both Charlemagne and Roland (see 7/4–7/5) to submit to the situation.

8/4

THE GUILT OF GANELON

Charlemagne's ominous dreams fail to reveal the exact nature of the threat, but they portend evil and point directly to its source. In answer to a question by Naimon, distressed by the emperor's care-worn appearance, the latter gives voice without concealment to his fear.

> 835   "Par Guenelun serat destruite France. ..."

Not only Charlemagne, but the entire Frankish army is oppressed by a foreboding of approaching disaster.

> 842   .c. millie Francs pur lui unt grant tendrur,
> E de Rollant merveilluse poür.
> Guen(e)s li fels en ad fait traïsun. ...

Although nothing specific has as yet occurred, the atmosphere is tense with premonition. The troops of the rearguard likewise develop a suspicion of evil at work to their detriment. Oliver is the first to give it voice when, from a vantage point on a small hill, he spies the advancing hosts of the enemy.

> 1024   "Guenes le sout, li fel, li traïtur,
> Ki nus jugat devant l'empereür."

More alert[9] than Roland to the implications of the situation, Oliver senses at once the connection between Ganelon's formal defiance (see 6/4) and the present ambush. Whether Roland's refusal to accept his stepfather's guilt at this time (see 5/4) is a sign of a lack of acuteness or, more likely, a demonstration of his strong family loyalty, it is wholly to his credit that he does not judge without proof. Evidence soon appears, however, of a kind

8. Jenkins, *La Chanson de Roland*, pp. 60–61.

sufficient to convince even Roland. Aelroth, Marsile's nephew and Roland's opposite number in the Saracen camp, taunts his opponent with the charge that he has been betrayed.

> 1191   "Feluns Franceis, hoi justerez as noz.
>   Traït vos ad ki a guarder vos out.
>   Fols est li reis ki vos laissat as porz. ..."

Aelroth cannot be accusing Charlemagne of betraying Roland by placing him in command of the rearguard and leaving him to the mercy of the Saracens, since the emperor was simply following the mandates of protocol in council and, indeed, Roland's own expressed wishes. The only plausible interpretation is that Aelroth is referring to the treachery of the renegade. As an envoy on a mission of public trust, Ganelon was under obligation to "guard" the interests of the Franks. This he had signally failed to do. There is no longer any reason for Aelroth to conceal the fact, since the victims cannot escape from the trap. Forced to accept as true the accusation that treachery has been committed, Roland must now face squarely the treason charge involving his mother's husband. His grief is sincere and natural.

> 1196   Quant l'ot Rollant, Deus! si grant doel en out!

Defending the propriety of his assignment to the rearguard by the emperor, Roland rushes furiously into combat, killing Aelroth; at the same time, he declares that Charlemagne will never condone the treason.

> 1207   "Ultre, culvert! Carles n'est mie fol,
>   Ne traïsun unkes amer ne volt.
>   Il fist que proz qu'il nus laisad as porz. ..."

After this speech, Roland begins to mention his stepfather's guilt, a fact which is henceforth impossible to overlook.

> 1457   "Guenes li fels ad nostre mort juree;
>   La traïsun ne poet estre celee. ..."

At this point, Roland announces the next great phase of the poem.

> 1459   "Mult grant venjance en prendrat l'emperere."

Before the poet actually turns his attention to the vengeance of Charlemagne, however, he gives Ganelon an opportunity to com-

---

9. *Ibid.*, p. 84: "It is Oliver who first suspects foul play, for he is more penetrating than Roland."

pound his guilt and to prove it indisputably to the Franks in the famous affair of the horn.

8/5

THE AFFAIR OF THE HORN

The scene, in which Roland first refuses and then insists on sounding the horn that might have saved his men from death in ambush, is divided, with the poet's customary skill, into two artistically parallel sections. The first part, a quarrel between Roland and Oliver, establishes those facets of character which engage the hero as the responsible architect[10] of his own fate; the second part, a quarrel between Charlemagne and Ganelon as they hear the horn on their way back to France, establishes, in complementary fashion, the criminal responsibility of Ganelon for treason.

As the scene opens, we recall that Oliver, viewing the approach of the Saracen hosts, at once suspects treachery. The overwhelming number of the enemy forces inspires him to request that Roland sound his horn at once, summoning back Charlemagne and the main army to their aid.

> 1051 "Cumpaign Rollant, kar sunez vostre corn:
> Si l'orrat Carles, si returnerat l'ost."

The request is wise: the safety of the rearguard hangs on Roland's assent. But the code of heroism,[11] in the extreme form espoused by Roland, rejects the slightest backward glance, the least hesitancy, which might be mistaken for cowardice. Roland therefore proudly replies that to sound the horn would be folly and mean the loss of his reputation in France. Wisdom counsels Oliver to repeat his request; this time, Roland responds that it would bring shame to his family. Even after Oliver's third request, Roland firmly insists, with more[12] than mere stubborn pride, that

10. Bédier III, 411: "... Roland et ses compagnons, loin de subir leur destinée, en sont les artisans au contraire, et les maîtres. ... Ce sont leurs caractères qui engendrent les faits et les déterminent, et mieux encore, c'est le caractère du seul Roland." Cf. Renoir, "Roland's Lament."

11. Jenkins, p. 86: "'Le refus de Roland d'appeler Charles à son secours est ... la vraie cause du désastre de Roncevaux: c'est un trait d'héroïque folie comme on en retrouve souvent dans l'histoire militaire de la France ... (G. Paris).'" Also Pei, "An Immortal Character in French Literature."

12. Pei, p. 193: "Roland is impetuous in speech, but clear-headed to the point of prophecy; had his original counsel been followed there would have been no betrayal, no ambush, no loss to the Franks. These details are lost sight of by those who see in Roland only the stubborn pride that leads him to refuse Charlemagne's offer of larger forces and Oliver's frantic plea that he call for reinforcements."

it will never be said that he has sounded the horn through fear of the pagans.

These two men, France's eternal symbol of friendship, are engaged in a quarrel wherein they personify respectively two allied human qualities in the heroic history of mankind: *fortitudo et sapientia*.[13] In the words of the poet:

> 1093   Rollant est proz e Oliver est sage. ...

Motivated by *sapientia*, wise Oliver foresees the great harm to come and blames Roland for his refusal.

> 1101   "Vostre olifan, suner vos nel deignastes;
>   Fust i li reis, n'i oüssum damage."

Brave Roland, prompted by *fortitudo*, is outraged by what appears to him, even in Oliver, to verge on cowardice.

> 1106   Respunt Rollant: "Ne dites tel ultrage!
>   Mal seit del coer ki el piz se cuardet!"

There is no doubt concerning the poetic value[14] of this first section of the scene. Essentially, however, from the functional point of view, it is a quarrel about reinforcements. Whether Charlemagne arrives in time to save his men or not, the next phase of the poem continues unaltered: the criminal must be punished. The real meaning of the horn incident must be sought elsewhere.

The first section is not yet complete, with Roland's refusal to sound the horn. Since the entire situation at Roncevaux is based on an act of treachery, the conflict of the poem will not be resolved by the outcome of the battle or the fate of its participants, important as these dramatic events may be to the superstructure. Functionally, the quarrel between Roland and Oliver gives the poet the opportunity to delineate his characters in the most moving fashion; but more vitally, it serves at the same time to foreshadow the moment when Roland does actually sound the horn. Interrupted temporarily by the pressing needs of battle action, the quarrel is once again resumed when the rearguard is all but wiped out. This time, reversing the preliminary roles, it is Roland who insists on sounding the horn, and Oliver who cries shame.

> 1705   Dist Oliver: "Vergoigne sereit grant
>   E reprover a trestuz voz parenz. ..."

Roland declares a second time that he will sound the horn. So

13. Nitze, "Two Roland Passages," pp. 236–37.
14. Bédier, III, 430–34.

deeply is Oliver affected that he threatens to break off Roland's engagement to his sister Aude. Although he is acting in good faith, with courage as his guiding force, his attitude wounds Roland deeply.

> 1722   Ço dist Rollant: "Por quei me portez ire?"

Oliver's reply, though ostensibly directed to Roland, must have struck home in many a knightly breast.

> 1725   "Mielz valt mesure que ne fait estultie.
>   Franceis sunt morz par vostre legerie."

Were this quarrel really essential to the substructure of the poem, it could easily have led to trouble at this point. Oliver's charges are very serious: Roland has caused the death of twenty thousand Franks not through heroic leadership worthy of the highest praise, but through a flaw in his character, *legerie*, the lack of the knightly quality of *mesure*. The poet permits this imposing criticism to pass unnoticed, because he has more important game in view.

The tenseness of the scene is dramatized by Roland's silence.[15] Sensitive to the implications of Oliver's harsh rebuke, the indomitable leader, known for his reckless and impulsive behavior, now hesitates. The impasse is resolved by Archbishop Turpin; sounding the horn, he tells them, will bring back Charlemagne to avenge them and give them decent burial. Roland may now do this without fear of misunderstanding. It is here that we see the true purpose of the horn incident; its function, from the standpoint of the substructure, is to call attention once more to Ganelon's responsibility, and his part in the developing story line.

The second section of the horn incident takes place thirty leagues away from Roncevaux; at this great distance, Roland's horn is heard. Charlemagne immediately recognizes its import.

> 1758   Ço dist li reis: "Bataille funt nostre hume!"

For Ganelon, who likewise hears it, too much is at stake to risk disruption of the ambush party. Vociferously, he tells the emperor that coming from anyone else, such a remark would have to be called a great lie.

> 1760   "S'altre le desist, ja semblast grant mençunge!"

15. *Ibid.*, p. 439: "A ces reproches, les plus durs qu'il puisse entendre ... et qui lui viennent de son plus cher compagnon, que répondra-t-il? ... Il se tait, et ce silence est la chose la plus sublime de la *Chanson de Roland*."

When Roland sounds the horn a second time, he does so with such force that his temples burst and the clear blood springs from his lips. The poet carefully stresses that he is heard this time not only by Charles (1766), but also by Naimon and the other Franks (1767). This can be nothing other than a device of the narrator to set Ganelon irrevocably against the whole Frankish army in a manner too obvious for them to ignore. The emperor declares with firm conviction that the horn would not have been sounded unless the men were engaged in combat. It is of course impossible for Ganelon to deny that which the whole army has heard. He must therefore attempt to deny its meaning.

> 1770 Guenes respunt: "De bataille est il nient!
> Ja estes veilz e fluriz e blancs;
> Par tels paroles vus resemblez enfant. ..."

This is dangerous ground that Ganelon treads. Taking the offensive, with a boldness greater even than his challenge to Marsile (see 7/4), he does not hesitate to beard the respected emperor to his face. His apparent composure, at this decisive moment which may spell success or failure for his plans, compels unwilling admiration. It is no trifling matter to tell Charlemagne that he is talking childish nonsense.

The explanation which Ganelon offers to account for the sounding of the horn is a subtle mixture of reason and humor

> 1773 "Asez savez le grant orgoill Rollant;
> Ço est merveille que Deus le soefret tant."

It is Roland's excessive vanity, he declares, which causes him to commit all sorts of acts even without the emperor's permission, as in the conquest of Noples (1775). The most insignificant trifles, he adds, simply offer Roland the occasion for brag and bluster.

> 1780 "Pur un sul levre vat tute jur cornant.
> Devant ses pers vait il ore gabant."

Given the gravity of the situation, Ganelon's lighthearted and whimsical description of Roland sounding the horn all day long in pursuit of a single rabbit is perfect in its simplicity; a simultaneous indication of Ganelon's courage in the face of grave danger and skill in the art of persuasion. It is exactly the right note on which to offer his advice to resume the march home.

> 1783 "Car chevalcez! Pur qu'alez arestant?
> Tere Major mult est loinz ça devant."

Perhaps (who knows?) it might have succeeded, except for the fact that the horn is heard a third time. There can be no doubt now that a battle is in progress. It is Duke Naimon who states this as a certainty.

> 1790   Respont dux Naimes: "Baron i fait la p(e)ine!
>   Bataille i ad, par le men escientre. ..."

In the light of what has preceded, the implication of Ganelon's advice cannot be overlooked. Naimon publicly charges him with treason.[16]

8/6

THE CHARGE OF TREASON

In plain words which leave no further room for doubt, Duke Naimon points the finger of accusation at Ganelon, standing before the white-haired emperor and his men, in imminent disgrace.

> 1792   "Cil l'at traït ki vos en roevet feindre."

This man who urges you to hang back, he informs the emperor, is a traitor! The very advice itself, even aside from previous public threats, is a form of outright treachery, since it endangers the rearguard for every moment of time lost in debate. Coupled with Ganelon's well-known animosity toward his stepson, the conclusion is inescapable: the traitor is exerting his energies and eloquence against rather than in their interests. There is no longer any reason for Charlemagne to hesitate.

> 1816   Li reis fait prendre le cunte Guenelun,
>   Sil cumandat as cous de sa maisun.

Since the emperor is now convinced, with thorough justification, of Ganelon's guilt, he hands the criminal over into the custody of the cooks and kitchen-boys, with strict instructions to guard him until the day of retribution.

> 1819   "Ben me le guarde, si cume tel felon!
>   De ma maisnee ad faite traïsun."

With these words, Charlemagne recognizes Ganelon's act as an attack against the royal household[17] ("ma maisnee"); the traitor

---

16. Jenkins, p. 136: "in Charles' army, this is the first public accusation of Ganelon, and it is followed by swift action. ..."

17. *Ibid.*, p. 138: "This is exactly Charles' accusation at Ganelon's trial; see vv. 3750 ff."

is at this moment in a most difficult and unpleasant situation. The question now is: what form will the punishment take?

8/7

THE INITIAL PUNISHMENT

The cook who receives Ganelon turns him over to one hundred of his fellows for swift and immediate chastisement.

> 1821 Cil le receit, si met .c. cumpaignons
> De la quisine, des mielz e des pejurs.
> Icil li peilent la barbe e les gernuns;[18]
>
> . . .
>
> 1824 Cascun le fiert .iiii. colps de son puign;
> Ben le batirent a fuz e a bastuns;
> E si li metent el col un caeignun,
> Si l'encaeinent altresi cum un urs;
> Sur un sumer l'unt mis a deshonor.
> Tant le guardent quel rendent a Charlun.

This description is comparatively long and detailed. It shows that the traitor is being subjected to the utmost indignity possible to a Frankish noble: the lowest element in the Frankish army can work their will on him; they pull out the hair of his beard and moustache, beat him with blows of their fists and with clubs, place a chain around his neck like a bear, and force him to ride on a pack-horse – apparently no punishment is considered too brutal or humiliating for him. Why then is he not killed at once? It cannot be that Charlemagne is waiting for further evidence of his guilt, or he would not have treated him as he did. It cannot be that he is not angry enough to do so, since he is described repeatedly as being in a fury (1812, 1834, 1842). Least of all can it be that there is no one in the French camp capable of killing him for at the proper time the criminal will certainly die.

The poet has already informed us, if the passage is authentic,[19] why the traitor is not to be executed on the spot: he will be punished only after a legal trial in the imperial capital at Aix (1406–11; see 8/2). In any case, the necessity for speed to rescue the rearguard would make it difficult for the Franks to pause, even for

18. The verse between 1823 and 1824, in the Oxford version, appears to be misplaced; see Jenkins, p. 138.

19. *Ibid.*, p. 109: "Luquiens questions the authenticity of these six lines, on linguistic and artistic grounds; it is certain that Ganelon is not to be hanged (v. 1409), although that was the usual punishment for traitors, and v. 1411 has no support at all in the other versions."

a moment, to take any steps. On the other hand, it is easy to imagine the extreme provocation under which Charlemagne and his
Franks are suffering as they speed along in mingled sorrow,
anxiety and fury, in the desperate hope of reaching Roland in
time. The temptation must have been very strong to give vent to
their rage and kill him without further ado.

Ganelon's position becomes even more precarious when the
Franks reach Roncevaux. At the discovery of the bodies of Roland,
the Twelve Peers, and the annihilated rearguard, the grief of
Charlemagne and his men is overwhelming. Despite any personal
feelings, however, the law will take its course: Ganelon will have
his legal trial. There is still a war on, with battles yet to be fought;
Marsile and the Saracens must be overcome and punished for their
misdeeds. Thereafter, however, the emperor himself, personally
involved through the murder of his nephew and greatest paladin,
will initiate proceedings in due form against Ganelon. The first
step, properly, will be to call together the peers of the realm in a
royal council.

8/8
EPILOGUE: THE KING'S COUNCIL

A trial such as Ganelon's, in which a great noble of the realm is to
be charged with murder and treason, is a solemn affair. This note
is adequately conveyed by the poet, as he sets the historical background of the scene.

> 3742 Il est escrit en l'anciene geste
> Que Carles mandet humes de plusurs teres.
> Asemblez sunt ad Ais, a la capele.
> Halz est li jurz, mult par est grande la feste. ...

Having assembled his vassals from all his lands, the emperor
requests them to give judgment in the case of Ganelon.

> 3750 "Seignors barons," dist Carlemagnes li reis,
> "De Guenelun car me jugez le dreit!"

Charlemagne acts as plaintiff,[20] making an explicit charge that
Ganelon has betrayed the Franks for financial gain.

20. *Ibid.*, pp. 258–59: "It is to be noted that the King cannot punish by his
own authority one of his vassals (or 'men'), no matter how guilty the 'man'
may be, without having summoned him to justify himself before a court of
his peers. ..."

3752   "Il fut en l'ost tresque en Espaigne od mei,
Si me tolit .xx. milie de mes Franceis
E mun nevuld, que ja mais ne verreiz,
E Oliver, li proz e li curteis;
Les .XII. pers ad traït por aveir."

In reply to Charlemagne's accusation that he has caused the loss of Roland, Oliver, the Twelve Peers, and twenty thousand Franks, Ganelon proudly admits the charge.

3757   Dist Guenelon: "Fel seie se jol ceil!"

He has no wish to play the role of a scoundrel by denying what he has actually done. It is not, however, greed on his part, as Charlemagne charges (3756), but greed on the part of Roland, which is the root of the trouble.

3758   "Rollant me forfist en or et en aveir,
Pur que jo quis sa mort e sun destrait. ..."

This passage has been considered ambiguous; nothing anywhere in the poem itself gives Ganelon the right to declare that Roland has "outdone" or injured him in some manner with regard to wealth and possessions. For this reason, Jenkins has emended the reading[21] of "forfist" to "sorfist" [*sorfaire* "to be in excess, to be overweening"]. Thus Ganelon seems to be saying, in this version, that his anger has been aroused by Roland's *desmesure* in taking too much booty as his share of spoils and then being overbearing about it. Although this explanation is plausible, it does not offer an especially strong defensive argument for Ganelon. The Oxford reading, on the other hand, if it is correct, provides another of the poet's consistent counterplays: having been accused of greed, Ganelon counters by laying it to Roland's account, rather than his own. Whatever the case with regard to "aveir," the one charge that Ganelon boldly and bluntly denies is that the deed which he has committed is in truth an act of treason.[22]

3760   "Mais traïsun n'en i otrei."

21. *Ibid.*, p. 262; see also his article, "Why Did Ganelon Hate Roland?" pp. 125–26. Also, Nitze, pp. 236–37: "I believe that ... it is wise to cling to O. ... At the same time, a reading is acceptable when it reflects not merely the text ... but also the context. ... Judged by this standard, Jenkins' *sorfist* ... suits 3758 admirably."
22. See Le Gentil, *La Chanson de Roland*, p. 136: "Son crime – le procès d'Ais le démontre – est donc le résultat d'une erreur et d'un refus également impardonnables. Ganelon est parvenu à se convaincre que sa vengeance n'était pas une trahison."

As Ganelon stands before his judges, he still presents a noble and imposing appearance, despite all his recent suffering.

> 3763 Cors ad gaillard, el vis gente color;
> S'il fust leials, ben resemblast barun.

His present disgrace is rendered all the sharper in contrast to what "might have been" had he only remained loyal to his trust. In his own eyes, however, he feels completely justified in all his acts, as he prepares an able defense of his case.

There is no doubt or confusion in his mind, as Ganelon confidently addresses himself to his defense, speaking to the assembled peers in a "loud voice."

> 3767 Puis s'escriat haltement, a grant vociz:
> "Pur amor Deu, car m'entendez barons!"

Gaining their attention, he skilfully reminds them of his long, loyal service to the emperor.

> 3769 "Seignors, jo fui en l'ost avoec l'empereür,
> Serveie le par feid e par amur."

Through no apparent fault of his own, this faithful servant of the king managed to arouse the hate of "Charlemagne's nephew," who, with malice aforethought, nominated him for a mission certain to lead to his death.

> 3771 "Rollant sis nies me coillit en haür,
> Si me jugat a mort e a dulur.
> Message fui al rei Marsiliun. ..."

It was only his own wisdom, continues Ganelon, that saved him.

> 3774 "Par mun saveir vinc jo a guarisun."

The pivot of Ganelon's defense is that he did not conceal his intentions; on the contrary, his public *desfiance* (6/4) of Roland and his companions was proper, open, and above board.[23]

> 3775 "Jo desfiai Rollant le poigneor
> E Oliver e tuiz lur cumpaignun;
> Carles l'oïd e si nobilie baron."

---

23. Monge, *Etudes morales et littéraires*, p. 117: "La guerre privée est considérée comme absolument légitime. On a le droit de venger ses injures personnelles. Ces idées sont inconciliables avec le christianisme; l'Eglise Romaine, qui n'admet pas la vengeance et qui réserve la justice humaine au pouvoir social, ne cessa jamais de les combattre. ..."

The whole affair, in short, is a matter of private vengeance, such as was his right, and not at all treason.[24]

> 3778 "Venget m'en sui, mais n'i ad traïsun."

This is no clear-cut case, with judgment and sentence settled upon even before the trial. The noble barons who are to render a decision do not answer immediately; they declare instead that they must take counsel with each other. While the judges are weighing the merits of Ganelon's defense, the latter is surrounded by thirty members of his household, hostages whose fortunes are so closely tied to his that, with him, their very lives are at stake. Among them is Pinabel, skilful in speech as well as arms (3784–85); to him, Ganelon turns for support. Pinabel, for whose strength and courage the Franks have the greatest respect, assures the defendant that his sword will guarantee the latter's safety. This strong "argument"[25] is overheard by the judges in consultation. As the poet ironically says:

> 3797 Pur Pinabel se cuntiennent plus quei.

The noble barons, moved in part by Pinabel's eloquent sword-arm, advise the emperor to be clement,[26] in view of Ganelon's previously unblemished record. In any event, Roland is dead; nothing they can now do will bring him back.

> 3803 "Morz est Rollant, ja mais nel reverreiz;"
>
> . . .
>
> 3808 Dient al rei: "Sire, nus vos prium
> Que clamez quite le cunte Guenelun,
> Puis si vos servet par feid e par amor.
> Vivre le laisez, car mult est gentilz hoem. ..."

Bound here by the customs[27] of his time, Charlemagne appears to be quite helpless. The poet shows him to be thoroughly angry.

> 3815 Quant Carles veit que tuz li sunt faillid,
> Mult l'enbrunchit e la chere e le vis;
> Al doel qu'il ad si se cleimet caitifs.

24. Taylor, *Medieval Mind*, I, 578: "His defense is feudal. ..." See also Le Gentil, pp. 109–11, 134–37, and Falk, *Etude sociale sur les chansons de geste*, p. 33: "Les trahisons, les attaques perfides, les guet-apens sont fréquents, et bien souvent ne paraissent pas être considérées comme indignes d'un chevalier de cette époque." (This is precisely what Charlemagne appears to be fighting.)
25. Bertoni, *La "Chanson de Roland,"* p. 125: "L'episodio non è privo di una certa comicità. ..."
26. Jenkins, p. 260.　　27. Bertoni, p. 124.

Bowing his head in presumed inability to counteract the decision,
and pouring forth his grief in the circumstances, all that Charlemagne can do is tell the judges how criminal[28] he considers them
to be.

> 3814   Ço dist li reis: "Vos estes mi felun!"

At this juncture, when all seems lost for the cause of justice, a
knight steps forward to support Charlemagne's role as plaintiff.

The young knight who proposes to act as Roland's champion is
not the heroic type, at least in appearance.

> 3820   Heingre out le cors e graisle e eschewid,
>   Neirs les chevels e alques bruns (le vis);
>   N'est gueres granz ne trop nen est petiz.

Courteously he addresses the emperor, telling him that he has at
all times faithfully performed his duties in the king's service. In
his judgment, he continues, whatever Roland may have done to
Ganelon, it was the duty of the latter to remember that so long as
Roland was on active duty for the king, he could not be touched.

> 3827   "Que que Rollant a Guenelun forsfesist,
>   Vostre servise l'en doüst bien guarir!"

Since Ganelon betrayed Roland under those conditions, he is
therefore a criminal guilty of perjuring and compromising himself,
by acting in opposition to the king's interests.

> 3829   "Guenes est fels d'iço qu'il le traït;
>   Vers vos s'en est parjurez e malmis.
>   Pur ço le juz jo a pendre e a murir. ..."

The young knight, Thierry of Anjou, is prepared to back his
judgment – that Ganelon be hanged as a traitor – with his sword.
As a result of this new development, the other Franks in council
agree to a judicial combat, to determine Ganelon's guilt or inno-
cence on the charge of treachery. Ganelon furnishes hostages, the
thirty members of his household; Pinabel will be his champion, as
Thierry is Roland's, and the rest is up to God.

8/9

THE JUDICIAL DUEL AND FINAL PUNISHMENT

The solemnity of the proceedings is intensified by the manner in
which the protagonists prepare for combat, first confessing them-

28. Jenkins, p. 266.

selves, then hearing mass and donating rich offerings to the church.

> 3858 Puis que il sunt a bataille justez,
> Ben sunt cunfes e asols e seignez;
> Oent lur messes e sunt acuminiez;
> Mult granz offrendes metent par cez musters.

The poet then describes the rich trappings, the beautiful armor and weapons, and the swift steeds of the fighters. The sympathies of the Franks are all on the side of Roland's champion; but the air is filled with suspense – no one knows what the judgment of God will be save He alone.

> 3870 Idunc plurerent .c. milie chevalers,
> Qui pur Rollant de Tierri unt pitiet.
> Deus set asez cument la fins en ert.

Mounted on their spirited chargers, both of the combatants display their nobility and fighting spirit. The battle is fierce, with mighty blows given and taken. Charlemagne prays only that the right may be made manifest.

> 3891 "El Deus," dist Carles, "le dreit en esclargiez!"

In the midst of the battle, Pinabel calls upon Thierry to yield. If the latter will but attempt to reconcile Charlemagne and Ganelon, Pinabel will become his man, give him his wealth!

> 3892 Dist Pinabel: "Tierri, car te recreiz!
> Tes hom serai par amur e par feid,
> A tun plaisir te durrai mun aveir.
> Mais Guenelun fai acorder al rei!"

Pinabel's is indeed a surprising offer since it is he who gives every appearance of being the stronger fighter with the better chance of success. Yet Pinabel will, if Thierry agrees to say one word to Charlemagne, sacrifice himself and all his possessions. His family loyalty[29] to Ganelon is extreme, especially since the offer in itself implies his uncertainty that justice is on the side of Ganelon.

In contrast, Thierry is just an average type of fighter, medium in size, slight in build (3820–22) and surely no formidable opponent for Pinabel. He would perhaps have been well advised to accept the latter's generous offer, considering the dangers involved in

29. Jenkins, p. 272: "Pinabel's code of family honor is exactly that of Roland and Oliver. ..."

combat. He is so clearly convinced, unlike Pinabel, of the justice of his cause, however, that he does not hesitate for a moment.

> 3896 Respunt Tierri: "Ja n'en tendrai cunseill.
> Tut seie fel se jo mie l'otrei!
> Deus facet hoi entre nus dous le dreit!

Although Thierry will not halt the fight in response to a proffer of wealth, he is prepared to accept submission by Pinabel, with an agreement to reconcile the latter with the emperor and thus save his life. But the traitor himself is excluded from any bargain and he must be punished in exemplary fashion.

> 3899 Ço dist Tierri: "Pinabel, mult ies ber,
> Granz ies e forz e tis cors ben mollez;
> De vasselage te conoissent ti per;
> Ceste bataille, car la laisses ester!
> A Carlemagne te ferai acorder;
> De Guenelun justise ert faite tel,
> Jamais n'ert jur que il n'en seit parlet."

Thierry's return offer matches Pinabel's in generosity. He asserts quite plainly that the nature of Ganelon's crime requires punishment drastic enough to be unforgettable. At the same time, he points out that Pinabel's prowess is too well known to his peers for him to fear that withdrawal from the combat could evoke criticism. With impressive nobility of soul, however, Pinabel takes his loyal stand to the end.

> 3906 Dist Pinabel: "Ne placet Damnedeu!
> Sustenir voeill trestut mun parentet;
> N'en recrerrai pur nul hume mortel;
> Mielz voeill murir que il me seit reprovet."

It can readily be seen how much of the dramatic intensity might have been lost had the poet made this a battle of all good against all evil. Not only was Ganelon a man of stature, respected by his peers, but his champion also was a noble and virtuous knight. The emperor, the judges, and the spectators could not therefore be at all certain of the outcome. One can easily imagine how, with bated breath, every move of the duel was eagerly watched; not only for the usual pleasure of a great contest, but to ascertain the will of God. In the words of the poet himself, only death can now provide the solution.

> 3914 Seinz hume mort ne poet estre afinet.

Despite the suspense, the conclusion is inevitable. For all his great courage, Pinabel is slain. This is the sign from God which the Franks have been seeking.

> 3931   Escrient Franc: "Deus i ad fait vertut!
>   Asez est dreiz que Guenes seit pendut
>   E si parent, ki plaidet unt pur lui."

The decision has been rendered: the assembled barons are simply confirming the judgment in accordance with the manifest will of God.

The decision of the judges that Ganelon and his relatives be hanged calls for special discussion. By modern standards particularly, the inclusion of the hostages in the death penalty is harsh[30] indeed. As seen through the eyes of the poet, however, the thirty hostages are being hanged because they have "pleaded" (3933) in support of the criminal – so proved by act of God; instead of disowning him for cause, they have undertaken to associate themselves with him in his crime as accessories. The poet himself does see the nobility of Pinabel and those who are prepared to sacrifice themselves out of loyalty to the family; he sees and understands the tragedy of their dilemma; perhaps he even sympathizes deeply with them. Only this could account for his continually favorable descriptions of Ganelon and his supporters. At issue, however, in this case is the fundamental problem of dual loyalty: to the family or to the king.

The importance of family loyalty during the Middle Ages is well known.[31] It breathes through every line of the *Roland*, from Charlemagne's attitude to his nephew and Ganelon's toward his wife and son, to Roland's own defense of his hated stepfather. In Roland's case, this family loyalty to Ganelon persisted unchanged until there was reasonable evidence that the older man was guilty of treachery. Knowing the facts, Ganelon's relatives did not change their attitude and thus assumed his guilt as family accessories; they condemned themselves the moment they identified themselves with him in an act contrary to the king's interest.

> 3958   .xxx. en i ad d'icels ki sunt pendut.
>   Ki hume traïst sei ocit e altroi.

After the hanging of the hostages, the barons from all over the

---

30. Menéndez Pidal, *Poema de Mio Cid*, p. 70: "La venganza es cruelmente sanguinaria en el poema de los *Infantes de Lara* y en el *Roland*, donde Ruy Velásquez o Ganelón son muertos con treinta caballeros de los suyos. ..."
31. Farnsworth, *Uncle and Nephew in the Old French Chanson de Geste*.

kingdom then turn their attention to the execution of Ganelon. The plan is changed from hanging in his case to a more spectacular ceremony.

> 3960 Puis sunt turnet Bavier e Aleman
> E Peitevin e Bretun e Norman.
> Sor tuit li altre l'unt otriet li Franc
> Que Guenes moerget par merveillus ahan.

The participation of all the most important vassals from every section of the empire suggests the national character, and thus the transcendent nature, of the crime and its punishment. Almost lovingly, the poet describes the events, lingering on the details.

> 3964 Quatre destrers funt amener avant,
> Puis si li lient e les piez e les mains.
> Li cheval sunt orgoillus e curant;
> Quatre serjanz les acoeillent devant,
> Devers un'ewe ki est en mi un camp.
> Guenes est turnet a perdiciun grant;
> Trestuit si nerf mult li sunt estendant
> E tuit li membre de sun cors derumpant:
> Sur l'erbe verte en espant li cler sanc.
> Guenes est mort cume fel recreant.

That the lesson be not forgotten, the poet ends the scene by repeating its moral.

> 3974 Hom ki traïst altre, n'en est dreiz qu'il s'en vant.

In spite of the severity of the cruel and tragic punishment, it is difficult for the reader, modern or medieval, to conclude with anything other than "Amen!"

8/10

CHANSON DE ROLAND: SUBSTRUCTURE

The autonomous core system of the *Roland*, on the basis of the preceding functional analysis, contains a sequence of four narremes of the kind described above (2/7) as Type I. This must be modified, however, to take into account an epilogue,[32] which is an

---

32. It should perhaps be stressed that the description of the king's council, the judicial duel, and the final punishment as an "epilogue" to the autonomous core system, i.e. as a superstructural expansion of the narreme punishment, in no way detracts from the power and importance of these incidents for this individual poem, or any other among those analyzed. Just as we know from an examination of all the epics involved, that a traitor is punished

expansion (see 4/7) of the narreme of punishment. The substructural pattern might then be schematically outlined as follows:

I The Autonomous Core System
  1/ The family quarrel, between Roland and Ganelon.
  2/ The insult, Roland mocks and laughs at Ganelon.
  3/ The act of treachery, Ganelon arranges a Saracen ambush.
  4/ The initial punishment, Ganelon is beaten, chained, and held for trial.
II Expansion: The Epilogue
  a/ The king's council, the assemblage of the peers as judges.
  b/ The judicial duel, Roland's champion as proxy.
  c/ The final punishment, the execution of the traitor.

The *Chanson de Roland* differs in one important respect from the other epics previously analyzed: it contains an epilogue of a special kind, devoted to trial and punishment in the king's name. The structure of the poem may now be compared, by a similar functional analysis, with that of the *Cantar de Mio Cid*.

whether his victim lives or dies, so we know that this punishment seldom takes the form of a king's council and judicial duel. These incidents are therefore the special devices of an individual poet, and not organic slots used by all the poets in a shared system.

CHAPTER NINE

Cantar de Mio Cid: Prologue and Family Quarrel

9 Cantar de Mio Cid: Prologue and Family Quarrel

THE CID AS MILITARY HERO AND FATHER

The initial difficulty in analyzing the *Cid*, which has been described above (1/6–1/9), stems from the fact that the poem is a fusion of two distinct elements. It is at the same time the biography[1] of a military hero and the narration of a family incident. In great part, the beauty of the poem lies precisely in the skill with which the poet has welded these two outwardly contradictory themes into one unified structure.[2] The power and fame of the hero add immeasurably to the interest in the family episode; this, in turn, supplies the chief motive for recounting the military exploits of the man.

A poet is clearly entitled to organize[3] his material in his own fashion. The author of the *Cid* has chosen to portray a man capable of achieving phenomenal success. At the beginning of the poem, in the "Cantar del destierro," the hero is a penniless exile, forced to leave home and family behind, the future dark before him. His worth as a man, his warm family relationships,

1. Battaglia, *Poema de Mio Cid*, pp. 24–25: "... quel carattere biografico ... soprattutto ... questo precipitare del "cantare" da una rievacazione guerresca alla narrazione d'un episodio famigliare, qual è quello delle nozze e dell'affronto delle figlie del Cid." Cf. Hatzfeld, "Esthetic Criticism Applied to Medieval Literature," p. 312: "... I would prefer Northup's interpretation of it as an Odyssey of a medieval businessman. ..."

2. Battaglia, p. 25: "Ma la contradizzione è soltanto apparente ... il poeta ha inscritto e ha magnificato nella sua virtù il destino della Spagna, ma non ha mai obliato il Cid vive anche per sé, per la sua famiglia, per la sua orgogliosa e avventurosa potenza." See also Menéndez Pidal, *Poema de Mio Cid*, p. 75: "Nada más distinto, empero, que la unidad del Poema del Cid y la del Roland." Also, with regard to language, see Corbató, "La sinonimia y la unidad del *Poema del Cid*," p. 347. "... es evidente que el vocabulario del poema tiende a confirmar la opinión de unidad de autor." However, cf. *supra*, chap. 1, n.11.

3. The words of Bédier, intended for the *Roland*, are equally applicable to the author of the Cid; *Les Légendes épiques*, III, 448–49: "... il lui a fallu se mettre à sa table de travail, chercher des combinaisons, des effets, des rimes, calculer, combiner, raturer, peiner." That he succeeded, there seems little doubt; Castro, "Poesía y realidad," pp. 13–14: "El Poema es una composición lograda, y su autor sabía lo que aspiraba a crear. ..."

his loyalty to his sovereign under adverse conditions, his military conquests and ever increasing wealth and renown, these are the details of an indispensable portrait, and the reader shares and approves his growing happiness.

Against the background of military adventure, new clouds begin to gather for the Cid, who has been no stranger to enemies. In the past, however, their strength has been pitted against him directly; they have been successful in turning his liege lord Alfonso against him and in forcing upon him the loss of his lands and citizenship. But despite their worst efforts, they have succeeded only in increasing his stature. An entirely different situation arises when the blows are struck against the daughters whom he loves.

The brutal act of injury inflicted on the daughters of the Cid by their husbands, the Infantes de Carrión, is the first incident in the poem which indicates the existence of a story plot.[4] The affront, which can scarcely be overlooked by the Cid, entails as a corollary the punishment of the culprits. On a structural basis, therefore, this is the central core[5] of the action. As it happens, this central scene does not take place until verse 2735, where the actual mistreatment of the girls begins. In a poem which ends at verse 3730, this would appear at first glance a little late for the allegedly vital action to commence, unless there is good reason for the delay. In fact, the structural sections are more gracefully proportioned than appearance indicates, since the Cid's role as father – his role in the main plot – begins at verse 1085 (see 9/4); and analysis will show that there is indeed a very good reason for the uncommonly long introduction[6] because of the special nature of the crime.

9/2

THE NATURE OF THE CRIME AND THE POSITION OF WOMEN

The Infantes de Carrión, with malice aforethought, disrobed their young wives, beat them viciously, and left them to the mercies of

4. Entwistle, "Remarks Concerning the Order of the Spanish Cantares de Gesta," p. 115: "Historical matter is always accessory; it is the plot that characterizes the epic, and the kernel of the plot is personality."
5. Milá y Fontanals, *Tratados doctrinales de literatura*, pp. 215–16: "La unidad, necessaria á la epopeya, tiene mayor ó menor cohesión en los más famoso poemas. ... Nuestro cantar de "El mío Cid" (incompleto al principio) es más bien un fragmento de la vida poética del héroe, aunque en el domina el casamiento de las hijas del héroe, con sus consecuencias."
6. Menéndez y Pelayo, *Historia de la poesía castellana,*" I, 140: "... toda su primera mitad está narrada con suma rapidez y cierta sequedad, como si

wild beasts in the lonely forest. The poet, a gentleman in the true sense of the word, is opposed to this kind of activity, and says so plainly.

> 3706   Qui buena dueña escarneçe e la dexa después,
>   atal le contesca o siquier peor.

It is difficult to tell from this statement, however, just how seriously he views the crime itself, since his suggested punishment is that the men who beat and deserted their wives should be treated in "like fashion or even worse." This could mean either mildly or severely, depending on his philosophy in this respect. In point of fact, the ultimate punishment of the Infantes appears quite mild, even according to modern standards; and in this, we have the clue to his technique.

Considering the legal position of women during the Middle Ages, fully reflected in the literature of the period,[7] it becomes clear that the narrator is selecting a revolutionary motif as the pivot of his action. In all the other Spanish epics analyzed, the woman has been the evil genius, planning, directing, and supporting the acts of treachery against the hero. The mistreatment she undergoes – Doña Lambra burnt alive, Countess Aba forced to take poison – is merited punishment for her crimes, meeting with the full approval of the audience. This is certainly not the case in the *Cid*.

The task facing the poet under these conditions is making the mistreatment of the two young wives credible to a medieval audience as a major literary theme. This effect is achieved by giving the beating of the girls a wider context than the normal relationship between husbands and wives: it is an indirect assault on the honor of the Cid, involving a quarrel between the Infantes and their father-in-law. Since the force of this indignity is in direct proportion to the audience interest in the welfare of the hero, it

en el propósito de su autor estuviese destinada *meramente á servir de introducción* á la historia del primer casamiento de la hijas del Cid de la venganza que éste toma de sus infames yernos ..." (my italics).

7. Quinn, "Development of Domestic Institutions," p. 627: "The feudal world was a man's world, in which woman lost a considerable number of the rights which had been gradually accruing to her." See also Painter, *French Chivalry*, pp. 102–3: "The *chansons de geste* show very clearly the attitude of the twelfth-century knight toward women. As these works were obviously composed with a male audience chiefly in mind, they emphasized what the nobleman liked. For the most part they dealt with war and feudal intrigue, but occasionally a woman slipped into the story. ... They were the victims of savage indignities. If a wife opposed her husband, his usual reply was to hit her on the nose so that it bled." For the changing status of women in the literature of this period, see Dorfman, *Women in the Epic and Romance* (Columbia Master's essay).

is essential that the remarkable career of the latter be exploited to the full limits of its potentiality.

9/3
PROLOGUE: THE QUEST, THE TEST, AND THE INITIAL REWARD

Skilfully the poet sketches the portrait of a superlative[8] individual. This man belongs to the most modest ranks of the nobility, yet he stands his ground with the most haughty. Ill-served by his king, he turns enmity into respect and friendship through loyal service. An exile torn from his home, he yet manages to keep his family together and protected, arranging carefully for their welfare, worrying about them in his own dark hours. His quest for vindication, his valor in meeting the test of courageous action, and the initial reward which is his due are succinctly summarized by Rose and Bacon in *The Lay of the Cid* (p. viii): "The Cid, an exile from Castile and flouted by his enemies at home, must vindicate himself. The discomfiture of the Moor is not an end in itself but the means of vindication and, be it said, of support. When he is restored to favor, the marriages of his daughters to the Heirs of Carrión under Alphonso's auspices is the royal acknowledgment."

Rose and Bacon seem surprised that the poet did not choose[9] to focus major attention on the Cid's military glory: "The poet either from ignorance or choice has disregarded the historical significance of the campaigns of the Cid. He fails to mention his defeat of the threatening horde of Almoravides at the very moment when their victory over Alphonso's Castilians had opened to them Spain's richest provinces, and turns the crowning achievement of the great warrior's life into the preliminary to a domestic event which he considered of greater importance. We are grateful to him for his lack of accuracy, for it illustrates how men thought about their heroes in that time." We have reason to be more grateful than Rose and Bacon imagine, since the greater importance attached to the "domestic event" illustrates clearly that the poet is consciously aware of an epic substructure in the poem, and that he is acting from choice rather than ignorance, as revealed in the first verse of the "Cantar de las bodas."

8. Del Río, *Historia de la literatura española*, I, 11: "... Rodrigo Diaz y las gentes de su acompañamiento pertenecen a la nobleza más modesta y el juglar los enfrenta constantemente, para realzar su calidad humana, con la soberbia de representantes de la alta nobleza." See also Cabal, *Héroes universales de la literatura española*, p. 28.

9. Rose and Bacon, pp. vii–viii; see also *infra*, chap. 12. n.21.

9/4

"HERE BEGINS THE GESTE OF THE CID. ..."

The introductory nature of the "Cantar del destierro" as prologue is incontrovertibly marked by the first verse of the second section, the "Cantar de las bodas," which states[10] explicitly:

> 1085 Aquis conpieça la gesta de mio Çid el de Bivar.

It is at this point that the main plot truly begins.

As the title indicates, the "Cantar de las bodas" deals primarily with the marriages of the Cid's daughters, a project near to his heart. This particular alliance, though not sought by the Cid, is a favorable one, since the family of the Infantes is superior to his in the scale of nobility. It is the king's wish that the marriages take place, in token of reconciliation and as a tangible reward fully earned; from it the Cid may expect to derive honor and glory. The shock will be the greater when, in the third section, the "Cantar de Corpes," it brings grief instead of joy.

Thus, because of the poet's skill in maintaining a high order of interest as he sets the scene and channels the action along, there can be no valid objection to the considerable attention devoted to preliminaries. These serve as the background necessary for the significance and cogency of the brutal act of treachery. As in many of the other epics of the period, the act of treachery is the central core of the action; therefore, the functional analysis of the *Cid* must begin with an examination of the marriages of the Cid's daughters, as the starting-point for the family quarrel which gives rise to the rest of the main action.

9/5

THE MARRIAGES

The Cid's plans for his beloved daughters run like a bright thread through the whole fabric of the poem. Almost at the very beginning of the "Cantar del destierro," in the prologue presumably devoted to the military background of the Cid, these plans are already made known. As the Cid, about to depart into exile, takes

---

10. Menéndez Pidal, *Cantar de Mio Cid*, III, 1067 (*Cid* citations are from this critical ed. The editor's definition ("compeçar, activo, 'comenzar, dar principio á una cosa,'") citing this specific verse, leaves no room for doubt (also *ibid.*, II, 584). In contrast to the explicit nature of the first verse of the second *cantar*, the first verse of the third *cantar* says nothing about a "beginning," though the second *cantar* itself does have a coda bringing it to a close (vv. 2276–77); the first leaf of the first *cantar* is missing, making it impossible to tell how the poem actually opened (*ibid.*, p. 909).

a sad and affectionate farewell of his family, he permits himself the significant hope that the future will allow him to arrange "with his own hands" suitable marriages for his daughters.

> 282 "Plega a Dios e a santa María,
> 282b que aun con mis manos / case estas mis fijas. ..."

There is a certain irony[11] in the expression *con mis manos*. It is perfectly justified, since it is precisely by means of his hands, that is to say, by his sword, that the Cid acquires the fame and wealth which induce the Infantes de Carrión to request his daughters in marriage. Yet, when the time comes, the Cid will be so little pleased at the prospect of this particular union that he will insist on the bestowal of the girls not by his own hands but by those of the king. But this is still all in the future;[12] at the moment, the Infantes have plans of their own.

It is in the "Cantar de las bodas" that the plans for the marriages begin to take shape. The Infantes de Carrión, carried away by exciting reports of the Cid's military exploits and calculating mentally the probable sum of his accumulating property, start to weigh the material advantages of a family alliance with the great warrior.

> 1372 Aquí entraron en fabla   iffantes de Carrión:
> "Mucho creçen las nuevas   de mio Çid et Campeador,
> "bien casariemos con sus fijas pora   huebos de pro.

The Infantes, however, are not yet ready to speak openly about their project.

> 1375 "Non la osariemos   acometer nos esta razón.
> "mio Çid es de Bivar   e nos de comdes de Carrión."

As Menéndez Pidal has justly remarked (chap. 1, n.22), the tragedy of the poem is born through the presumption of the Infantes who believe that their high birth entitles them to wed the daughters of kings or emperors. Here, with the first intimation of

---

11. Menéndez Pidal, III, 744: "La *mano* significa el 'poder, potestad, mando' que se tiene sobre algo. ... El padre no quiere casar por sí mismo sus hijas con los infantes de Carrión, pues éstos no son de su agrado, *non gelas daré yo con mi mano* 2134 (y eso que al salir desterrado exclamaba: *plega a Dios ... que aun con mis manos case estas mis fijas* 282). ..." Like a good father, the Cid sincerely hopes to give his daughters in marriage himself; it is ironic that his prayer will eventually be followed by a marriage alliance on the highest levels of nobility, in which his distaste for his prospective sons-in-law, greater than his pleasure in the anticipated event, will compel him to forgo the no less keen desire to marry the girls "with his own hands."

12. See *infra*, 9/11.

their marriage plans, the Infantes disclose their haughty disdain[13] for the house of Bivar. For them, this is an alliance not to be entered into lightly; despite the manifest material advantages, they decide temporarily to maintain a discreet silence.

> 1377　Non lo dizen a nadi,　e fincó esta razón.

To all intents and purposes, the line of future plot development is already suggested. If the marriages do take place, there will be an easy possibility of family conflict between the high-born Infantes de Carrión and their father-in-law, the lowly *infanzón*.[14] Having introduced the Infantes as potential sons-in-law, the poet turns his attention to the prospective brides.

Won over at last by the conquering hero, Alfonso has graciously given permission for Jimena and the daughters to rejoin the Cid in his newly won domains. The latter receives them joyfully, doubly happy at the unexpected opportunity for them to observe with their own eyes how he "gains his bread" in battle:

> 1643　"afarto verán por los ojos　cómmo se gana el pan."

In reply to their anxious questions, the Cid informs them that this is the way the great wealth is won which will serve the useful purpose of seeing his daughters well married.

> 1648　"Riqueza es que nos acreçe　maravillosa e grand;
> 　　　"a poco que viniestes,　presend vos quieren dar:
> 　　　"por casar son vuestras fijas,　aduzenvos axuvar."

After a successful battle, and a magnificent dowry earned for his daughters, the Cid returns to his wife Jimena with an interesting proposal. He suggests that the worthy ladies whom she has brought in her train be married to his vassals.

> 1764　"Estas dueñas que aduxiestes,　que vos sirven tanto,
> 　　　"quiérolas casar　con de aquestos mios vasallos;

It is significant that the Cid feels called upon to add immediately that these multiple marriages will not include their daughters.

> 1768　"Lo de vuestras fijas venir se a más por espacio."

13. Battaglia, p. 29: "Il clima psicologico del Poema è constituito da questa rivalità familiare e politica fra il signore di Bivar e i conti di Carrión, con i loro feudi confinanti e con la loro potenza in conflitto."

14. Menéndez Pidal, II, 718: "yfançon, masc., individuo correspondiente á la segunda clase de la nobleza, colocada bajo la de los *ricos omnes* y sobre, la de los simples *fijos dalgo* (véase); todo caballero era hidalgo, pero no infanzón."

Whether the delay is due to the extreme youth of the young ladies, or to the fact that the Cid is awaiting a more favorable match, is not made clear. In any case, the path is left open for the Infantes to continue weighing the matter in secret.

Emphasizing the importance of the plans of the Infantes for the development of the plot, the narrator calls attention to them in the first person.

> 1879   D'iffantes de Carrión   yo vos quiero contar,
> Fablando en so conssejo,   aviendo su poridad:
> "Las nuevas del Çid   mucho van adelant,
> "demandemos sus fijas   pora con ellas casar;
> "creçremos en nuestra ondra   e iremos adelant."

With these great advantages in mind, the young men decide to approach Alfonso for aid. The king appears to be in no great rush to satisfy their desire. There is good reason, too, for his hesitation; he is none too certain that the Cid will relish the proposal.

> 1892   "del casamiento   non sé sis abrá sabor; ...

The Cid is, of course, grateful to the king for being gracious enough to think of him in connection with so important a matter as the marriage of his daughters. He is not happy, however, with the choice of in-laws, and gives a specific reason for his antipathy.

> 1938   "ellos son much urgullosos   e an part en la cort, ...

Diego and Fernando, the Infantes de Carrión, belong to the court party,[15] the Cid's personal enemies responsible for his previous exile; they are, in addition, given to pride and arrogance. It is the king who counsels the marriage, but only God knows what is best.

> 1940   "mas pues lo conseja   el que más vale que nos,
> "fablemos en ello,   en la poridad seamos nos.
> "Afé Dios del çielo   que nos acuerde en lo mijor."

In accordance with the king's wishes, the Cid agrees to a rendezvous at a designated place, where the matter may be fully discussed. The Infantes, overjoyed, already begin to live as though they were in fact being supported on the bounty of their future father-in-law.

---

15. Menéndez Pidal, *Poema de Mio Cid*, pp. 24–25: "Los hijos de este conde don Gonzalo, Diego y Fernando Gonzáles, ... son personajes históricos, pues aparecen al lado de los otros enemigos del Cid ... como confirmantes en diplomas reales, entre los años 1090 y 1109. ..."

1975   Iffantes de Carrión   mucho alegres andan,
          lo uno adebdan   e lo otro pagavan;
          Quantos quisiessen   averes d'oro e da plata.

When the king's party meets the Cid and his retainers, the greetings are warm and sincere. After the salutations, Alfonso proposes the alliance between the Cid's daughters and the Infantes.

2075   "Vuestras fijas vos pido,   don Elvira a doña Sol,
          "que las dedes por magieres   a ifantes de Carrión.
          "Semejam el casamiento   ondrado e congrant pro,
          "ellos vos las piden   e mándovoslo yo.

According to the king's words, this is a request on the part of the Infantes; on his own behalf, however, it is a command! To this unmistakable order of Alfonso's, the Cid makes a very strange reply: he does not have, says he, any daughters to give in marriage!

2082   "Non abría fijas de casar,"   respuso el Campeador,
          ça non ha grant hedad   e de días pequeñas son.

Since it is obvious that he does have daughters, marriageable or not, he must hasten to explain: they are not nubile. Is the Cid indulging in diplomatic prevarication when he states that otherwise the match would be quite satisfactory?

2084   "De grandes nuevas son   ifantes de Carrión,
          "perteneçen pora mis fijas   e aun pora mejores.

Unless he is speaking with tongue in cheek, the Cid shows plainly that he recognizes the superiority of the Infantes in point of birth, since he is prepared to admit that they are worthy of an even better marriage alliance; assuredly he does not mean that they could find better girls than his daughters anywhere in Spain. In the circumstances, nevertheless, he is prepared to submit to the wishes of his liege lord.

Torn between paternal premonitions and his feudal duty to the king, the Cid unreservedly places the welfare of his daughters in the royal hands.

2086   "Hyo las engendré amas   e criástesles vos,
          "entre yo y ellas   en vuestra merçed somos nos;
          "afellas en vuestra mano   don Elvira e doña Sol,
          "dadlas a qui quisiéredes vos,   ca yo pagado so."

Pointedly, the Cid emphasizes that the king may bestow his daughters as he sees fit, but asks that he accept them from the Cid as his responsibility. Alfonso unhesitatingly agrees to this understanding.

> 2097 "Daquí las prendo por mis manos   don Elvira e doña Sol,
> "e dólas por veladas   a ifantes de Carrión.

Alfonso patently regards the marriage as one between equals, since the girls are specifically to be recognized as in the category of wives known as *veladas*.[16] At the same time, he gives the Infantes into the paternal power of the Cid, who has not lost his daughters but gained two sons.

> 2106 "los yernos e las fijas   todos vuestros fijos son:
> "lo que vos ploguiere,   dellos fet, Campeador."

The Cid bows to necessity: he accepts the situation, together with his prospective sons-in-law. He does not, however, forget to remind the king of his responsibility.

> 2110 "Vos casades mis fijas, ca non gelas do yo."

Just as significantly, the king repeats that the Infantes are now members of the Cid's family, and should be treated as such.

> 2121 El rey a los ifantes   a las maos les tomó,
> metiólos en poder   de mio Çid el Campeador:
> "Evad aquí vuestros fijos   quando vuestros yernos son;
> "de oy mas, sabed   qué fer dellos, Campeador. ..."

The continued repetition has an underlying effect which cannot be ignored. It shows the profound meaning of the family relationship to both Alfonso and the Cid; and it anticipates that this relationship will play a vital role in the development of the poem. This is made clear by the Cid's insistence that the king assume full responsibility for the marriage. With all due respect to his liege lord, the Cid thanks Alfonso for the great gift bestowed upon him, but repeats yet again that the marriage is of the king's making and that logically, therefore, the king should appoint someone to give his daughters away in marriage in the royal name.

---

16. Menéndez Pidal, *Cantar de Mio Cid*, p. 889: "velada, fem., 'mujer legítima'"; cf. 886: "varragana, fem., 'manceba, concubina,' "... el Cantar opone esta palabra á la de *pareja* ó mujer *velada*, y muestra que la barragana era de condición social inferior á la del que se unía á ella. ..."

2131   "Yo vos pido merçed a vos, rey natural:
           "pues que casades mis fijas, así commo a vos plaz,
           "dad manero a qui las dé, quando vos las tomades;
           "non gelas daré yo con mi mano. ..."

Without hesitation, Alfonso turns to Alvar Fáñez, the Cid's nephew[17] and loyal supporter, making him his proxy in the affair. All then withdraw, with the king's permission, to Valencia, hard-won prize of the Cid, to prepare for the nuptials.

For better or worse, the Cid is prepared to go on with the wedding of his daughters. Returned to Valencia, he gives orders that the Infantes be lodged in his own palace, and that they be well treated. It is apparent that he is doing his utmost to show good-will and cordiality to the young men. This feeling is strengthened by the first words which the Cid addresses to Jimena.

2187   – "Grado al Criador vengo, mugier ondrada!
         "hyernos vos adugo de que avremos ondrança; ...

This cheerful approach of the Cid to the forthcoming wedding, and his explicit statement that honor will accrue to them from it, is matched by the positiveness of the remark he addresses directly to the girls.

2189   "gradídmelo, mis fijas, ca bien vos he casades!"

The young ladies, as might be expected, are elated at the prospect, since they will now be "rich ladies" (2195) in the double[18] sense of the word. Repeating that their marriages will bring them honor, however, the Cid again emphasizes that Alfonso is personally responsible.

2196   – "Mugier doña Ximena, grado al Criador.
         "A vos digo, mis fijas, don Elvira e doña Sol:
         "deste vuestro casamiento creçremos en onor;
         "mas bien sabet verdad que non lo levanté yo:
         "pedidas vos ha e rogadas el mio señor Alfons,
         "atan firme mientre e de todo coraçón
         "que yo nulla cosa nol sope dezir de no.
         "Metivos en sus manos, fijas, amas ados;
         "bien me lo creades, que el vos casa, ca non yo."

17. Menéndez Pidal, *Poema de Mio Cid*, pp. 19–20.
18. Menéndez Pidal, *Cantar de Mio Cid*, II, 826–29. (Even more than wealth, the word implies great nobility of rank.)

The reluctance of the Cid could not be more plainly revealed nor the powerful conflict of loyalties that must have animated him than is expressed in these few words. Since the matter is settled, however, arrangements are made for the festivities. As the Cid himself says, with as good grace as possible: if it has to be done anyhow, why wait?

> 2220 "Pues que a fazer lo avemos, por qué lo imos tardando?

The same note of reluctance, visible here is maintained throughout the proceedings. The Cid nevertheless gives the order for the ceremony to begin by calling upon Alvar Fáñez to officiate, in accordance with the king's instructions. The latter obeys, addressing the Infantes directly in the king's name.

> 2231 "Por mano del rey Alfons, que a mí lo ovo mandado,
> "dovos estas dueñas, – amas son fijas dalgo, –
> "que las tomassedes por mugieres a ondra e a recabdo."

It is thus made clear to the Infantes that the Cid's daughters, members of the nobility ("fijas dalgo"), are to be treated with the honor and consideration which is their due; this, by order of the king. The Infantes accept their responsibility with love and gladness.

> 2234 Amos las reçiben d'amor e de grado. ...

After mass at the church of Santa María under the ministrations of Bishop Don Jerome, the wedding party returns to the palace at Valencia for fifteen days of joyous celebration. In the beginning, at least, the situation is very pleasant for the Infantes.

9/6

THE FAMILY GROUP AT VALENCIA

Celebrated magnificently, the wedding has been a great success; the guests have departed for Castile, laden with untold wealth in gifts. The Infantes cannot fail to be happy with their lot.

> 2267 Mucho eran alegres Didago e Ferrando; ...

Accepted as part of the family, treated with love and affection, the young men remain with the Cid, their father-in-law and new lord, for the space of two years.

> 2270 el Çid e sos hyernos en Valencia son restados.
> Hy moran los ifantes bien cerca de dos años,
> los amores que les fazen mucho eran sobejanos.

This happiness is shared by the Cid and all his vassals.

> 2273   Alegre era el Çid   e todos sos vasallos.

Before bringing this introductory part of the story to a close, the narrator produces one fugitive, shadowy note. Against the background of such happiness as he describes, he interposes the pious hope that the Holy Family may be pleased to see the Cid contented with the marriage.

> 2274   Plega a santa María   e al Padre santo
> ques pague des casamiento   mio Çid o el que lo ovo âlgo.

On this note, the poet terminates the second *cantar*, bringing the long prologue to a close.

> 2276   Las coplas deste cantar   aquis van acabando.

From the structural point of view, this is the logical place to end the introduction. It is from this point on that the internal chain of narremes will begin to unfold a linked sequence of epic incidents. We have been eagerly following until now the herculean[19] efforts of a courageous knight on a mighty quest to vindicate himself and retrieve his place in society. We have seen him meet the test, his efforts crowned with superb success. In token of his achievements and the merited reconciliation with his sovereign, to whom he has maintained unswerving fidelity, he has attained an initial reward, the glorious marriage of his daughters. It is this marriage which brings him two new sons, with whom he has had a quarrel in the past. And up to this point we have observed the family group, parents and children, as well as vassals, dwelling together in happiness and amity.

---

19. Battaglia, p. 15: "Ora ricominciare daccapo, quando si vedono annullate di colpo le ragioni della propria vita, e rifarsi i modi di una nuova esistenza, questo è l'eroismo più originale del Cid."

CHAPTER TEN

Cantar de Mio Cid: The Insult

10 Cantar de Mio Cid: The Insult

THE LION INCIDENT

The first incident of the "Cantar de Corpes," the escape of a lion from his cage in the Cid's palace at Valencia, supplies a clue concerning the way in which a conflict will develop. Whether this episode[1] was taken from local tradition connected with the Cid historically, a strong possibility, or borrowed from folklore, it serves an essential[2] function at this juncture of the poem. It reveals not only to the Cid's retainers but to the Infantes themselves just what manner of men they are.

The Cid and his sons-in-law have been living together in Valencia, it will be recalled, for a happy period of two years.

> 2278　　En Valençia sedi　mio Çid con todos los sos,
> 　　　　con elle amos sos yernos　ifantes de Carrión.

Suddenly one day, as the Campeador lies slumbering on his couch, a lion breaks out of his cage.

> 2280　　Yazies en un escaño,　durmie el Campeador,
> 　　　　mala sobrevienta,　sabed, que les cuntió:
> 　　　　saliós de la red　e desatós el león.

The ensuing panic is shared by all those present.

> 2283　　En grant miedo se vieron　por medio de la cort; ...

In a mad rush to escape the lion, Fernando, finding neither chamber nor tower to hide in, seeks safety under the couch, shaking with fear.

---

1. Menéndez Pidal, *Cantar de Mio Cid*, II, 731: "Es frecuente el caso de leones domesticados, como el del Cid, mantenidos en una casa." See also Ford, *Main Currents of Spanish Literature*, p. 29: "It is not improbable that the poet found in local tradition, already associated with the name of the Cid, certain of the episodes which he has woven into his narrative; but it is also fair to assume that he had sufficient ability to take them from the universal stock of folk-lore, where they are found, or even from other literary documents, and apply them to the general enhancement of his subject matter. In this connection, one thinks naturally of the incident of the chests full of sand, and that of the escape of the lion, both of which are easily paralleled elsewhere in literature and in folk-lore."
2. Barahona, *Al margen de Mio Cid*, pp. 111–33.

> 2286 Ferrant Gonçálvez, ifant de Carrión,
> non vido allí dos alçasse, nin cámara abierta nin torre;
> metiós sol escaño, tanto ovo el pavor.

At the same time, Diego rushes headlong through the open door and hides behind a winepress, where his costly garments become stained and filthy.

> 2288 Díag Gonçálvez por la puerta salió,
> diziendo de la boca "non veré Carrión!"
> Tras una viga lagar metiós con grant pavor;
> el manto e el brial todo suzio lo saco.

In the confusion, the Cid awakes, and inquires concerning the disturbance. Fearlessly, he makes for the lion.

> 2296 Mio Çid fincó el cobdo, en pie se levantó,
> el manto trae el cuello, e adelinó pora' león; ...

This time it is the lion who cowers in shame before the man.

> 2298 el león quando lo vió, assi envergonçó,
> ante mio Çid la cabeça premió e el rostro fincó.

Seizing the lion by the mane, the Cid returns him to his cage. Once more, the Cid has added a marvelous exploit to his fame.

> 2302 A maravilla lo han quantos que i son. ...

Solicitously, the Cid looks about for his sons-in-law, but they are nowhere in sight.

> 2304 Mio Çid por sos yernos demandó e no los falló;
> maguer los están llamando ninguno non responde.

The honeymoon period between the Cid and the Infantes is meeting its first sharp test.

10/2

THE DERISION OF THE COURT

Once the lion is safely caged, the Cid seeks his sons-in-law. They do not respond to calls for them, but are eventually discovered, pale and bloodless in appearance.

> 2306 Quando los fallaron, assí vinieron sin color; ...

At the sight of them, the Cid's retainers, probably in reaction to their own great fear of the escaping lion, burst forth into merriment such as was never heard before.

> 2307   non vidiestes tal juego   commo iva por la cort; ...

The keen delight of the court in the discomfiture of the Infantes is not shared by the Cid. In deference to the husbands of his daughters, he orders his people to halt their derisive laughter.

> 2308   mandólo vedar   mio Çid el Campeador.

It was of course impossible for the Cid to have stopped the laughter before it began. Although he does his best to stop it at once, the Infantes are nonetheless deeply wounded.

> 2309   Muchos tovieron por enbaídos   ifantes de Carrión,
>   fiera cosa les pesa   desto que les cuntió.

We can only speculate on the precise significance attached by the poet to the word "enbaídos." These verses are translated by Huntington[3] as:

> The Lords of Carrión esteemed them grieved
> Most deeply. What befell them sorely weighed.

Menéndez Pidal glosses[4] *enbayr* as "avergonzar, confundir," that is, "to shame, humiliate," for the verse in question; he also glosses the same word in other contexts as "atropellar, maltratar," that is, "to insult, abuse." In the same paragraph, he quotes a *Curlu de Sancho V*, in which the connotation of "damage" is unmistakable: "... si algun ombre de linage envayere o feriere o matare a otro ombre de linage, así que primero non desafiase a eyll ante mi e cinco cavaylleros otros, ... sea atal traydor. ..." In its strongest sense, *enbayr* implied an assault on a level with physical injury or death, which normally had to be preceded by the act of *desafiar*[5] or "declaration of war" between the persons concerned.

There is obviously nothing in the lion incident which calls for *desfiance* – as there was, for example, in the dispute between Roland and Ganelon – except, perhaps, in the warped minds[6] of the Infantes, acting under severe tension such as ridicule can produce. At the least, the word *enbaídos* carries the implication that the

3. *Poem of the Cid: Translation*, II, vv. 2309–10.
4. Menéndez Pidal, II, 637–38.
5. *Ibid.*, II, 622.
6. Barahona, p. 130.

idea of vengeance is being born in this very moment of humiliation, when the Infantes conceive themselves as having been deeply
insulted. Quickly, this seed begins to mature, nurtured by another
incident following hard upon the heels of the lion.

10/3

THE MOORS ATTACK VALENCIA

While the Infantes are still smarting under their recent humiliation, they observe the approach of King Búcar, come with his
mighty hosts to attack Valencia.

> 2311   Ellos en esto estando,   don avien grant pesar,
>   fuerças de Marruecos   Valençia vienen çercar; ...

The sight of fifty thousand Moorish tents (2313) arouses joy in
the hearts of the Cid and his brave followers, at the thought of all
the booty to be gained.

> 2315   Alegravas el Çid   e todos sos varones,
>   que las creçe la ganançia,   grado al Criador.

But the Infantes take no delight in the fearsome display.

> 2317   Mas, sabed, de cuer las pesa   a ifantes de Carrión;
>   ca veyen tantas tiendas de moros   de que non avien sabor.

Taking counsel with each other, the brothers wonder how they
might extract gain rather than loss from this war, which otherwise
bodes well to make widows of the Cid's daughters.

> 2320   "Catamos la ganançia   e la pérdida no;
>   "ya en esta batalla   a entrar abremos nos'
>   esto es aguisado   por non veer Carrión,
>   bibdas remandrán   fijas del Campeador."

Their secret mutterings are overheard by Muño Gustioz, who
reports them to the Cid, with the advice that he spare his "brave"
sons-in-law both the battle and the booty.

> 2326   "Evades vuestros yernos   tan osados son,
>   "por entrar en batalla   desean Carrión.
>   "Hidlos conortar,   sí vos vala el Criador,
>   "que sean en paz   e non ayan i raçión."

For whatever reason, whether at the wit of Muño Gustioz in his
advice to "comfort" (2328) the Infantes, or at the "wisdom" of

the latter, who prefer to have wives rather than widows, or both, the Cid smiles as he goes on his errand:

2331 Mio Çid Don Rodrigo   sonrrisando salió:

Well he knows the love of the Infantes for his daughters.

2332 "Dios vos salve, yernos,   ifantes de Carrión,
"en braços tenedes mis fijas   tan blancas commo el sol!

Since he looks forward to the fight, as they do to Carrión, he gives them permission to stay at leisure as long as they like in Valencia.

2334 "Hyo desseo lides,   e vos a Carrión;
"en Valencia folgad   a todo vuestro sabor.

It is he who has had previous experience of the Moors and is well able to handle them

2336 "ca d' aquellos moros   yo so sabidor;
"arrancar me los trevo   con la merçed del Criador."

At this vital point, there is a leaf missing[7] from the manuscript. There is no means of knowing the poet's actual description of the Infantes' immediate reaction to these words of their father-in-law; but the implications of the Cid's attitude are obvious enough. His sons-in-law prefer the ease and comfort of Valencia (or Carrión) and the pleasant companionship of their lovely young wives to the dangers of combat. Since he is an expert in the task at hand, he has no real need of them. The young men are not brave, but they are not stupid either. The fact that it is their own fault in no way mitigates the situation for them; they know when they have been insulted.

Filling the gap of the missing leaf from other sources, Menéndez Pidal reports that the Infantes ask to be placed in the front line of battle!

Los infantes de Carrión pidiéronle estonces la delantera. ...[8]
In the fight, however, Don Fernando, who has attacked the Moor Aladraf, suddenly flees before him in great fear. Coming to his rescue, Pero Vermúdez slays the Moor and gives his captured steed to Don Fernando, urging him to claim credit for the victory and promising to support him in this. His reason, as he explains

7. Menéndez Pidal, III, 1114; also p. 978, of the paleographic ed. in the same volume.
8. *Ibid.*, III, 1114.

himself, in the first verse where the poem resumes, is the hope
that the Cid may yet live to find the Infantes worthy men.

> 2338   "aun vea el ora   que vos meresca dos tanto."

The news is indeed pleasing to the Cid and his men as they
advance into battle. There is some justification for the pious hope
of the Cid that, just possibly, the Infantes might distinguish themselves on the field of honor.

> 2341 · Plogo a mio Çid   e a todos sos vasallos;
>   "Aun si Dios quisiere   e el Padre que está en alto,
>   "amos los mios yernos   buenos serán en canpo."

That this is not likely, however, the poet himself tells us at once;
for as the Christians marvel at the unprecedented might of the
enemy, the Infantes marvel even more — by their own free will,
they would never have come here!

> 2348   Mas se maravillan   entre Díago e Ferrando,
>   por la su voluntad   non serien allí llegados.

In his solicitude for the welfare of the Infantes, the Cid com-
mends them to the special care of his beloved nephew, Pero Vermúdez.

> 2351   "¡Ala, Per Vermudoz,   el mio sobrino caro!
>   "cúriesme a Dídago   e curiesme a Fernando,
>   "mios yernos amos a dos,   la cosa que mucho amo. ..."

Pero Vermúdez, who frankly has no love for the Infantes, turns
down the request.

> 2355   – "Hyo vos digo, Çid,   por toda caridad,
>   "que oy los ifantes   a mí por amo non abrán;
>   "cúrielos que quier,   ca dellos poco m'incal.

This is the same Pero Vermúdez who has just vouched for Don
Fernando's gallantry in action; now he pleads the need to concentrate on his fight in the vanguard of battle.

> 2358   "Hyo con los mios   ferir los quiero delant. ...

Mighty are the deeds and frightful the carnage. All participate
in the action, even Bishop Don Jerome. The Moors are routed and
flee to the sea. In hot pursuit, the Cid overtakes King Búcar and
slays him. On his victorious return, laden with tremendous spoils,
the Cid encounters the Infantes on the field of battle.

Unaware that the Infantes have comported themselves in any

but the most courageous manner, pleased and happy about the glorious victory over the Moors and the death of their chief, Búcar, the Cid is even more content when he sees his sons-in-law among his fighting-men.

> 2440   e vido venir   a Díago e a Fernando;
>   amos son fijos   del comde don Gonçalvo.
>   Alegrós mio Çid   fermoso sonrrisando.

Smiling pleasantly, he congratulates them on their performance, calling them not only his sons-in-law but his *sons*, and assuring them that good reports of their deeds will go to Carrión.

> 2443   "¿Venides, mios yernos,   mios fijos sodes amos!
>   "Sé que de lidiar   bien sodes pagados;
>   "a Carrión de vos   irán buenos mandados.

Alvar Fáñez joins the Cid in praising the Infantes on their baptism of fire, which has tested their mettle.

> 2460   "E vuestros yernos   aquí son ensayados,
>   "fartos de lidiar   con moros en el campo."

The Cid can only add that if they have proved themselves worthy now, the future will bring them great esteem.

> 2462   Dixo mio Çid: "yo desto so pagado;
>   "quando agora son buenos,   adelant serán preçiados."

On the surface, these words appear to have been uttered in good faith. The poet himself specifies that all this is well meant:

> 2464   Por bien lo dixo el Çid ...

Knowing the truth about themselves, however, the Infantes take it ill:[9]

> 2464   ... mas ellos lo touieron a escarnio.

If trouble comes, however, it will be through no fault of the Cid as he doles out to each his fair share of the spoils.

The Cid shows his good faith by distributing to the Infantes their share of the spoils, six hundred silver marks each (2467), as though they had actually earned it in battle. With such wealth, the sons-in-law of the Cid believe that never again will they want for anything.

9. Alonso, Dámaso, *Ensayos sobre poesía española*, 87: "... pero ellos, que saben en su corazón la verdad, no pueden por menos de creer que el Campeador habla con ironía."

2468   Los yernos de mio Çid   quando este aver tomaron
        desta arrancada,   que lo tenien en so salvo,
        cuydaron que en sos días   nunqua serien minguados.

In his prayers, giving thanks for his new possessions, the Cid
does not fail to include his sons-in-law, and their part in the great
battle.

2477   "Grado a Cristus,   que del mundo es señor,
        "quando veo   lo que avia sabor,
        "que lidiaron comigo en campo   mios yernos amos a dos;
        "mandados buenos irán   dellos a Carrión,
        "commo son ondrados   e aver nos han grant pro."

Enumerating his achievements, from a penniless start to his present wealth, the Cid counts his sons-in-law among his great gains.

2494   "Antes fu minguado,   agora rico so,
        "que he avers e tierra   e oro e onor,
        "e son mios yernos   ifantes de Carrión; ...

The wealth gained is indeed beyond counting; when all is included, the steeds and the camels and the rest, all who shared in
the fighting will receive not less than five thousand marks each –
the Infantes are now very wealthy men.

2507   grandes son los gozos   de sos yernos amos a dos:
        valía de çinco mill marcos   ganaron amos a dos;
        muchos tienen por ricos   ifantes de Carrión.

10/4
THE REPETITION OF DERISION AT THE COURT

The Infantes return with the others to the palace at Valencia. At
their entrance, they are welcomed to the court as kinsmen by
Alvar Fáñez, in the name of the Cid.

2517   "Acá venid, cuañados,   que mas valemos por vos."

The Cid is himself well pleased to see them.

2518   Assí commo llegaron,   pagós el Campeador.

Joyfully bringing his little family together, the Cid advises his
daughters to embrace and serve their husbands well.

2519   "Evades aquí, yernos,   la mie mugier de pro,
        "e amas las mis fijas,   don Elvira e doña Sol;
        "bien vos abraçen   e sírvanvos de coraçón."

It is still the Cid's apparently firm conviction that his daughters will gain great honor from their marriage.

> 2525 "destos vuestros casamientos   vos abredes honor.
> "Buenos mandados irán   a tierras de Carrión."

At these words, Don Fernando feels impelled to thank God and the Cid for all that he and his brother have obtained through their good graces.

> 2528 "Grado al Criador   e a vos, Çid ondrado,
> "tantos avemos de averes   que no son contados.

Had Don Fernando stopped here, all might yet have been well, though there would have been no epic. Instead, the lying braggart must go on to describe how "we fought for you, we conquered the Moors on the battlefield and we killed the traitor, Búcar."

> 2530 "por vos avemos ondra   e avemos lidiado,
> "vençiemos moros   en campo e matamos
> "a aquel rey Búcar,   traydor provado.

The members of the Cid's court, faced with this boastful outburst of wishful thinking,[10] cannot keep from smiling.

> 2532 Vassallos de mio Çid   sediense sonrrisando:

They know very well that where the fighting was hardest, the Infantes were most conspicuously absent.

> 2533 quien lidiara mejor   o quien fora en alcanço;
> mas non fallavan í   a Dídago ni a Ferrando.

Who can blame the Cid's vassals for their scornful jests, lasting days and nights? Once again, the Infantes are the butt of derision at court, and this time, they determine to take action.

> 2535 Por aquestos juegos   que ivan levantando,
> elas noches e los días   tan mal los escarmentando,
> tan mal se consejaron   estios ifantes amos.

On a former occasion, the Cid had put an immediate stop to the pleasantries; now they continue without ceasing. Rightly or wrongly, the Infantes consider themselves insulted[11] and they hold the Cid responsible. The next step is for them to seek retaliation for the humiliation they have endured.

10. Ford, p. 25.
11. Alonso, p. 86: "Los infantes se tienen por afrentados, el antiguo rencor renace en su alma."

CHAPTER ELEVEN

Cantar de Mio Cid: The Act of Treachery

11 Cantar de Mio Cid: The Act of Treachery

11/1

THE INFANTES PLAN VENGEANCE

The crime of the Infantes begins with its first formulation into words. The young men, their pride deeply injured, consider themselves intolerably humiliated by the laughter, jokes, and derision of the Valencian courtiers. Consulting with each other in secret (2538), the brothers plan a miniature feudal war.[1] They will ask the Cid for permission to take their wives on a trip to Carrión, in order to show them the estates which are now their heritage.

> 2543 — "Pidamos nuestras mugieres al Çid Campeador,
> "digamos que las llevaremos a tierras de Carrión,
> "enseñar las hemos do ellas heredadas son.

The true reason for the trip, however, is quite explicitly to remove the girls from the protective power of the Cid, so that no one can hinder them from working their will on their helpless wives.

> 2546 "Sacar las hemos de Valençia, de poder del Campeador;
> "después en la carrera feremos nuestro sabor. ..."

The duplicity and treachery of the Infantes is revealed in these few lines. They will start with a lie about their purpose, and carry out their crime in secret, far from the avenging reach of their father-in-law. The goad that spurs them is a festering rancor going back to the lion incident, which they fear their wives may some day throw up to them; their crime will be, in a sense, a preventive act to forestall this possibility.

> 2548 "ante que nos retrayan lo que cuntió del león.

As nobles of their rank, Infantes de Carrión, they believe they should never have been subjected to the kind of treatment they

---

1. Huizinga, *Waning of the Middle Ages*, p. 13: "In the feudal age, the private wars between two families have no other discernable reason than rivalry of rank and covetousness of possessions. Racial pride, thirst of vengeance, fidelity, are their primary and direct motives."

received; in payment, they will retain all the wealth they have obtained from the Cid.

> 2550 "Averes levaremos grandes   que valen grant valor; ..."

But even more important, they will repay in kind the insults they have received by insulting the daughters of the Cid.

> 2551 "escarniremos   las fijas del Canpeador."

Crowning their presumption, the Infantes foresee a still greater insult for the Cid and his daughters, which is at the same time the greatest reward for their nobility of blood: with their great wealth, they will now be able to marry daughters of kings and emperors (see chap. 1, n. 22.)

> 2552 "D' aquestos averes   sienpre seremos ricos omnes,
> "podremos casar con fijas   de reyes o de enperadores,
> "ca de natura somos   de comdes de Carrión.

In a manner reminiscent of the parallel passages in the *Roland*, the poet selects the salient points for emphasis through repetition. The main issue for the Infantes is retaliation: they will accomplish this by insulting the Cid's daughters, and by making it impossible for them to recall the humiliating lion episode.

> 2555 "Assí las escarniremos   a fijas del Campeador,
> "antes que nos retrayan   lo que fo del león."

The underlying cause of the desire for vengeance is revealed, in the verses just quoted, as a complex mixture of cupidity, arrogance, and shame.[2] Which feature is paramount? The Infantes have known all along that they would not be satisfied with the daughters of the house of Bivar as wives, since to them this is a marriage below their standing. Nothing but the certain expectation of untold wealth could have induced them to undertake such a project, and testifies to their greed.

Now that they have the wealth, their arrogance, perhaps a manifestation of an "inferiority complex," suggests to them that they can make good use of their gains by wooing the "daughters of kings and emperors"; surely a sign that cupidity plays no small

2. In private conversation Mario A. Pei has called to my attention how strikingly this parallels the motivation of Ganelon. Like the Infantes, he also suffers from an "inferiority complex" vis-à-vis his antagonist. His primary need is also to wipe out a public insult and yet, he too finds it compatible with his honor to acquire great wealth – the bribes of Marsile – as part of his act of treachery. The analogy is not absolutely complete, however, since Ganelon conspires only after issuing a formal *desfiance*, whereas the Infantes maintain a cowardly appearance of friendship until the very moment of their deed.

role in their plans. And yet, by placing the reference to the lion in the very last verse (2556) of the secret conversation, in repetition of the same remark made just a few lines earlier (2548), the poet reveals that the strongest motivation of the Infantes is neither cupidity, nor arrogance, strong as these are, but the derision of the court following the escape of the lion.

The Cid's daughters are not only to be repudiated as wives; they are to be insulted and disgraced. They have been witness to scenes in which their husbands have made themselves ridiculous and, being wives, they may be tempted some day to bring up the subject. Thus it is clear to the Infantes themselves that their primary motive is a direct reflex to the insult which they feel has been inflicted upon them.

The fact that the Cid had halted the jeering of the court (see 10/2) acts as nothing in his favor; and his very words of praise after the battle with the Moors, we recall (see chap. 10, n. 9), are taken as an insulting gibe.

> 2464   Por bien lo dixo el Çid,   mas ellos lo touieron a escarnio.

That the Cid's daughters are personally blameless in the whole affair means nothing either; they were present during the worst humiliation and are therefore, to minds like those of the Infantes, guilty by association. The expectation of future profit through a more desirable marriage serves mainly to lend wings to their plans; for the moment, they are concentrating on repaying insult with injury.

The honeyed words of the Infantes leave nothing to the imagination. Maintaining an outward demeanor of true "sons" and loving husbands, they call down God's care on the Cid.

> 2559   'Sí vos vala el Criador,   Çid Campeador!

Begging the Cid's indulgence and the favor of Doña Jimena and Alvar Fáñez, they humbly request permission – as they had planned – to take their wives to Carrión, these wives whom they had taken in *holy wedlock*.

> 2562   "dadnos nuestros mugieres   que avemos a bendiçiones; ..."

Knowing the plans of the Infantes, the reader can only be appalled at the viciousness of their statement: not only will the Cid's daughters see the great possessions into which they have married, but their children's share as well!

> 2567   "verán vuestras fijas   lo que avemos nos,
> "los fijos que oviéremos   en qué avrán partiçión."

The Cid has no hesitation in handing over his daughters; more, he bestows priceless gifts on his sons-in-law: three thousand silver marks, palfreys, steeds and mules, rich clothing, and two fine swords, Colada and Tizón, won in manly combat. The Infantes are his sons, since he has given them his daughters, the substance of his heart.

> 2577   "mios fijos sodes amos,   quando mis fijas vos do;
> "allá ne levades   las telas del coraçón.

There is bitter irony in his promise that if they serve his daughters well, he will reward them greatly.

> 2582   "si bien las servides,   yo vos rendré buen galardon."

The Cid's daughters take affectionate farewell of their parents and friends. Since it is their parents' wishes that they go, they are willing to do their filial duty.

> 2597   "Agora nos enviades   a tierras de Carrión,
> "debdo nos es a cunplir   lo que mandáredes vos."

They pray that their parents will have good news of them in Carrión.

> 2600   "que ayades vuestros menssajes   en tierras de Carrión."

The Cid does not betray by word or sign to his daughters the anxiety he feels for their future; but he has seen in auguries that somehow the marriage of his daughters will be stained. In spite of that, there is nothing he can do, for he has already given them in wedlock.

> 2615   Víolo en los auueres   el que en buena cinxo espada,
> que estos casamientos   non serién sin alguna tacha.
> Nos puede repentir,   que casadas las ha amas.

There is one precaution he can take, however. He can send his nephew, Félix Muñoz, to escort the party to Carrión, observe the situation of the young wives, and report everything back to the Cid.

With tears and lamentation, father and daughters part from each other.

> 2631   Grandes fueron los duelos   a la departiçión.
> El padre con las fijas   lloran de coraçon.

In a poetic simile foreshadowing the pain to follow, the poet describes the parting as the nail torn from the flesh.

> 2642   Quomo la uña de la carne   ellos partidos son.

Before the Infantes are given an opportunity to consummate their act of treachery against their wives, the poet interposes an odd[3] incident: the affair of the Moor Abengalbón. This scene requires detailed analysis concerning its relationship to the narremic substructure of the poem.

Knowing that the travel party would be passing near Molina, the home of his loyal friend, the Moor Abengalbón, the Cid has instructed Félix Muñoz, accompanying the group, to convey his greetings and request shelter for his daughters, their husbands, and their retinue. Happily acceding to the Cid's request, the Moor grants them lavish hospitality.

> 2648 El moro quando lo sopo, plógol de coraçón;
> saliólos recibir con grandes avorozes;
> Dios, que bien los sirvió a todo so sabor!

The next day, he accompanies them partly on their way, with an escort of two hundred knights. Showing his love for the Cid, the Moor bestows gifts on the girls and fair steeds on the Infantes.

> 2654 A las fijas del Çid el moro sus donas dió,
> buenos seños cavallos a ifantes de Carrión;
> tod esto les fizo el moro por amor del Çid Campeador.

The conduct of the Moor has been exemplary. He has received strangers into his house; but sent by a friend, they are treated as his own. He has spared nothing to make them happy and has even showered them with gifts. How will the Infantes repay their kind host?

Aroused by the display of the Moor's wealth, with no sense of gratitude for his kindness, the Infantes put their scheming minds to work on the possibilities of foul play.

> 2659 Ellos vedien la riqueza que el moro sacó,
> entramos hermanos conssejaron traçión.

Since they are about to desert the Cid's daughters, they obviously need feel no loyalty to the Cid's good friend. If they can kill the Moor, the wealth they will thereby gain will be enormous.

> 2661 "Hya pues que a dexar avemos fijas del Campeador,
> "si pudiéssemos matar el moro Avengalvón,
> "quanta riqueza tiene aver la yemos nos."

3. Barahona, *Al margen de Mio Cid*, p. 123: "Con base en las anteriores observaciones no es fácil hallar la explicación de la conducta que observan con el moro Abengalbón. Esta traición no se explica con el complejo de timidez épica, pues sus fines y antecedentes no guardan relación con éste."

The motive given here so far, omitting for the moment the implications of the first verse, is pure and simple cupidity. Enough has been said by the poet to give some color to his interpretation.

Barahona, taking these verses to mean that this is indeed the chief motive of the Infantes in this affair, notes[4] shrewdly that their greed acts here mainly as a stimulant; but that, in reality, the psychological base of the planned murder is the desperate need of the Infantes to recapture some measure of self-esteem. This is indeed a powerful driving force and no doubt enters into the situation. Before considering the probable psychological motivation, however, we must first return to the more tangible facts cited by the poet himself.

In their secret discussion of their plot, the Infantes had mentioned they would slay the Moor, now that they were going to desert their wives. The purpose of the plot against the Moor is not concealed; they state it specifically.

2664 "Tan en salvo lo abremos   commo lo de Carrión;
"nunqua avrié derecho   de nos el Çid Campeador."

The Infantes well know that their planned mistreatment of the Cid's daughters may entail dangerous consequences. The Moor's wealth will so increase their own power as to place them far beyond the reach of the Cid. From the poet's point of view, this is apparently a motive strong enough to steel their hand for the bloody task.

Although the narrator does not make them explicit, other motives present themselves as possibilities to support the chief one. Abengalbón is a personal friend of the Cid; the Infantes, together with the others, are his guests only because the Cid has requested it. Thus the murder of the Moor would be a blow against the Cid himself and would even involve him obliquely in the crime, since the Moor's trust of the Cid has made the deed possible. Nothing, assuredly, except the cruel treatment of his daughters, could wound the generous heart of the Cid more deeply, as the Infantes must have known.

One fact which seems strange and unexplained is that the Infantes, as described thus far by the poet, have as yet given no indication that they possess within themselves the strength[5]

4. P. 125: "La envidia de las riquizas se presenta como ocasión y estímulo, el crimen como medio para dar paso al egoismo, conquistador invertido, que busca sin peligros el bienestar personal."

5. *Ibid.*: p. 125: "... ¿de dónde salen todas estas fuerzas negativas, destructoras y antiegoístas, que mueven a los infantes para tramar la incalificable traición? ¿Cómo explicarse esta anomalía en dos hombres tímidos? Nada se

necessary to conceive and carry through so bold a deed as the murder of the Moor. In every scene, they have been consistently cast in a negative role: hesitating to ask Alfonso for his intercession in the marriage, repressing their true feelings while living with the Cid in his palace, fleeing the lion in a frantic rush before mocking spectators, avoiding the danger zones on the field of battle. But this is perhaps where the true significance of the Abengalbón incident really lies. It is precisely because the Infantes have not as yet demonstrated a capacity for active, criminal conduct that the poet is constrained to develop their growing power in the performance of evil. Traitors such as these will have no compunction about carrying through their coming act of treachery with the Cid's daughters.

There is another ramification to this important scene. It must be remembered that Félix Muñoz, the Cid's nephew, is also with the party. Unless the Infantes plan to kill him too – and this has not been at all intimated   word will inevitably get back to the Cid. Even in this case, if they wanted to suppress the news entirely – and thereby lessen rather than increase the insult to the Cid – they would have to kill all of the Moor's retainers, an unlikely occurrence. Since the Cid is bound to learn of the affair in one way or another – and the deeper his discomfiture, the greater their revenge – the slaying of the Moor would in itself cut off any retreat from and simultaneously steel them for their projected assault of their wives. Whatever they do, they are going to face the possibility of punishment; as it happens, the discovery of the plot, followed by Abengalbón's's public and contemptuous dismissal of them serves the very same purpose. The Infantes are too much committed to enmity toward the Cid ever to draw back now.

There is a certain incredibility about the capacity of the Infantes, even two against one, to face a great warrior and attempt to kill him. This is not in character for them, and certainly not to be compared to the easy challenge of two helpless young wives. But it is not out of character for them, in their arrogance and self-hypnosis, to believe themselves capable of any violence. The poet could not have intended, by any stretch of the imagination, to allow the Infantes to carry through their plot against Abengalbón; the ground has not been sufficiently prepared for that. The discovery of the plot, with its implications for the Cid when he learns of it, is something else again; it is a highly skilful structural device

puede contestar que satisfaga. ..." (For a possible answer to these questions, see 11/2.)

to keep the Infantes strong enough, through their very fear of the Cid, from backing down on their original plans.

In the act of conspiring against their host, the Infantes are overheard by a Moor who understands their speech.

> 2666 Quando esta falssedad   dizien los de Carrión,
>   un moro latinado   bien gelo entendió;

The latter hastens to his master, to inform him of the plot against his life.

> 2668 non tiene poridad,   díxolo Avengalvón:
>   "Acáyaz, cúriate destos,   ca eres mio señor:
>   "tu muert odi conssejar   a ifantes de Carrión."

The brave Moor, Abengalbón, in his castigation of their traitorous conduct, informs the Infantes that, were it not for his love of the Cid, he would chastise them in such manner that the news would be heard throughout the world, after which he would return the girls to their father; never again would they see their home in Carrión.

> 2677 "Si no lo dexás   por mio Çid el de Bivar,
>   "tal cosa vos faría   que por el mundo sonás,
>   "e luego levaría sus fijas   al Campeador leal;
>   "vos nunqua en Carrión   entrariedes jamás."

It is once again ironic that his very consideration for the Cid holds Abengalbón back from carrying out his threat, an act which could have spared the Cid the suffering which will be his; ironic, that now, in addition to fine wives, great wealth, and long hospitality, the Infantes owe their very lives to the father-in-law for whom their bitter hate can only increase. As an opposing parallel to the tender parting of the Cid with his children, the Moor, standing as surrogate for his friend, tells the Infantes:

> 2681 "Aquim parto de vos   commo de malos e de traydores.

With his last words to them, Abengalbón gives an intimation of unhappiness to come.

> 2684 "Dios lo quiera e lo mande,   que de tod el mundo es señor,
>   "d' aqueste casamiento   ques grade el Campeador."

A pious hope: "God grant the Cid joy from this marriage!" A wish doomed to disappointment, as was the equally ironic prayer of the Cid on the field of battle, that time would alter the young men for the better. The act of treachery is now sufficiently motivated; the Infantes are committed to do their worst.

11/2

CORPES WOOD

The Infantes cannot hasten too quickly away from this further humiliation; to put as much distance as possible between them and their enemies, they travel day and night.

> 2690   acójense a andar   de día e de noch;...

After much journeying, they eventually arrive at Corpes Wood, a lonely forest, with trees whose branches reach the clouds and wild beasts everywhere.

> 2697   Entrados son los ifantes   al robredo de Corpes,
>   los montes son altos   las ramas pujan con las nuoves,
>   elas bestias fieras   que andian aderredor.

This is the place the Infantes have selected for their triumph. Their despicable character is perhaps as fully revealed by their preparations for the crime as by anything they do thereafter. Perhaps they sense some suspicion in their wives concerning what is in store for them; the young women were, after all, witnesses of Abengalbón's public revelation of their plot, and must have understood the ominous nature of his prayer for their welfare. Possibly, also, their greed extends to possessions of another sort: their wives are still their property, though not for long. It may be, moreover, that the young men are greatly aroused, violence and passion so often going hand in hand, by the sadistic pleasure of anticipation. Whatever the basis, nothing is so well calculated to disarm the young women and render their awakening all the ruder than their last night of love.

In a well chosen location, probably an orchard,[6] near a limpid spring, the Infantes make camp for the night.

> 2700   Fallaron un vergel   con una linpia fuont;
>   mandan fincar la tienda   ifantes de Carrión,
>   con quantos que ellos traen   i yazen essa noch, ...

In these idyllic surroundings, the Infantes play their tender love scene; the rising sun will show a different story!

> 2703   con sus mugieres en braços   demuéstranles amor;
>   ¡mal gelo cunplieron   quando salie el sol!

6. Curtius, "Antike Rhetorik und vergleichende Literaturwissenschaft," p. 29: "Menéndez Pidal gibt zu *vergel* die Erklärung: "... una mancha de floresta. ..." Liegt es nicht näher, in dem französischen Lehnwort *vergel* den *verger* zu erkennen, der in der französischen Epik so beliebt ist (*Roland*, 11, 103, 501)?"

The next morning, after their pleasant interlude in the orchard, the Infantes start the final preparations for their big moment. First they order the packing of their many possessions for the continuation of the journey. Then they send away all their retainers temporarily, with the plea that they wish to disport themselves a while with their wives.

> 2708   assí lo mandaron   ifantes de Carrión,
> que non i fincás ninguno,   mugier nin varón,
> si non amas sus mugieres   doña Elvira e doña Sol:
> deportar se quieren con ellas   a todo su sabor.

The masters have spoken, the servants obey, leaving the four alone.

> 2712   Todos eran idos,   ellos quatro solos son, ...

With no one to stop them, the Infantes reveal the type of sport they have in mind; they are going to insult their wives, here in the wild and lonely woods.

> 2714   "Bien lo creades   don Elvira e doña Sol,
> "aquí seredes escarnidas   en estos fieros montes."

They are going to desert their wives, who will never have any share in the estate of Carrión.

> 2716   "Oy nos partiremos,   e dexadas seredes de nos;
> "non abredes part   en tierras de Carrión.

They are not reluctant to explain their motive for shaming their wives in this manner.

> 2718   "Hirán aquestos mandados   al Çid Campeador;
> "nos vengaremos aquesta   por la del león."

The two chief elements which move them, eloquently summarized in these two verses, are the facts that news of the insult will be intentionally reported to the Cid, and that this is therefore personal vengeance against the Cid, required in order to wipe out the insulting stain of the lion incident, which is ever present in their minds. The unfortunate victims have been chosen for two main reasons: because of his love for them, an attack upon them can hurt[7] the Cid more deeply than any direct blow, and, vitally important, this is the kind of retaliation which holds the least

7. Barahona, p. 129: "La venganza personal. Figuras singulares, los infantes dan en la idea de ejercer represalias en las hijas del Cid; es decir, buscan como victimas las personas más próximas al causante de la deshonra. ..."

danger for themselves.[8] Thus in splendid isolation, the Infantes commit their vicious act of treachery, an act which takes the form of a severe beating administered to their wives, followed by desertion.

The nature of the crime, previously discussed (9/2), is such that some attention should be given to the poet's description of it. The Infantes proceed in business-like fashion, stripping their wives of their rich outer garments.

> 2720   Allí les tuellen   los mantos e los pelliçones,
> páranlas en cuerpos   y en camisas y en çiclatones.

Wearing their sharp spurs, they take in hand the strong and heavy saddle-girths.

> 2722   Espuelas tienen calçadas   los malos traydores,
> en mano prenden las çinchas   fuertes e duradores.

The cowardice of the Infantes makes a powerful contrast with the bravery of the girls. Whereas the former are ready to wreak their vengeance on defenseless women, the latter, true daughters of the Cid, beg to be slain with the swords given to the Infantes by their father, rather than be subjected to insult.

> 2725   "Por Diós vos rogamos,   don Díago e don Ferrando, nos!
> "dos espadas tenedes   fuertes e tejadores,
> "al una dizen Colada   e al otro Tizón,
> "cortandos las cabeças,   mártires seremos nos."

Warning their husbands that villainous treatment will bring shame upon the perpetrators themselves, they predict, in a scene reminiscent of the foreshadowing of Ganelon's trial at Aix during the battle of Roncevaux (8/2), that the traitors will be called to a reckoning by the *cortes*.

> 2732   "si nos fuéremos majadas,   abiltaredes a vos;
> "retraier vos lo an   en vistas o en cortes."

The Infantes are not to be diverted from their monstrous deed. With spur and girth, they strike their wives, tearing their sole remaining undergarments, and their delicate flesh, so that the clear blood flows.

> 2736   con las çinchas corredizas   májanlas tan sin sabor;
> ronpien las camisas e las carnes   a ellas amas a dos;
> linpia salie la sangre   sobre las çiclatones.

8. *Ibid.*, p. 132: "... una verdadera agresión diferida, en la que se ha buscado el mayor daño para el enemigo y el menor riesgo para sí mismos. ..."

The beating continues until the husbands are too fatigued to strike further; their only concern, to see which one can deliver the hardest blows.

> 2745 Cansados son de ferir   ellos amos a dos,
>   ensayandos amos   quál dará mejores colpes.

At long last, the girls lose their very power of speech, and are left for dead in the forest.

> 2747 Hya non pueden fablar   don Elvira e doña Sol,
>   por muertas las dexaron   en el robredo de Corpes.

For greater emphasis, the poet repeats twice again, within the next few verses, that the girls are left for dead.

> 2752 Por muertas las dexaron, sabed, que non por bivas.
>
>   . . .
>
> 2754   Ifantes de Carrión   por muertas las dexaron,
>   que el una al otra   nol torna recabdo.

Contemplating the results of their ferocity, the Infantes feel no remorse, but they do indulge in some self-justification.

11/3
THE SELF-JUSTIFICATION OF THE INFANTES

The beating over, the Infantes, not to be cheated of their due, take away their wives' fine cloaks and ermine wraps, leaving them exposed to the savage birds and beasts of the forest.

> 2749   Leváronles los mantos   e las pieles armiñas,
>   mas déxanlas marridas   en briales y en camisas,
>   e a las aves del monte   e a las bestias de la fiera guisa.

On the way back home, the Infantes begin to boast of the vengeance they have taken; it is a vengeance for their ill-considered marriage.

> 2757   por los montes do ivan,   ellos ívanse alabandro:
>   "De nuestros casamientos   agora somos vengados.

There is, however, more than a touch of self-justification in their boasts. Completely forgetting, in their self-hypnosis, the Cid's reluctance (9/5), and their own approach to a similarly reluctant Alfonso (9/5), they now claim that they never would have taken the Cid's daughters even as *varraganas* or "concubines" (chap. 9, n.16), had they not been begged to do so!

> 2759   "Non las deviemos tomar por varraganas,   si non fossemos
> rogados. ..."

Girls such as their wives are simply not worthy of so high an estate.

> 2761   "pues nuestras parejas   non eran pora en braços.

It is the next verse, however, which repeats again the true source of the worm eating away at their soul.

> 2762   "La desondra del león   assís irá vengando."

In order for the vengeance to be complete, it is necessary that the Cid hear of it, and hence necessary that the victims be found.

11/4
THE DISCOVERY OF THE VICTIMS

The Cid's nephew, Félix Muñoz, commissioned by the Cid to keep a protective eye on his daughters, had been forced, against his will, to go on ahead with the others, when the Infantes had asked to be left alone with their wives. (11/2).

> 2765   sobrino era   del Çid Campeador;
> mandáronle ir adelante,   mas de so grado non fo.

Gnawed by anxiety for the welfare of his cousins, Félix Muñoz draws aside from the others, hiding in a coppice to wait for the coming of the Infantes and their wives.

> 2767   En la carrera do iva   doliól el coraçon,
> de todos los otros   aparte se salió,
> en un monte espesso   Félez Muñoz se metió,
> fasta que viesse venir   sus primas amas a dos
> o que an fecho   ifantes de Carrión.

Hidden as he is, Félix Muñoz eventually sees the Infantes riding alone and hears their conversation. Knowing that it would be death if he were discovered (2574), he waits until they have passed, and hastens in search of the girls, only to find them both at death's door.

> 2776   Por el rastro   tornós Félez Muñoz,
> falló sus primas   amorteçidas amas a dos.

The condition of the girls, who cannot speak a word, is heart-breaking.

> 2784   tanto sonde traspuestas   que nada dezir non puoden.
>   Partiéronselo las telas   de dentro del coraçón, ...

The task of Félix Muñoz, once he has seen the girls to safety, is to see that the Cid is informed of what has happened, so that, as the victims themselves have predicted (11/2), the attempt can be made to punish the traitors.

CHAPTER TWELVE

Cantar de Mio Cid: The Punishment and Epilogue

12 Cantar de Mio Cid: The Punishment and Epilogue

12/1

THE ALTERNATIVES FOR PUNISHMENT

As the Infantes are at the very height of the brutal treatment of their wives, the poet interposes not once but twice the fervent wish[1] that the Cid were there to witness the incident.

2741   ¡Quál ventura serie esta,   si ploguiesse al Criador,
       que assomasse essora   el Çid Campeador!

. . .

2753   ¡Quál ventura serie   si assomas essora el Çid Roy Díaz!

Were the Cid actually present in Corpes Wood – assuming the unlikely eventuality that the Infantes would still have the forti-tude to proceed – it would not have been possible for him to observe in silence and without immediate retaliation the cruel mis-treatment of his daughters. It would have been too much to expect of any man that he content himself with threats of future punish-ment through the organized channels of legal justice.

Except where the aim is the accurate reporting of known his-torical facts, a rare concern in the *Cid* (see 9/1, 9/3), an imagina-tive narrator always has a ready stock of literary devices to achieve his purpose. It would have been a simple matter to bring the Cid to the scene; a legitimate suspicion on the part of an anxious father, a hurried message from the outraged Abengalbón, these might have enabled the Cid to intercept the Infantes just before, during, or directly after the crime. The poet must certainly have considered the possibility of the Cid's presence at the scene of the crime, since he himself repeated twice the wish that the Cid might be there. If the arrangement of the story is otherwise, it is because of the obvious intention of the poet to find an alternative form of punishment.

The fact that Félix Muñoz, the Cid's nephew, is actually a

1. This is very much like the way in which the author of the *Roland* inter-poses the wish that the Franks, marching home with Charlemagne, might have some inkling of the terrible ambush: 716 "Deus! quel dulur que li Franceis nel sevent!"

member of the travel party, and thus available, gives the poet another opportunity – if he wishes – to punish the Infantes immediately. The sly manner in which he has been temporarily separated from his cousins and his caution in spying on the Infantes have already been described (11/4). Félix Muñoz, chosen by the Cid for this mission, is, one must assume, a courageous man. Yet he hides from the Infantes because, says the poet, were they to see him, it would surely mean his death.

> 2774   sabed bien que si ellos le vidiessen,   non escapara de muort.

This, it must be admitted, is somewhat strange. Seldom have two proven cowards been assumed so readily to be the equal of one brave man. The odds were certainly not insuperable had Félix Muñoz – or the poet – been intent upon immediate reprisals. Not that Félix Muñoz is without fear; it is striking to observe as a social phenomenon that the poet includes fear as a warrior's trait which requires neither evasion nor explanation. During his attempt to revive his cousins, after their beating, he exhorts them to hurry; he is afraid, he tells them, that wild beasts may devour them all or that the Infantes, discovering his absence, may come back to seek him.

> 2792   "Esforçadvos, primas,   por amor del Criador!
> "De que non me fallaren   ifantes de Carrión,
> "a grant priessa   seré   buscado yo;
> "si Dios non nos vale,   aquí morremos nos."

It is not an avenger that the exigencies of the plot require here, but a messenger to inform the Cid of what has occurred. Since this is the essential, Félix Muñoz must take no chances, despite the provocation. He must hasten first of all to provide for the safety and well-being of the girls, who are in extreme danger. Then he must set in motion the processes of retribution. As quickly as possible, he escorts the girls to the town of Saint Stephen, where they may recuperate their strength.

News such as this spreads quickly. Even before the Cid is informed of the events, King Alfonso learns of it and is grieved to the heart.

> 2825   de cuer pesó esto   al buen rey don Alfons.

This is an important interpolation on the part of the narrator; the king, as the sponsor of the marriage, is directly involved in the outcome, and must share the grief of the Cid.

When the Cid hears what has happened to his daughters, he assumes a pose characteristic[2] of Charlemagne; raising his hand to his beard, he ponders long and carefully.

> 2827 quando gelo dizen   a mio Çid el Campeador,
> una grand ora   penssó e cómidió;
> alçó la su mano,   a la barba se tomó; ...

Nowhere does the poet reveal more starkly than here the potential insufficiency of the type of crime selected as an act of treachery and the central focus of action. The loving father, having just learned that his beloved daughters have been beaten almost to death and left to be mangled by savage beasts in a lonely forest, ponders the situation in all calmness![3]

The Cid's carefully controlled emotions are close enough to the surface, however, to permit a sarcastic prayer of thanks for the "honor" paid to him by the Infantes.

> 2830 "Grado a Cristus,   que del mundo es señor,
> "quando tal ondra me an dada   ifantes de Carrión; ..."

With these words, the Cid shows that he recognizes the intent of the Infantes' action: an insult directed at him, through the repudiation of his daughters. Touched to the quick, he swears that the Infantes will yet be foiled in their plans – the past apparently washed away – not through being forced to take back his daughters but, more effectively, seeing them wed elsewhere in a desirable marriage.

> 2833 "non la lograrán   ifantes de Carrión;
> "que a mis fijas   bien las casaré yo!"

The poet continually emphasizes, as opposed to the physical mistreatment, the repudiation implied by the crime. Thus when Pero Vermúdez speaks to the girls about their terrible ordeal, he congratulates them on being alive and well and otherwise unharmed.

> 2865 "Don Elvira e doña Sol,   cuydado non ayades,
> "quando vos sodes sanas   e bivas e sin otro mal.

---

2. In this same manner, hand on beard and listening for some time in silence, Charlemagne gives his attention to Roland: 215 "Si duist sa barbe, afaitad sun gernun / Ne ben ne mal ne respunt. ..."

3. Castro, "Poesía y realidad," p. 25: "El Cid reprime todo impulso violento, no exterioriza ningún sentimiento elemental."

He tells them that they need not worry; though they have lost a good marriage, they will yet find a better.

> 2867 "Buen casamiento perdiestes,   mejor podredes ganar.

Be it observed that the marriage to the Infantes is still considered a good one, based as it is on the rank of the married partners, rather than on any such immaterial considerations as personal relationships. It is not the beating and near murder that is to be avenged, but the desertion; this is made explicit by the very next verse which sees the hoped-for new marriage as the proper form of vengeance.

> 2868 "Aun veamos el día   que vos podamos vengar!

The Cid himself, when he meets his daughters again, first declares apologetically that he was compelled to accept this marriage against his will, but that he will find a better one for them and thus be avenged on his sons-in-law.

> 2891 "Hyo tomé el casamiento,   mas non osé dezir al.
> "Plega al Criador,   que en çielo está,
> "que vos vea mejor casadas   d' aquí en adelant.
> "De mios yernos de Carrión   Dios me faga vengar!"

The insulting act of treachery has thus far called for some form of punishment, abstractly considered. What exactly shall it be? The Cid and his men take counsel to this end.

The alternative possibilities for immediate reprisals against the Cid have not been taken; nor does the Cid leap to precipitate action even when word reaches him concerning the suffering of his daughters. After quiet deliberation with his men, the Cid determines to refer the matter, without further delay, to King Alfonso of Castile.

> 2898   El que en buen ora nasco   non quiso tardar,
> fablós con los sos   en su poridad,
> al rey Alfons de Castiella   penssó de enbiar.

There is in this calm decision a cool impersonality, which has been taken as a reflection of the Cid's — or the poet's — unawareness of aristocratic concepts.[4] It may very well be true that when

4. Petriconi, "Das Rolandslied und das Lied vom Cid," p. 224: "Was ein Roland, was ein spanischer Held späterer Zeit unter solchen Umständen getan haben würde, steht ausser Zweifel – sie hätten sich persönlich Genugtuung verschafft, das wären sie ihrer Standesehre schuldig gewesen. Unser Dichter dagegen denkt noch nicht in aristokratischen Begriffen. ..." What the critic overlooks here is the literary result of this decision; an extra-

a knight is in the presence of injustice, his reaction should be aimed toward instant, violent, personal satisfaction. On the other hand, when circumstances permit the mind time for thoughtful deliberation, as here, it is precisely then, according to Menéndez Pidal,[5] that conduct based soundly on the juridical code may be considered the mark of a perfect knight.

There is another reason, perhaps even more important, to account for the Cid's failure to react to the affront with private vengeance. He is convinced that it is the king's honor which has been more besmirched[6] than his own. This is made absolutely clear in the message which the Cid, through his vassal Muño Gustioz, transmits to Alfonso. Let him remind the king that it was he who gave the girls in marriage, not the Cid.

> 2906 "desta desondra que me an fecha ifantes de Carrión
> "quel pese al buen rey d'alma e de coraçon.
> "Elle casó mios fijas, ca non gelas di yo; ..."

Therefore, if there is any dishonor, great or small, attaching to the Cid through this desertion, it is all the king's affair.

> 2909 "quando las han dexadas a grant desonor,
> "si desondra y cabe alguna contra nos,
> "la poca e la grant toda es de mio señor.

Contributing heavily to the legal aspect of the case, and therefore to the juridical responsibility of Alfonso, is the question of the great wealth which the Infantes had acquired as his sons-in-law and had borne off under false pretences.

> 2912 "Mios averes se me an levado, que sobejanos son;
> "esso me puede pesar con la otra desonor.

For these reasons, the Cid is entitled to appeal to the king for reparation through a meeting, interview, or king's council.

> 2914 "adúgamelos a vistas, o a juntas o a cortes,
> "commo aya derecho de ifantes de Carrión.

ordinary resemblance to the structural sequence – a narremic sequence – of the *Roland*, where the autonomous core system is expanded by means of an epilogue: The king's council, the judicial duel, and legal punishment.

5. *El Cid en la historia*, p. 28: "El ser entendido en materias jurídicas era, pues, una elevada necesidad y una de las dotes preeminentes que debía poseer el perfecto caballero."

6. Ford, *Main Currents of Spanish Literature*, p. 27: "The news of the infamous insult put upon him by his sons-in-law is brought to the Cid, who at once demands vengeance of the king, reminding Alphonsus that he, the monarch, had assumed responsibility for the marriage. This the king admits."

12/2

THE JUDICIAL QUARREL

In the last verse of his instructions to Muño Gustioz, to be transmitted to Alfonso, the Cid adduces the fundamental reason for his appeal to the king's justice.

> 2916   "ca tan grant es la rencura   dentro en mi coraçón.

The key word, *rencura*, was used once before by the Cid's daughters, while they were describing their just resentment against the Infantes.

> 2862b   "toda nuestra rencura   sabremos contar nos."

Defined[7] by Menéndez Pidal as "... queja, resentimiento, origen de una querella judicial ...," a definition supported by Castro, the acknowledgment of *rencura* contrasts the basic difference between the situation of the Cid and that of the Infantes; it posits the consequent need for a different kind of response on their several parts.

Had the Infantes had a legitimate cause for complaint, they would not have hesitated to ask for a public airing of their "dispute" with the Cid. By employing the stab in the back, delivered at a distance to avoid observation, they were confessing the baselessness of their desire for vengeance.

The Cid, on the contrary, defends a cause too firmly grounded on justice to have to play the game in this way. For what they have done to him and his, the Infantes must be punished; but when they are, there will be no question of justification for the act: the judicial quarrel is open and above board. The Cid is not restraining his natural impulse of indignation and anger unnaturally; he is reasonably taking the proper course for a medieval man solemnly convinced of the justice of his cause.[8]

This is all the more true in the case of the Cid, since the latter,

7. *Cantar de Mio Cid*, II, 825. See also Castro, p. 24: "*Rencura* no es aquí tanto el rencor moderno como la 'queja que da base a una querella judicial.'"

8. Castro, p. 25: "El Cid no es un ser virtuoso, sanctificado, que perdona las injurias; dentro del Poema asume la postura más elevada que para el contemporáneo podía ofrecer un hombre en el horizonte vital: ser sostenido por Dios en el juicio solemne que va a ser abierto ante la corte regia, en esa corte que el juglar se inventa." Castro's final words here may be taken as additional support for the contention that the poet has the choice of several alternatives for punishment and deliberately selects the measures leading to the king's council epilogue.

though personally affected by the crime, is satisfied that the attack more closely concerns the king than himself. Under these conditions, as a knight conscious of his duty to uphold the right,[9] the Cid has a major responsibility in seeing that justice take its proper course. This is precisely the point of the message which Muño Gustioz delivers to the king, as he makes his public charges against the Infantes.

The dignity of the Cid is enhanced by the power of the mighty monarch, before whom his representative, Muño Gustioz, has come to make his accusation.

> 2923   Rey es de Castiella   e rey es de León
>   e de las Asturias   bien a San Çalvador,
>   fasta dentro en Santi Yaguo,   de todo es señor,
>   ellos comdes gallizanos   a él tienen por señor.

Recognizing Muño Gustioz, the king receives him well. Kneeling, the messenger pays his respects and affirms the loyalty of the Cid to his liege lord.

> 2936   "Merçed, rey, de largos reynos   a vos dizen señor!
>   "Los piedes e las manos   vos besa el Campeador;
>   "elle es vuestro vasallo   e vos sodes so señor."

Obeying his instructions, Muño Gustioz quickly reminds Alfonso that it was he who married the Cid's daughters to the Infantes.

> 2939   "Casastes sus fijas   con ifantes de Carrión,
>   "alto fo el casamiento   ca lo quisiestes vos!"

The king is aware, Muño Gustioz tells him, how the Infantes have paid honor to the Cid's family by their insult.

> 2941   "Hya vos sabedes la ondra   que es cuntida a nos,
>   "quomo nos han abiltados   ifantes de Carrión":

In specific detail, the accuser describes the vicious beating, and the desertion of the young wives, left to the mercies of the wild beasts and savage forest birds.

> 2943   "mal majaron sus fijas   del Çid Campeador;
>   "majadas e desnudas   a grande desonor,
>   "desenparadas las dexaron   en el robredo de Corpes,
>   "a las bestias fieras   e a las aves del mont."

---

9. Krauss, *Das tätige Leben und die Literatur*, pp. 27–28: "Die Sicherung des Rechtes wurde für die wichtigste Sendung der Ritter gehalten. ..."

Because of this, the Cid is officially requesting a royal[10] adjudication, either through a meeting, interview, or king's council.

> 2948 "Por esto vos besa las manos, commo vassallo a señor,
> "que gelos levedes a vistas, o a juntas o a cortes.

Alfonso is himself deeply involved, the accuser declares, since whatever dishonor falls to the Cid, his is all the greater, and sufficient cause to grieve him.

> 2950 "tienes por desondrado, mas la vuestra es mayor,
> "e que vos pese, rey, commo sodes sabidor;"

There is but one answer possible, Muño Gustioz concludes, and that is that the Cid receive justice in his complaint against the Infantes.

> 2952 "que aya mio Çid derecho de ifantes de Carrión.

King Alfonso, matching the Cid's calm reception of news in which the element of insult is all too apparent, deliberates carefully before speaking.

> 2953 El rey una grand ora calló e comidió; ...

Unhesitatingly, he affirms his own grief at the unexpected turn of events.

> 2954 "Verdad te digo yo, que me pesa de coraçon, ...

The king makes no difficulty about accepting as true the claim that the responsibility is his.

> 2955 "e verdad dizes en esto, tú, Muño Gustioz,
> "ca yo casé sus fijas con ifantes de Carrion";

In his own justification, Alfonso assures the Cid through his messenger Muño Gustioz that he, the king, had intended the marriage for the Cid's advantage.

> 2957 "fizlo por bien, que ffosse a su pro.

---

10. Menéndez Pidal, II, 901: "vistas, fem. plur., 'reunión con carácter judicial' semejante á la junta ...;" pp. 435–36: "aiunta, 'entrevista,' ... 'sesión de la asamblea judicial de distrito, presedida a veces por el rey' ...;" 598: "cort, 'reunión de la corte del rey, presedida por éste, para tratar algún asunto importante'; en este sentido úsase también el plural *cortes* 2914, 2949. Era la Cort, ó Curia Regia, rueda importantísima en el mecanismo político de León y Castilla. ..." Once again the weakness of the crime is emphasized (see 9/2, 12/1); the three types of judicial assembly listed above are in ascending order of importance, and the plaintiffs do not know which is most appropriate; the decision is left to King Alfonso.

Associating himself completely with the Cid in his hour of tribulation, Alfonso announces his decision: he will give every aid possible toward obtaining justice for him.

> 2959   "Entre yo e mio Çid   pésanos de coraçón.
> "Ayudar lê a derecho,   sín salve el Criador!

Without delay, arrangements are made for *porteros* to travel through the length and breadth of the kingdom, summoning counts and *infançones* to a special court to be held in seven weeks' time at Toledo. The Infantes will be summoned there, to render justice to the Cid and, hopefully, eliminate the basis for the judicial quarrel.

> 2965   "mandaré commo i vayan   ifantes de Carrión,
> "e commo den derecho   a mio Çid el Campeador,
> "e que non aya rencura   podiéndolo vedar yo."

The Infantes had thought to humiliate the Cid through their insulting behavior toward a man of lower rank than theirs. Counteracting this, the king declares that this will be a court set up especially for love of the Cid and through it, despite what has happened, he will yet be honored.

> 2971   "Por amor de mio Çid   esta cort yo fago.
> "Saludádmelos a todos,   entrellos aya espaçio;
> "desto que les abino   aun bien serán ondrados."

The solemn nature and peculiar importance of the trial is underscored by the fact that it is a full king's council; the summons goes throughout the entire kingdom, to León and Santiago, to the Portuguese and the Galicians, to the lords of Carrión and Castile. All loyal vassals must attend, or forfeit their status.

> 2982   qui non viniesse a la cort   non se toviesse por so vassallo.
> Por todas sus tierras   assí lo ivan penssando,
> que non falliessen   de lo que el rey avié mandado.

The Infantes de Carrión are about to have their arrogance put to a real test.

12/3

THE INITIAL PUNISHMENT

Pride, arrogance, and cowardice are the besetting sins of the Infantes: pride, which persuades them that they are superior to the Cid and entitled to behave toward him and his daughters as they wish (2549–51); arrogance, which induces in them the illusion that they have been tricked into marriage with inferiors (2759–61), they who might wed the daughters of kings and emperors (2553); and cowardice, which seeks satisfaction through helpless women, isolated from any possibility of aid (2546–47). It is through these, their own flaws of character, that the Infantes will be punished.

The first inkling that the Infantes have miscalculated, in their pride and arrogance, is the remark by Alfonso, once he has acknowledged his responsibility for the marriages, that he wishes they had never taken place.

> 2958 "¡Si quier el casamiento fecho non fosse oy!

What is significant here is the recognition by the king that the Cid, not the Infantes, has suffered from a misalliance.

Winner of the first round, the Cid takes the second also: he has but to request a simple trial, and the king outdoes himself in preparation for an extraordinary king's council, to the glory of the Cid and the discomfiture of his enemies. The point is not lost on the Infantes, who find cause for alarm in the coming developments.

> 2985 Hya les va pesando a ifantes de Carrión,
> por que en Toledo el rey fazie cort; ...

Not the least of their woes is the cowardly fear of coming face to face with the man they have affronted, but beyond whose reach they had confidently expected to be.

> 2987 miedo han que i verná mio Çid el Campeador.

In their understandable anxiety, the Infantes once more put their overbearing pride to the test: they request the king to rescind the order for the council.

> 2988 Prenden so conssejo assí parientes commo son,
> ruegan al rey que los quite desta cort.

The third round in this preliminary skirmish again goes to the Cid. The king rebuffs the plea of the Infantes with a decisive refusal.

> 2990 Dixo el rey: "No lo feré, sín salve Dios!

The Infantes are obligated to meet the Cid, since he has just cause for a judicial quarrel.

> 2991 "ca i verná mio Çid el Campeador;
> "darlêdes derecho, ca rencura ha de vos."

This initial punishment of the Infantes is firmly reinforced by Alfonso who warns them that failure to comply with his orders will result in exile.

> 2993 "Qui lo fer non quisiesse,   o no irâ mi cort,
> "quite mio reyno,   ca dél non he sabor."

12/4

EPILOGUE: THE KING'S COUNCIL

On the day set for the trial, the lords of the realm appear on schedule, all except the Cid and his men who are nowhere to be seen. Not pleased by the delay, Alfonso nevertheless greets them warmly when the latter eventually arrive, five days late. In solemn preparation for the trial, the Cid follows the customary religious procedure of mass, candles at the altar, and prayerful vigil.

The preliminaries over, the Cid girds himself for his day in court. Calling his good men about him, he warns them of the treacherous propensities of the Infantes. They are to wear their strongest arms, but over them, munificent garments for disguise; in this way they will go to court to demand justice.

> 3077 "so los mantos las espadas   dulçes e tejardores;
> "d' aquesta guisa   quiero ir a la cort,
> "por demandar mios derechos   e dezir mie razón."

With one hundred men as guard, he need not fear the capacities of his enemies for evil.

> 3080 "Si desobra buscaren   ifantes de Carrión,
> "do tales çiento tovier,   bien seré sin pavor."

At his magnificent entrance into court, the noble lords who are to judge the issue rise to their feet to do him honor.

> 3107 Quando lo vieron entrar   al que en buen ora naçió,
> levantós en pie   el buen rey don Alfons
> e el comde don Anrric   e el comde don Remont
> e desí adelant, sabet,   todos los otros de la cort:
> a grant ondra lo reçiben   al que en buen ora naçió.

The only ones who fail to honor him in this way are the men of Carrión, led by Crespo de Grañón.

> 3112 Nos quiso levantar   el Crespo de Grañón,
> nin todos los del bando   de ifantes de Carrión.

While all gaze with admiration at the Cid, at his magnificent beard and manly appearance, the Infantes are compelled to turn away in shame.

> 3126   Nol pueden catar de vergüença   ifantes de Carrión.

Alfonso opens the proceedings by proclaiming that in all his previous reign there had been only two such trials.

> 3128   "Oíd, mesnadas,   sí vos vala el Criador!
> "Hyo, de que fu rey,   non fiz mas de dos cortes: ..."

This third one in Toledo has been called for love of the Cid, that he may receive justice in his complaint against the Infantes. Great wrong has been done him, as everyone knows.

> 3134   "Grande tuerto le han tenido,   sabémoslos todos nos; ...

The king asks only that the judges apply their wisdom to discover the right, since that, and not injustice, is what he wishes.

> 3137   "Todos i meted i mientes,   ca sodes coñosçedores,
> "por escoger el derecho,   ca tuerto no mando yo.

The trial itself is now ready to begin, and without further ado Alfonso requests the Cid to state his case, that they may learn what reply the Infantes wish to make.

> 3143   "Agora demande   mio Çid el Campeador:
> "sabremos que responden   ifantes de Carrión."

Thanking Alfonso for his favor in holding the trial, the Cid is prepared to make his demand.

> 3148   "Esto les demando   a ifantes de Carrión:

First, however, a disavowal: the Cid denies that in deserting his daughters, the Infantes dishonored him; the king himself, who requested the marriage, will know what to do about that.

> 3149   "por mis fijas quem dexaron   yo non he desonor,
> "ca vos las casastes, rey,   sabredes que fer oy; ..."

It was when the Infantes were about to depart for Carrión with his daughters that, in his love for them, the Cid gave them two fine swords, Colada and Tizón, with which to win honor for themselves and serve the king well. When they deserted his daughters in Corpes Wood, however, they showed that they wished nothing from him and forfeited his love.

3156 "quando dexaron mis fijas   en el robredo de Corpes,
       "comigo non quisieron aver nada   e perdieron mi amor; ..."

This then is his demand: since they are no longer his sons-in-law,
let them return his swords.

3158 "denme mis espadas   quando mios yernos non son."

The judges agree at once that his demand is just.

3159 Atorgan los alcaldes: "tod esto es razón."

The Infantes, doubtlessly waiting in fear for the grave charge of
treachery, are overjoyed at this mild request. They believe that, in
accordance with legal formula,[11] this will be the only charge
against them; once they return the swords, the case will be over
and the court will depart, leaving the Cid forever without justice.

3167 "Démosle sus espadas,   quando assí finca la boz,
       "e quando las toviere,   partir se a la cort;
       "hya mas non avrá derecho   de nos el Çid Canpeador."

Turning to the king, the Infantes give their answer: they cannot
deny that the Cid gave them the swords, and if he wants them
back, he may have them.

3172 "Non lo podemos negar,   ca dos espadas nos dió;
       "quando las demanda   e dellas ha sabor,
       "dárgelas queremos   delant estando vos."

Taking the swords, which he recognizes as his own, and swear-
ing by his beard in the manner of Charlemagne,[12] the Cid avers
that thus will his daughters be avenged.

3186 "par aquesta barba   que nadi non messó,
       "assís irán vengando   don Elvira e doña Sol."

These swords he now gives to his own true men, Pero Vermúdez
and Martín Antolínez, "better men," as he calls them. Thanking
God and Alfonso for the favorable decision about Colada and
Tizón, concerning which he declares himself satisfied, he is ready
now to discuss a second *rencura*.

3201 "hya pagado so de mis espadas,   de Colada e de Tizón,
       "Otra rencura he   de ifantes de Carrión: ..."

11. Hinojosa, "El Derecho en el Poema del Cid," p. 565: "Revela la exis-
tencia de la práctica formalista, en cuya virtud el demandante debía exponer
consecutivamente y en un solo acto todos los puntos de la demanda, so pena
de perder su derecho. ..."
12. When Duke Naimon, in the *Roland*, volunteers to go as an envoy to
Marsile in place of Ganelon, Charlemagne responds: 249 "Par ceste barbe
e par cest mun gernun, / Vos n'irez pas. ..."

The Cid has a second, more serious complaint. As a parting gift to the Infantes, about to leave with his daughters for Carrión, he had given them three thousand marks in silver and gold. In spite of what he had done for them, they were still capable of repaying him as they had.

> 3203   "quando sacaron de Valençia   mis fijas amas a dos,
> "en ora e en plata   tres mill marcos les dîo;
> "hyo faziendo esto,   elles acabaron lo so; ..."

He demands, now that they are no longer his sons-in-law, that they return to him his wealth.

> 3206   "denme mios averes,   quando mios yernos non son."

The Infantes reply that they have returned the swords in order to put an end to the trial. But the king commands that they meet this demand also. The Infantes having already spent all the wealth received, offer to pay in property from their estate in Carrión.

> 3223   "pagar le hemos de heredades   en tierras de Carrión."

The judges are not opposed to this solution, if the Cid is willing to accept it, but it is their judgment that full restitution be made to the Cid here in court.

> 3225   "Si esso ploguiere al Cid,   non gelo vedamos nos;
> "mas en nuestro juvizio   assí lo mandamus nos,
> "que aquí lo enterguedes   dentro en la cort."

All that remained of the three thousand marks, a mere two hundred, the Infantes gave to King Alfonso; these are now returned to the Cid as his property. Above this amount, the Infantes are forced to borrow; they hand over considerable property in the form of war-steeds, palfreys, mules, and swords, which the Cid accepts according to the court's valuation.

> 3242   Veriedes aduzir   tanto cavallo corredor,
> tanta gruessa mula,   tanto palafré de sazón,
> tanta buena espada   con toda guarnizón;
> recibiólo mio Çid   commo apreçiaron en la cort.

Compared to their former confident selves, the Infantes are coming off a sorry sight.

> 3229   Mal escapan jogados,   sabed, desta razón.

But worse is yet to come. Now that the Infantes have restored Colada and Tizón, and have gone deeply into debt to make restitution for the wealth they had carried off, the Cid begs leave to present his chief complaint.

There is mounting tension as the Cid addresses the court on his final and major complaint, which he is not prepared to forget. Begging all present to join with him in his affliction, the Cid now affirms that for the great dishonor which the Infantes visited upon him, nothing short of a challenge will suffice.

> 3254 "La rencura mayor   non se me puede olbidar.
> "Oídme toda la cort   e pésevos de mio mal;
> "ifantes de Carrión,   quem desondraron tan mal,
> "a menos de riebtos   no los puedo dexar.

With bitter eloquence, he asks the Infantes directly wherein he has offended them, in jest or in earnest? For any fault of his, he is willing to make amends, as the court decide.

> 3258   "Dezid ¿qué vos merecí,   ifantes de Carrión,
> "en juego o en vero   o en alguna razón?
> 3259b "aquí lo mejoraré   a juvizio de la cort.

At this point, the Cid makes the specific charge of treachery. If the Infantes, traitorous dogs, did not want his daughters any longer, why did they take the girls away from Valencia, laden with untold wealth?

> 3261 "A la salida de Valençia   mis fijas vos di yo,
> "con muy grand ondra   e averes a nombre;
> "quando las non queriedes,   ya canes traidores,
> "¿por qué las sacávades   de Valençia sus honores?

Why did they beat the girls with girths and with spurs, leaving them alone to the savage beasts and birds of Corpes Wood? For what they have done to his daughters, it is themselves they have shown to be less in worth.

> 3268 "Por quanto les fiziestes,   menos valedes vos.

And it is for this that he demands redress, from the Infantes or from the court.

> 3269 "Si non recudedes,   véalo esta cort."

In this court scene, the Cid demonstrates an admirable legal dexterity[13] in the submission of his claims. Historically, it seems

13. Entwistle, "Remarks Concerning the Order of the Spanish Cantares de Gesta," p. 119: "Thus the known legal skill of the Cid appears in the conduct of his case before Alfonso, both in the scrupulous observance of the forms of

to violate normal trial procedure, which presumably required that all charges be preferred at once (see n. 11); Castro is very likely correct in assuming that it was invented out of the whole cloth (n. 8). If so, the poet is to be congratulated on a skilful and effective literary arrangement, a triple variation[14] which leads the Infantes step by step deeper into the trap.

Similar in pattern to the triple variation of the initial punishment (12/3), the Cid's trial technique begins by first establishing the guilt of the Infantes; their initial agreeableness in restoring Colada and Tizón is in itself a confession. Next, the Infantes are forced, against their will, to restore the Cid's wealth; as a result of the judge's decision against them, they are plunged in debt, a sign of even deeper guilt. When finally the charge of treachery is preferred against them and they are challenged to fight, their backs are against the wall.[15] Nevertheless, they attempt to defend their conduct.

The defense of the Infantes is divided into two parts: a preliminary verbal duel between Count Don García and the Cid; and a triple set of challenges to judicial duel addressed to the Infantes, Fernando and Diego, and to Asur González. Don García, sworn enemy of the Cid and once before humiliated by him, is the first to speak. In the best military tradition, which favors offense as the best defense, Don García begins by making light of the Cid's appearance in court, with his overgrown beard which fills some with fear and others with wonder.

> 3272 "Vezós mio Çid a llas cortes pregonadas;
> "dexóla creçer e luenga trae la barba;
> "los unos le han miedo e los otros espanta."

The case for the defense is simple: the Infantes – so claims Don García – are so superior to the Cid by birth that they should never have accepted the daughters as concubines, much less as wives and equals.

justice, and the dexterous arrangement of his claims." See also Hinojosa, pp. 580–81: "La fidelidad con que retrata el Autor las instituciones conocidas por las fuentes jurídicas, es garantía segura de su exactitud respecto á las que conocemos solamente por el *Poema*."

14. The triple-variation technique is almost a keynote of the *Roland*; e.g., Roland refuses three times to sound the horn at Oliver's request; then he insists three times that he will sound it against Oliver's will; Roland tries three times to break his sword Durendal (vv. 2300–51).

15. Entwistle, p. 119: "By reserving his most serious charge to the end he is able to secure restitution of property and chattels, before he compels his opponents to fight to the death on an accusation of *menos valor*."

3275 "Los de Carrión,   son de natura tan alta,
   "non gelas devién querer   sus fijas por varraganas,
   "¿o quien gelas diera   por parejas o por veladas?"

Therefore, the Infantes had every right to act as they did, and the Cid's complaint is worthless.

3278 "Derecho fizieron   por que las han dexadas.
   "Quanto él dize   non gelo preçiamos nada."

There is a certain (probably unconscious) humor to the scene in which the Cid, informed that his beard is overgrown, his daughters not fit for concubines, their desertion fully justified, and his own words of little value, concentrates nevertheless on first problems first. This note is caught in Huntington's translation:

3280 The Campeador laid hand upon his beard.
   "My Thanks to God who heaven and earth commands!
   'Tis long, for while it grew, 'twas cared for well.
   What moves you, Count, to thus attack my beard?
   For since it grew it every care received.
   Ne'er son of woman born laid hand thereon,
   Nor ever plucked it Christian's son nor Moor's,
   As I did yours in Cabra's castle, Count,
   When took I Cabra and you by your beard,
   No boy was there but plucked a thumb's length forth,
   Not yet the part I plucked hath even grown."

It is possible that the Cid may have had more to say on this growing subject, but one of the Infantes, Fernando, apparently impatient for the trial to end, cannot help interrupting the Cid with the request to stop this talk!

3293 "Dexássedes vos, Çid,   de aquesta razón; ..."

Fernando wishes to speak for himself.

Observing the failure of Don García's offense, Fernando González tries, to the best of his ability, the path of reasonableness. The Cid has, after all, had all his wealth restored to his satisfaction. What further need is there for a *varaja*,[16] or legal argument, between them?

3294 "de vuestros averes   de todos pagados ssodes.
   "Non creçiés varaja,   entre nos e vos."

16. Menéndez Pidal, p. 884: "varaia, fem., 'alegación de dos partes litigantes ante el juez', 3295; en el Cantar, la baraja es en materia criminal ..., pero lo era también en materia civil, respondiendo al carácter de lucha entre las dos partes que tenía el procedimiento germánico primitivo. ..."

Repeating the lines of their basic defense, Fernando again affirms that nobles of their quality have the right to marry the daughters of kings and emperors; that the daughters of *infançones* are simply not proper mates for them (3296–98). In deserting their wives, the Infantes were doing no more than the right thing; it is an act they are proud of, rather than ashamed.

> 3299   "Por que las dexamos   derecho fiziemos nos;
>   "más nos preçiamos,   sabet, que menos no."

Restraining himself with an effort, the Cid bids Pero Vermúdez make the reply; the latter would not, otherwise, have the right to issue the challenge to arms. Pero Vermúdez is slow and halting of speech; at the Cid's court they call him Pero the Mute.

> 3309   "Dirévos, Çid,   costunbres avedes tales,
>   "siempre en las cortes   Pero Mudo me llamades!

But he is well capable of doing what is required; addressing Fernando directly, he gives him the lie to his face.

> 3313   "Mientes, Ferrando,   de quanto dicho has.
>   "por el Campeador   mucho valiestes más."

The eloquence of the dumb pours in a flood once it is unloosed. Pero Vermúdez calls attention to the instances in which Fernando had acted in cowardly fashion: the time he pleaded to go into battle only to turn tail before the Moor, whom Pero himself had to kill to save his life – a story kept secret until now; and the lion incident, when Fernando cowered beneath the couch, nowhere in sight when he was sought. Fair he might be in appearance, but in reality he, Fernando, is nothing but a *mal varragán*,[17] a coward.

> 3327   "E eres fermoso,   mas mal varragán!
>   "¡Lengua sin manos,   quomo osas fablar?"

There is a delightful double parody in these two verses. The Infantes, who have judged the Cid's daughters as less than *varraganas*, are themselves now judged as less than *varragán*. And the man who so labels them, a mute warrior in arms – without a tongue, so to speak – calls his opponent a "tongue without hands."

Pero Vermúdez is not yet through, however. Boldly, he defies the traitor and challenges him to a duel, here before King Alfonso.

17. *Ibid.*, p. 886: "varragán ó *barr-*, masc., 'mozo'; y aludiendo al vigor que trae consigo la mocedad: *buen barragán* 2671 'valiente' (comp. "buen mozo" 'hombre de aventajada estatura y conformación), *mal varragán* 3327 'cobarde'. ..." (The Moor Abengalbón was desecribed by the poet as a 'buen barragán, 2671.)

3343 "Riébtot el cuerpo   por malo e por traidor.
     "Éstot lidiaré aquí   ante rey don Alfons.

In combat he will prove that the Infantes did wrong in deserting
their wives; though the latter are women and the former men,
they are their better in every way.

3346 "por quanto las dexastes   menos valedes vos;
     "ellas son mugieres   e vos sodes varones,
     "en todas guisas   más valen que vos.

                    . . .

3350 "tú lo otorgarás   a guisa de traidor;
     "de quanto he dicho   verdadero seré yo."

It is now the turn of Diego González to take up the defense, the
first line of which is the utter purity of their blood-stream; it was
definitely not fitting for them to become the sons-in-law of the
Cid.

3354 "De natura somos   de los comdes más linpios;
     "¡estos casamientos   non fuessen apareçidos,
     "por consagrar   con mio Çid don Rodrigo!"

In view of their lineage, so superior to the Cid's, the brothers
"still" do not repent their desertion.

3357 "Porque dexamos sus fijas   aun no nos repentimos; ..."

According to Diego, it is not for the Infantes, but for the Cid's
daughters to sigh during their lifetime; what happened will be a
permanent reproach to the girls.

3558 "mientra que bivan   pueden aver sospiros:
     "lo que fiziemos   seer les ha retraydo."

This he is prepared to defend against the fiercest fighter, that in
deserting their wives, the Infantes have honored themselves.

3559b "Esto lidiaré   a tod el más ardido:
      "que por que las dexamos   ondrados somos venidos."

Martín Antolínez replies by asking Diego to recall the lion
incident, in which he had covered himself with wine-stains instead
of glory, to the point where he could never wear those garments
again.

3362 "Calla, alevoso,   boca sin verdad!
     "Lo del león   non se te deve olbidar; ..."

Contrary to the belief of the Infantes, they had no right to desert their wives, who are worth more than they. From his own mouth, after the fight, Diego will confess himself a traitor and a liar!

> 3370 "Al partir de la lid   por tu boca lo dirás,
> "que eres traydor   e mintist de quanto dicho has."

The defendants, Diego and Fernando González, sons of Count Don Gonzalo Ansúrez, and heirs of Carrión, stand committed to prove with arms the legitimacy of their defense. There is a third, however, ready to enter the lists and fight for his kin, the Infantes; Asur González, presenting a slightly comic, if sacrilegious, appearance, now comes into the palace, trailing his ermine cloak, his face flushed from feasting in obvious betrayal of his fast.

> 3374 manto armiño   e un brial rastrando;
> vermejo viene,   ca era almorzado.
> En lo que fabló   avie poco recabdo: ...

There is little enough sense in what he has to say, as he rhetorically asks those about him if ever anyone saw as evil a thing as this complaint.

> 3377 "Hya varones,   ¿quien vido nunca tan mal?"

Contemptuously, he calls for information about the Cid, "picking at his mills for his miller's toll corn."

> 3378 "¿Quién nos darie nuevas   de mio Çid el de Bivar!
> "¡Fosse a Rio d'Ovirna   los molinos picar
> "e prender maquillas,   commo lo suele far!"

Whoever told the Cid, Asur González would like to know, that he should contract marriage with the house of Carrión?

> 3381 "¿Quil darie   con los de Carrión a casar?"

It would appear that, in addition to their other failings, the house of Carrión may also be accused of short memories. In the poem, it was the Infantes who begged for the intercession of the king in arranging the marriage; and it was the king who compelled the Cid, against his better judgment, to yield. Without making use of this argument, Muño Gustioz contents himself with calling Asur a liar and traitor.

Muño Gustioz scornfully charges Asur González with breaking his fast before prayer; he is a man false to friend and lord, but above all false to God.

3384 "Antes almuerzas   que vayas a oración,
"a los que das paz,   fártaslos aderredor.
"Non dizes verdad   âmigo ni ha señor,
"falsso a todos   e más al Criador."

The truth of this Asur González will be forced to admit.

3389 "Fazer telo he dezir   que tal eres qual digo yo."

At this point Alfonso calls for a cessation of the arguments. Those who have issued the challenges will have to fight.

3390 Dixo el rey Alfons: "Calle ya esta razón,
"Los que an reptado   lidiarán, sín salve Dios!"

But before the judicial duels actually begin, there is an extraordinary interruption.

12/5

THE JUDICIAL DUEL

Before the judicial combats are permitted to begin, the poet interposes a remarkable scene; one which, because of its effect on the morale of the Infantes, can easily be understood as part of their coming ordeal by battle. Two knights enter the court, kiss the hands of King Alfonso, and request of the Cid that he give his daughters in holy and honorable matrimony to be queens of Navarre and Aragón.

3398 piden sus fijas   a mio Çid el Campeador
por seer reínas   de Navarra e de Aragon,
e que gellas diessen   a ontra e a bendiçión.

It is not difficult to imagine the hush that settles on the court as all pause to listen with careful attention to the new development.

3401 A esto callaron   e ascuchó toda la cort.

The Cid thanks God for this happy request from Navarre and Aragón but Alfonso is his liege, and his daughters, as before, are in the king's hands, to do as he commands.

3406 "Vos las casastes antes,   ca yo non,
"afé mis fijas,   en vuestras manos son:
"sin vuestro mandado   nada non feré yo."

Out of love for the Cid and in the interest of increasing his honor, his lands, and his fiefs, the king proposes that the marriage

of the Cid's daughters to the Infantes of Navarre and Aragón be
seen to this very day.

> 3412   "este casamiento   oy se otorgue en esta cort,
> "ca creçevos i ondra   e tierra e onor.

This new turn of events pleases most heartily most of the spectators at the court, but naturally, not the Infantes.

> 3427   A muchos plaze   de tod esta cort,
> mas non plaze   a ifantes de Carrión.

Hardly has the matter of the new marriage between the Cid's
daughters and the heirs of Navarre and Aragón been settled, when
a second interruption occurs, to the further discomfiture of the
Infantes of Carrión. Alvar Fáñez rises to denounce them on his
own account; he too has a *grand rencura* (3437) against them, and
for good reason. It was he who gave away his cousins, by the
delegated authority of the king, into honorable and holy wedlock.

> 3438   "Hyo les di mis primas   por mano del rey Alfons,
> "ellos las prisieron   a ondra e a bendiçión; ..."

Because of their dishonorable conduct in bearing away the Cid's
great gifts, and then deserting their wives, despite their free acceptance of the marriage, Alvar Fáñez is determined to "defy
their bodies as evil-doers and traitors."

> 3442   "Riébtoles los cuerpos   por malos e por traidores."

Although Gómez Peláyet, of the Carrión party, is ready to
accept this additional challenge, King Alfonso forbids expressly
any further dispute. Why then does the poet bother to bring in
an abortive challenge? There would seem to be several literary
purposes served by this incident.

Dramatically, Alvar Fáñez, through his interruption, has introduced a delaying tactic which deeply intensifies the eagerness for
combat. In the second place, from the point of view of literary
form, the incident seems to indicate that the poet is consciously
intent on keeping to a triple variation pattern; this is clearly evident from the words of Alfonso insisting on three challenges.

> 3465   "Cras sea la lid,   quando saliere el sol,
> "destos tres por tres   que rebtaron en la cort."

The most important purpose served by the incident, however,

is functional: Alvar Fáñez, in his remarks, is announcing in advance the real and final punishment of the Infantes. Formerly, he declares, the Infantes could hold the Cid's daughters in their arms as wives and equals.

3449 "antes las aviedes parejas   pora en braços las dos, ..."

Now that the girls will be queens of Navarre and Aragón, their former husbands will have to kiss their hands, call them ladies, and serve them, no matter how this might grieve them.

3450 "agora besaredes sus manos   e llamar las hedes señores,
"aver las hedes a servir,   mal que vos pese a vos."

The Infantes, having repudiated their wives with the intention of forming a better alliance, discover that it is not they who will wed the "daughters of kings and emperors," but their discarded wives who are marrying kings' sons. Too shaken to submit at once to the judicial duels, which Alfonso had scheduled for sunrise the next morning, the Infantes plead for a delay.

It is the Infantes themselves who interpose the third[18] interruption of the proceedings. The punishment they have been taking is intense. Forced to stand trial brought by an inferior, deprived of their good swords Colada and Tizón, depleted of their steeds, armor and other property, their humiliation of the Cid's daughters turned upon themselves, they are in no position to fight. They beg the king for permission to return to Carrión to replace the arms and steeds they have given to the Cid.

3468 "Dandos, rey, plazo,   ca cras seer non puode.
"Armas e cavallos   diémoslos al Canpeador.
"nos antes abremos a ir   a tierras de Carrión."

Alfonso agrees to abide by the Cid's decision in this. The latter prefers his own home to Carrión and expresses his wish to return to Valencia. The king then schedules the judicial combat for three weeks hence, on the fields of Carrión; unconditionally, he guarantees the safety of the Cid's champions, promising to protect them

18. The pattern of triple variation (see n. 14) pervades this entire portion of the poem: after the triple aspect of the initial punishment (12/3), there are three complaints at the trial, the three accepted challenges, the three interruptions before combat, and eventually the three duels. For an elaborate formal – not functional – analysis of the tripartite construction of an epic and the constant prevalence of triple variation, see Keller, "Structure of the *Poema de Fernán González*."

from harm or treachery. In taking leave of the Cid, who has showered all with fabulous gifts, Alfonso swears that there is no better man in the entire kingdom.[19]

> 3509 "Hyo lo juro   par sant Esidre el de León
> "que en todas nuestras tierras   non ha tan buen varón."

King Alfonso greatly admires the fleet Babieca, the Cid's own war-steed. With his proverbial generosity, the latter offers it to the king, who declines the gift, however, stating that master and horse were meant for each other, in the great task of chasing Moors from the battlefield.

> 3517 "si a vos le tollies, el cavallo   no havrie tan buen señor.
> "Mas atal cavallo cum ést   pora tal commo vos,
> "pora arancar moros del canpo   e seer segudador; ..."

Meanwhile, the Cid gives his final instructions to his champions, bidding them show themselves men in battle, so that good reports will come back to him in Valencia.

> 3525b "firmes seed en canpo   a guisa de varones;
> "buenos mandados me vayan   a Valençia de vos."

They promise that he may hear they have been killed, but not conquered.

> 3529 "podedes odir de muertos,   ca de vencidos no."

Satisfied, the Cid departs for Valencia, to await the three weeks and the final outcome.

After the departure of the Cid for Valencia, his three champions, accompanied by Alfonso, in whose protection they are, arrive at the appointed location in Carrión, where they await the Infantes for two days beyond the designated time. On their own home grounds, the treacherous Infantes had been planning to decoy and murder their opponents.

> 3538 Mucho vienen bien adobados   de cavallos e de guarnizones;
> e todos sos parientes   con ellos acordados son
> que si los pudiessen apartar   a los del Campeador,
> que los matassen en campo   por desondra de so señor.

19. These words recall the manner in which Ganelon praises the emperor Charlemagne to the Saracen Marsile: 532 "Tant nel vos sai ne preiser ne loer / Que plus n'i ad d'onur e de bontet. / Sa grant valor, kil purreit acunter?"

Only their great fear of Alfonso prevented the attempt.

> 3542 El cometer fue malo, que lo al nos enpeçó,
> ca grand miedo ovieron a Alfonsso el de León.

Since the first trick did not work, the Infantes are prepared for a second. Seriously regretting the swords, Colada and Tizón, which they now fear in the hands of their enemies, on the advice of García Ordóñez, they request Alfonso to forbid the use of them in the fight, a demand which he rejects. Instead, the king tells them that honor will accrue to them if they win; but if they are defeated, they will have no one to blame but themselves.

> 3565 "si del campo bien salides, grand ondra avredes vos;
> "e ssi fuéredes vençidos, non rebtedes a nos,
> "ca todos lo saben que lo buscastes vos."

Bitter is the regret that bites into their souls; well might they fear that right is not on their side. Although it is not their treacherous deeds which they regret, but their present danger, not all the wealth in Carrión could have induced them to do what they did, had they foreseen that it would come to this.

> 3568 Hya se van repintiendo ifantes de Carrión,
> de lo que avien fecho mucho repisos son;
> no lo querrien aver fecho por quanto ha en Carrión.

Well knowing the perfidy of the Infantes, the Cid's champions remind the king that no one can tell what treachery the brothers have in mind, and that the Cid has placed them in his hands to see that justice is done.

> 3578 "non sabemos qués comidrán ellos o qué non;
> "en vuestra mano nos metió nuestro señor;
> "tenendos a derecho, por amor del Criador.!"

This responsibility Alfonso fully accepts, as he warns the Infantes to defend their right honorably and to attempt no tricks.

> 3598 "Estos tres cavalleros de mio Çid el Campeadore
> "hyo los adux a salvo a tierras de Carrione;
> "aved vuestro derecho, tuerto non querades vose,
> "ca qui tuerto quisiere fazer, mal gelo vedaré yove,
> "en todo mio reyno non avrá buena sabore."

The Infantes are sad indeed to hear these words:

> 3603 Hya les va pesando a ifantes de Carrión.

Nothing remains now to delay the final judgment.

The first to enter the lists in combat are Pero Vermúdez and Fernando González. After a sharp battle, Fernando is wounded by a lance thrust. Seeing Pero Vermúdez coming at him with the sword which he recognizes as Tizón, Fernando fearfully admits defeat, without waiting for the final blow.

> 3643   quando lo vido Ferrán Gonçálvez,   conuvo a Tizón;
>   antes que el colpe esperasse   dixo: "vençudo so."

The second fight is between Martín Antolínez and Diego González. Their lances shattered, Martín strikes Diego a mighty blow with Colada. Knowing he cannot otherwise escape with his life, Diego turns his horse's head and flees the field, without even attempting to reply with his own sword.

> 3665   "valme, Dios glorioso,   Señor, cúriam deste espada!"
>   el cavallo asorrienda,   e mesurandol del espada,
>   sacol del mojón;   don Martino en el campo fincava.

The third and last duel, between Muño Gustioz and Asur González, is a little more dramatic than the combat with the cowards. Asur, like Pinabel and the thirty hostages of Ganelon, is guilty of no crime except, perhaps, family loyalty to traitors; this may be why the poet gives him an opportunity to strike Muño, piercing the shield, though not the flesh. The issue is not long in doubt, however; Asur himself is soon so badly wounded that the onlookers take him for dead. The last defender of the house of Carrión now confesses himself vanquished.

> 3690   dixo Gonçalvo Anssuórez: "nol firgades, por Dios!
>   "vençudo es el campo,   quando esto se acabó!"

The Cid has been vindicated by judgment of God. His honor restored, he may now enjoy with clear conscience the fruits of his glorious victories. The Infantes, on the other hand, have confessed defeat, acknowledging their guilt as traitors, and the justice of their punishment.

12/6

THE FINAL PUNISHMENT

The final punishment of the Infantes takes two forms: utter disgrace for the cowardly traitors, supreme vindication for the aggrieved victim. The preliminary punishments were hard enough to bear: the Infantes have lost not only the support of King Alfonso to an inferior in rank, but also the wealth for which they had contracted their "misalliance" in the first place. These are as nothing, however, compared with the soul-searing loss of pride faced by the arrogant young men, brought low by judgment of God in their judicial ordeal.

The official seal of legal punishment consists in the statements of the judges in council, certifying individually the defeats of the Carrión defendants and the victories of the Cid's champions. When Fernando, to save his life, admits that he is vanquished, the judges yield the victory to Pero Vermúdez.

> 3645   Atorgaróngelo los fideles,   Per Vermudoz le dexó.

Diego's flight from the field of battle draws from Alfonso the remark that Martín Antolínez, by his deed, has indeed conquered:

> 3669   "por quanto avedes fecho   vençida avedes esta batalla."

And to this, the judges give their unhesitating assent:

> 3670   Otórgangelo los fideles   que dize verdadera palabra.

The surrender of Asur González to Muño Gustioz, admitting defeat, is also acknowledged by the judges to be a legal fact.

> 3692   Dixieron los fideles: "esto odimos nos."

There can henceforth be no question that the Infantes are legally guilty as charged.

When the Cid's champions are at length ready to leave, they follow Alfonso's suggestion and travel at night, in order to avoid a possible treacherous attack. Deep is the joy in Valencia, for the Infantes have been left behind in complete disgrace as convicted evil-doers.

> 3702   por malos los dexaron   a ifantes de Carrión,
>
> . . .
>
> 3705   Grant es la biltança   de ifantes de Carrión.

This shame of lost honor, solemnly revealed by God's judgment, accomplished in open combat before the eyes of peers from all corners of the realm, and sealed by legal decision of the royal judges, makes a punishment of no mean proportions: it is a fundamental lesson which the poet has tried to teach.[20] In a sense, it is a fate worse than the death which could have been their lot, had the Infantes not groveled abjectly and been reprieved. Remaining

---

20. Castro, p. 27: "Después de lo escrito se ve distintamente que lo jurídico y lo didáctico no es ganga que arrastre el Poema, sino elemento esencial de cierta concepçión de la vida, base de la civilización coetánea."

alive, they keep their punishment alive by being forced to defer to the new glories of their former wives. As the poet phrases his moral lesson, whoever mistreats a lovely lady, shaming and deserting her, deserves the like or worse (see 9/2). And now, continues the poet, let us leave the Infantes to rue their deed and the fate they have so richly earned.

The obverse of punishment for the Infantes – perhaps more accurately its crowning aspect – is the intense joy in the Cid's camp, because of the corresponding honor they have won.

> 3711 Grandes son los gozos   en Valençia la mayor,
>   porque tan ondrados   foron los del Canpeador.

The Cid considers himself thoroughly avenged for the mistreatment of his daughters and is ready to give thanks.

> 3714 "Grado al rey del çielo,   mis fijas vengadas son!
>   "Agora las ayan quitas   heredades de Carrión!"

All taint of shame removed, the Cid can now marry his daughters once again, whoever likes it or not.

> 3716 "Sin vergüença las casaré   o a qui pese o a qui non."

With the approval of Alfonso, the Cid's daughters, Doña Elvira and Doña Sol, are married to the heirs of Navarre and Aragón. The former marriages to the Infantes de Carrión were good, but these are even better.

> 3719 Fizieron sos casamientos   don Elvira e doña Sol;
>   los primeros foron grandes,   mas aquestos son mijores;
>   a mayor ondra las casa   que lo que primero fo.

Thus with his daughters married into the royal houses of Navarre and Aragon, the Cid is related to the kings of Spain.

> 3724 Oy los reyes dEspaña   sos parientes son, ...

With these words, the poet completely justifies his choice of a "domestic event" (see 9/3) as the central pivot of action. His revolutionary motif, the mistreatment of women as a major literary theme, is completely successful: in context, the deed of the Infantes has proved to be an act of treachery on a scale to challenge God and king, fully worthy of their intervention. In his self-vindication, the Cid serves a higher purpose as well, reaching the zenith of his glory with the triumph of justice.

12/7

CANTAR DE MIO CID: SUBSTRUCTURE

The autonomous core system of the *Cid*, like that of the *Roland* (see 8/10), contains a sequence of four narremes which we have labeled Type 1 (2/7). Its substructural framework, however, is subject to a little greater modification than that of the *Roland*, because of a double expansion (see 4/6–4/7): a prologue[21] to the family quarrel, as well as an epilogue to the punishment. The schematic narremic pattern of the expanded core system thus shows the following parts in the *Cid*:

1 Expansion: The Prologue

  a/ The quest, the exiled hero seeks vindication and glory.

  b/ The test, the hero worthily achieves wealth and fame.

21. Huerta, *Poética del Mio Cid*, pp. 103–4: "Los tres Cantares se refieren al mismo protagonista y tienen por unidad interna el triúnfo del héroe. ..." Despite this, Huerta notes a structural difference in the relationship of the three *Cantares* to each other: "Con todo, esta unidad moral o mítica permite que el asunto se agrupe con cierta independencia en los tres sucesivos Cantares, particularmente en el primero. En efecto, nada evidente indica, a lo largo del Cantar del *Destierro*, que su autor hubiera proyectado los otros dos cuando lo estaba componiendo." To this sweeping statement, we except only one verse, (282), a barely noticeable link to the coming marriage (see 9/5). Regarding the other two *Cantares*, he continues: "En cambio, la separación entre el Cantar de las *Bodas* y el de la *Afrenta de Corpes* es una ficción artística."

De Chasca, *Estructura y forma*," pp. 30–33, differentiating between "acción principal" ("El sistema total de incidentes ocasionados por las exigencias de la honra del Cid constituye la acción principal"), and "incidentes y episodios" ("La acción principal consta de incidentes y episodios"), considers the marriage "... el mas importante de los incidentes intermedios, esto es, de los incidentes que contribuyen al engrandecimiento del Cid y que entrelazan el medio con el principio y el fin." The marriage is the Cid's crowning achievement of all that has preceded: "El casamiento es, pues, la mayor honra que el Campeador ha logrado hasta ahora. ..." It is also the focal point of the poem, and the cause of what is to follow: "Desde el punto de vista de la estructura, reducir las bodas al mínimo de espectacularidad es un gran acierto, porque así resalta más su importancia como resultado culminante y forzoso de todo lo que ha ocurrido hasta entonces, y como ocasión de lo que va a ocurrir hasta el desenlace final."

We may accept this analysis as recognizing the *preparatory* nature of the events leading up to the marriage (which we call the prologue); and as recognizing this marriage as the *first cause* of what follows (thus introducing the family quarrel and the rest of the narremic chain). No less than the epilogue (see chap. 8, n. 32), the prologue, even if structurally outside the autonomous core system (i.e. the *obligatory* incidents of the substructure), has an important function not to be underestimated. It raises the status of a "domestic event" to epic proportions, making it possible in turn to clothe the act of wife-beating with the dread qualities of an act of treachery and an attack on the king's honor (see chap. 1, n. 15, 9/1–9/4, 12/2).

      c/ The initial reward, the king reconciles himself with the hero and marries his daughters to princes.

II   The Autonomous Core System: The Main Plot

      1/ The family quarrel, between the Cid and his sons-in-law.

      2/ The insult, the Cid's court derides and jeers the Infantes.

      3/ The act of treachery, the Infantes mistreat their wives.

      4/ The initial punishment, the Infantes lose the support of Alfonso and are compelled to go on trial for their act.

III Expansion: The Epilogue

      d/ The king's council, the assemblage of peers as judges.

      e/ The judicial duel, the three trials by combat.

      f/ The final punishment, the Infantes are forced to relinquish their gains, are branded infamous cowards and traitors, and must serve their former wives who are now their superiors in rank.

This functional analysis of the *Cid* warrants two main, though tentative, conclusions. Since the type of substructural pattern in the medieval narrative can vary in the nature and sequence of its narremes, the author of the *Cid* is consciously following a definite substructural pattern. The substructural pattern of the *Cid* reveals a special and remarkable parallel with that of the *Roland*, showing a closer relationship with it than with that of other contemporary epics. It is this relationship which must be examined now in specific detail.

CHAPTER THIRTEEN

The Roland and the Cid: Comparison

13 The Roland and The Cid: Comparison

FUNCTION AND STRUCTURE IN COMPARATIVE LITERARY ANALYSIS

Those things only may be fruitfully compared which share some common characteristic. There is little to be gained from a comparison of Lincoln's Gettysburg Address and the street and number of his residence at the time; and not too much more from a detailed comparison of the Song of Songs and the story of the Exodus, though the possibilities are indubitably greater. In the author's view, the first step toward a satisfactory literary comparison of the medieval epics is a thorough-going, clear-cut description of the structural base that they share in common, that is, their autonomous core system.

A comparison which stops at a mere description of the common base, however, is far from complete. The purpose and method of narremic analysis is not merely to isolate and take inventory of the least common denominator elements of the narremes as structural units, but to illuminate their functional relationship to each other. In this task, the marginal incidents of the superstructure shed an additional helpful light. They serve, first of all, to point out the central nature of the narremes; but, equally important, they give that individuality to each work of art without which there would be little need for comparison with others at all.

To determine the functional units in the substructural framework of the *Roland* and the *Cid*, the act of treachery was selected as the central element of the autonomous core system. The examination of the French and Spanish medieval epics disclosed that *Gormont et Isembart*, *Fernán González*, and the *Infantes de Lara* utilized the same central element. The *Fernán González*, however, employed a variation of the pattern: a murder inspired blood vengeance and this led to an act of treachery which produced a family quarrel. In terms of unified structure and narremic sequence, therefore, *Gormont et Isembart* and the *Infantes de Lara* are the only surviving reasonably contemporary epics – known to us in reconstructions – which are close enough in type to require comparison with the *Roland* and the *Cid*.

13/2

THE FAMILY QUARREL: FUNCTIONAL SIMILARITY AND SUPERSTRUCTURAL DIFFERENCES

Functionally, the act of treachery in the *Roland* was made possible by a family quarrel: the major antagonists, Roland and Ganelon, are in-laws. At every opportunity, they employ the expressions *parrastre* and *fillastre* ("stepfather" and "stepson"), indicating that this relationship is a vital one to them. Ganelon appears to claim that Roland is sending him to his death for no other reason than this. Although there may well be other points of contention, the family problem gives powerful impetus to the developing tensions between them. It sets the background and supplies the motivation for the all-important insult to follow.

Like the *Roland*, the *Cid* also revolves around a family quarrel. This is indeed, functionally, a major incident, foreshadowed in the first section where the Cid prays for a suitable marriage for his daughters; and dominating the second and third sections. There is a basic conflict between the families of Bivar and Carrión which rests on a solid foundation of mutual antipathy. The Cid dislikes his potential sons-in-law from the very beginning, since they are arrogant and belong to the faction of his enemies at court. On their side, the Infantes have a deep-seated contempt for the "miller," whose sole allure for them is the color of his gold and the phenomenal success of his military career.

Although there is apparent harmony between the Cid and the Infantes for a period of two years following the wedding, this is a surface harmony whose fissures are revealed the moment the first stresses appear. For reasons of their own, the Infantes have maintained tight control over the expression of their feelings. The sudden escape of the lion catches them off balance; they act like fools and cowards. Although it is the Cid's courtiers who mock and deride them, it is the Cid whom the Infantes hate. The reason their perverted logic makes him guilty of the insult inflicted by others is simply that they are ready to accept any excuse to justify their hate. This is strictly a quarrel among in-laws.

The functional impetus for *Gormont et Isembart* and the *Infantes de Lara* is, just as much as for the *Roland* and the *Cid*, the family quarrel. In all four of the poems – unlike, for example, the

Pèlerinage de Charlemagne or *Sancho II* – there is a common underlying current of conflict between the older and the younger generation, brought about by the evil consequences of a fateful marriage. Least is known about the antecedents of *Gormont et Isembart*, but there can be no question that young Isembart is the product of the marriage of Louis' sister: a nephew who finds himself in violent opposition to his uncle. The quarrel in the *Infantes de Lara* is even more definitely a conflict among in-laws, since the central problem arises from the marriage of Ruy Velásquez to Donña Lambra, who becomes embroiled with her husband's nephews. Establishing the functional similarity of this initial narreme in the four poems as a basis for structural comparison, however, should not obscure but rather help to illuminate the significance and value of the superstructural differences.

There are several differences in the treatment of the family quarrel in the *Roland* and the *Cid*; it is this which enables us to speak of *variants* of the same narreme. The background of the domestic conflict between Roland and Ganelon is very subtly suggested; there is no mistaking the central family nature of the difficulties in the *Cid*. The reason for this appears to be the different necessities of the story line in each case. The *Roland* deals with an historic event taking place in a foreign land, under conditions of military warfare on a national scale. There is little place, except incidentally, for domestic details, even though these furnish an essential feature of the structural framework. The main plot, however, pivots around an act of treachery, originating in a treasonable deal with the enemy which culminates in a pitched battle. The *Cid*, on the other hand, does no more than hint subtly at this quarrel during the prologue. It is only later that it becomes the major focus for the act of treachery in a domestic tragedy; but as such it shares heavily in the developing details of the story.

The type of family relationship, although involving in-laws in both cases, also differs somewhat. The *Roland* dispute embroils an antipathetic stepfather and stepson; the *Cid* quarrel concerns a father-in-law and his antagonistic sons-in-law. In the former poem, the responsibility for the crime belongs to the older generation; the latter shows the younger generation as the villains. The *Roland* creates its difficulties out of a bad second marriage; the *Cid*, out of a bad first marriage. The differences are even greater in the other two poems which have been selected for additional comparison.

Although the *Gormont et Isembart* – like the *Cid* – makes the younger generation the villain, and the *Infantes de Lara* – like the

Roland – the older generation, in neither of these two is there any talk of first and second marriages. The *Infantes de Lara,* moreover, departs especially from the others, which depend on long-standing family resentments based on jealousy and greed (possibly excluding *Gormont et Isembart*). This is not the cause of the conflict between Doña Lambra and her nephews; the hate is a direct result of a spontaneous fight and a murder. In fairness to Doña Lambra, forced to watch the shedding of her cousin's blood at her own wedding party, there is considerable justification for her resentment. In addition, the *Infantes de Lara,* unlike any of the others, includes in the family quarrel a person, Mudarra, who will play a major role in events to come, though he is as yet unborn at the time of initial conflict.

These are superficial differences, structurally speaking. In one all-important respect, with regard to the substructural organization of the poems, they play an identical functional role; they give color and body to the same core incident: a conflict between protagonists brought together in a family alliance through marriage, whose dislike of each other is sufficiently strong to create trouble and produce the ensuing events.

13/3

THE INSULT: FUNCTIONAL SIMILARITY AND SUPERSTRUCTURAL DIFFERENCES

The mutual antipathy of the respective protagonists in the *Roland* and the *Cid* eventually gives rise to what is known in diplomatic language as "incidents." During the imperial council at which the peace offer of Marsile is being discussed, Roland engages his stepfather in a game of wits. Ganelon is made to appear a fool in the eyes of the spectators. He is injured by the lack of respect shown him and he is insulted when it becomes plain that, unlike his peers, he is considered "expendable." The thrust plunges deeper when Roland roars at his discomfiture. Subjected to a high degree of emotional tension, Ganelon is unable to take the gloves and baton, symbols of his ambassadorial mission, without dropping them. For this embarrassment, we may be sure, full payment will be exacted.

In the *Cid,* two happy years, about which the poet has little to say, are interrupted by an embarrassing incident: a lion escaping from his cage in the palace puts the court to rout. The Infantes, in their frantic haste to flee, become a butt of public scorn. The

Cid must intervene to stop the jests and mocking derision of the courtiers. Shortly thereafter, the Infantes again reveal their cowardice by failing to take part in the battle against the Moor Búcar. With a smile, which the Infantes were quick to interpret in their own malicious way, the Cid permits them to remain out of the fight and "at their ease" in Valencia. When their father-in-law, under a false impression due to appearances, praises their conduct in battle, the Infantes are certain that he is joining in the fun against them. They may not be brave, but they are vain enough to resent the patronizing smiles of a "miller." These they interpret, rightly or wrongly, as deliberate insults which they cannot brook. Holding the Cid responsible for their terrible embarassment, the Infantes will eventually find a way to exact payment in revenge.

Corresponding to this narreme, or functional incident, in the *Roland* and the *Cid*, Isembart's motive for treachery is also an insult, administered by the uncle against the nephew; an insult strong enough to result in a renegade's betrayal of faith and country. Similarly, the *Infantes de Lara* makes use of the same functional device; there are in fact two insults, one on each side. After the youngest Infante de Salas kills Doña Lambra's cousin, peace is temporarily restored. The lady, however, is simply biding her time. She orders her servant to spill a skin full of blood on the murderer of her cousin. Enraged by the insult, the brothers kill the servant as he seeks protection under her mantle. Here he should have been inviolate – in killing him, the Infantes have insulted their aunt more grievously than she has them.

The insult thus adds the second link to the structural sequence in the poems. The protagonists, all of them antipathetic to each other as members of a family, believe themselves to be humiliated. Functionally, then, this incident is the same for all, in a substructural sense, despite the overt differences that do exist.

The variant natures of the narreme of insult in the *Roland* and the *Cid* may be seen clearly if we call the former "The Verbal Duel" and the latter "The Lion Incident." The verbal duel[1] between Roland and Ganelon, one of the most fascinating incidents

---

1. The use of words as effective weapons of attack is far more prominent in the *Roland* than in the other poems. In a few deft strokes during Ganelon's trial, Pinabel declares audibly (see 8/8) that his well-known sword will help the assembled judges to arrive at a favorable verdict. This is the strongest "argument" in favor of the defense which the judges have heard.

Again, there is a touching verbal duel between the champions of Roland and Ganelon, Thierry and Pinabel, described almost like David and Goliath, when the two fighters courteously request each other to give way (8/9). In all these examples, the narrator uses double-edged words which inflict wounds and raise a smile at the same time. He describes another type of

of the poem, lays bare the character of the two men with the utmost economy of expression. The brilliant repartee is like the parry and thrust of the sword, touching each time a vital part. This is a caustic humor with the cutting quality of a razor's edge (6/2–6/4), producing a delighted smile of approval with each blow, as Roland matches wits and words with his stepfather.

The humor in the *Cid*, especially in the lion incident which serves the comparable function of inspiring the act of treachery, is broader; burlesquing the weakness of the Infantes, it subjects them to overt and prolonged merriment and derision. With less economy, perhaps, but surely with equal success, it likewise starkly bares the difference in character between the protagonists; in this case, the brave Cid and the cowardly Infantes.

A comparison of the variants here – the verbal duel and the lion incident – discloses how widely different the superstructural events can be, while still serving the identical substructural function. The Infantes, for example, act through cowardice. This charge would be difficult to sustain against Ganelon. The latter does declare – openly – that he dislikes the mission for which he has been nominated, because it means certain death; but he also refuses to let Roland go in his place. Given the opportunity to remain in Valencia, safe from the battle, the Infantes hasten to accept. Ganelon's courage is never really questioned; not in the imperial councils, not at the camp of Marsile, not even during the great test of his trial. The poet never hesitates to show Ganelon's nobler qualities: a good man gone wrong. In contrast, the *Cid* ascribes no redeeming features to the Infantes who remain weaklings throughout the poem. Their plans to marry the Cid's daughters are first whispered in secret. They pretend to serve the Cid loyally while hating him in silence. Loathing the Cid they attack him through his daughters. At their trial, they hurriedly return the Cid's swords on request, and then appeal to Alfonso to prevent their opponents from using them. They yield abjectly in the judicial duel without striking a blow.

Louis' insult in *Gormont et Isembart* appears to have been verbal, though whether or not a verbal duel is difficult to say, in view

---

verbal duel, however, which serves the straight purpose of giving and accepting the challenge to fight (Thierry, 3834–36; Pinabel, 3841–44).

The author of the *Cid* exploits the humorous possibilities of the verbal duel in somewhat broader fashion, in the exchange between Don García and the Cid (12/4), as a prelude to the three separate instances of defiance. There is, however, an important variation to be noted: in the *Roland*, it is Ganelon's champion who calls the defender of justice a liar; in the Spanish poem, the champions of the right give the lie to the traitors. But the end result is the same in both; the real liars are resoundingly defeated and the truth rises triumphant.

of the fragmentary nature of the text extant. The insult inflicted by Doña Lambra's nephews on their aunt might be called "The Protective-Mantle Violation," thus indicating its combined ethico-physical nature. Despite all these surface differences, the underlying least common denominator is the same for all: Ganelon and the Infantes de Carrión, Isembart and Doña Lambra, driven by strong emotional pressures, conceive and perpetrate an act of treachery as the direct result of wounded pride.

Superstructurally, the *Cid* differs from the others most of all in intent; Roland, Louis, and the Infantes de Sala deliberately intend to hurt their antagonists, but the Cid does not. His self-esteem damaged, Ganelon must stand by to observe his stepson twist his own words to mockery; he who is noted for his sage counsel to the emperor, a skilful diplomat and orator, seconded in debate by the wise Nestor of the Franks, Duke Naimon. Isembart is insulted to his face by his uncle Louis; Doña Lambra has her mantle over the servant who is killed right there at her feet. How different all this from the noble courtesy of the Cid, who unfailingly gives his love and protection to his former enemies, once they have entered his family. It is the Infantes, arrogant in the blueness of their blood as lords of Carrión, and uneasy in the marriage to the daughters of an *infanzón*, who smart under the humiliation which grows as their own weaknesses are disclosed; they are in no condition to withstand anything that even resembles an insult, direct or indirect, from the man whom they consider an inferior. The net effect of these events — so outwardly different — is nevertheless functionally the same for all: the next step for all the "victims" is to contrive a suitable method of revenge.

13/4

THE ACT OF TREACHERY: NARREMIC VARIANTS

It would probably be difficult to find in literature two acts of treachery more ostensibly different than those in the *Roland* and the *Cid*. No comparison seems possible on the surface between a crime involving collaboration with the enemies of religion and the state, and a minor domestic quarrel in which two women are roughly handled and deserted. As a result of the first crime, thousands of men are destroyed, including the flower of Frankish chivalry; in the second, the two women not only live to tell the tale but come out of their predicament better than before. Ganelon, the envoy extraordinary, goads his hosts into fearful anger and then enlists their aid in a projected ambush designed to annihilate Charlemagne's rearguard; so intent is he on his scheme that he makes no attempt to contradict Marsile in his use of the word "treason." In contrast to this sensational crime, two unpleasant young men take their wives far from home and, in a lonly wood, strip them and beat them almost to death.

Superficially, it might appear that Isembart's crime is analogous to Ganelon's; he too collaborates with the enemies of religion and the state. On a smaller scale, Ruy Velásquez and Doña Lambra likewise arrange a Moorish ambush in which the Infantes de Salas are trapped and beheaded, while their father is sent on a false mission to become a prisoner of the Moors, unsuspectingly carrying instructions for his own death as well. The least common denominator which unites all these incidents, including the *Cid*, making them variants of each other, is the fact that they are all unquestionably acts of treachery. But certain differences among them call for special mention.

13/5
FUNCTIONAL DIFFERENCES AND SIMILARITIES

The thread which unites the traitors in the four poems is their assumption that, acting as individuals, they are engaged in the private warfare[2] for which the period is notorious. As crimes, the specific acts differ in detail; the attitudes they disclose toward the institutions of private feuds and family wars are identical. *Gormont et Isembart* and the *Infantes de Lara* do nothing to combat this concept; the crimes are directly performed and as directly punished, without subtle questions concerning their true nature.

The first touch of similarity between the *Roland* and the *Cid* in this respect, differentiating them from the other two poems, is the necessity of the traitors to justify and defend their conduct. The Infantes, like Ganelon, are convinced that they are perfectly within their rights in doing what they do; that is their defense. Ganelon claims the right to avenge himself for injuries received, since he has given formal *desfiance*. The Infantes claim that the right of birth justifies their treatment of an *infanzón*. The tie that binds these two crimes is the fact that they represent private vengeance to the perpetrators. The authors of the *Roland* and the *Cid*, possibly following the moral example of the Church,[3] appear to be condemning these practices in the most vigorous manner.

2. Sémichon, *La Paix et la trêve de Dieu*, p. vii: "... le xɪe siècle ... dans ce siècle, deux faits nous ont frappés: l'anarchie féodale se révélant principalement par l'abus des guerres privées: *la Paix et Trêve de Dieu*; un grand mal et un grand remède."

3. *Ibid.*, p. 317: "[L'Eglise] ... défendit à tous la violence, prêcha partout la paix. ..."

Whatever the actual accomplishments[4] of the Church in this direction, however, the main inspiration of the two poets seems to have been secular,[5] since neither one has used this excellent opportunity to cast his prelates in the role of pacifier; neither Turpin nor Don Jerome ever call upon the antagonists to desist from violence. Yet an unmistakable attempt is made in both poems to demonstrate the evils of private vengeance. Long in advance, the poets have prepared the public and civil agencies of retribution.

13/6

LÈSE-MAJESTÉ

The crimes of Ganelon and the Infantes, outwardly so different in superstructural detail, have a common core which separates them from all the other acts of treachery examined above. When Ganelon conspires with Marsile, his inducement to obtain the latter's aid is the declaration that Roland's death will end the war and force Charlemagne's return to France. During the trial afterward, Thierry argues that so long as Roland was actively in the king's service, he was inviolately under the royal protection.[6] Both these views are counter-aspects of the same problem: Ganelon must choose between his rights as an individual (feudal lord) and the king's interest. His statement to Marsile reveals that he is consciously deciding on the paramount nature of his personal right to private vengeance.

There is some justification for Ganelon's position, apparently, since the initial decision of the assembled judges is that Ganelon be freed and the trial dropped. Pinabel's pointed jibe that his sword might help the barons arrive at a favorable decision is just another indication that force, like possession, is nine-tenths of the law. In the face of Thierry's charge of *lèse-majesté* (high treason), nevertheless, it seems remarkable that the other barons are unaware of the terrible gravity of Ganelon's crime. The answer seems to be that a new lesson,[7] at least one not universally

4. *Ibid.*, p. 315: "L'institution de la paix et trêve de Dieu ... s'est offerte à notre examen comme la cause première des progrès accomplis dans la royaume de France et dans les contrées soumises à l'influence de la France, depuis le xe siècle jusqu'à la fin du xiie."

5. Owen, "Secular Inspiration of the *Chanson de Roland*," p. 390: "The religious setting may charge the emotional atmosphere, but it is otherwise irrelevant to the actual plot."

6. Monge, *Etudes morales et littéraires*, p. 133: "Pour avoir livré des Français à l'ennemi, Ganelon est odieux; il est infâme: il n'est légalement coupable que pour avoir trahi son seigneur Charlemagne. ..."

7. Internal evidence for the novelty of the lesson is the utter confidence of Ganelon and his partisans in the rights of private warfare. External support

accepted, is here being taught. Sly tricks and stratagems were apparently not inconsistent[8] with accepted knightly comportment, nor was the king's power,[9] as described in the *Roland*, sufficient to ensure the punishment of the traitor.

The purpose of the poet, in the *Roland*, becomes clear; he is proclaiming the majesty and overriding power of the king's authority. The evidence that he is consciously trying to teach this lesson is implicit in two facts: Ganelon has deliberately chosen to carry through his private feud at whatever cost to the king; and a mediocre champion like Thierry will be sufficient (with God's help) to prove that he has made the wrong choice.

Considered in this light, the situation in the *Cid* is, at its core, identical. The Infantes have mistreated and deserted their wives. From the standpoint of their rights as feudal lords and husbands, what is wrong with their act? Are they not of the highest ranks in aristocracy? Do the young ladies or their father compare with them in birth? In their view, they could and should have married the daughters of kings and emperors, and still may. The important question for the poet, however, is not whether the Infantes have the personal right, by birth or otherwise, to desert their wives; the essential fact is that Alfonso, as king, had assumed full responsibility for the marriages. The Infantes were fully aware of this. The Cid had clearly established this fact, with Alfonso and with the Infantes; and the wedding was performed directly in the king's name. Like Ganelon's crime, the act of the Infantes passed beyond the rights of the Infantes as individuals; as *lèse-majesté*, it breached the king's authority, and called for a public accounting, in the king's name.

13/7

THE KING'S JUSTICE

There is a question difficult to answer, but one which should at least be asked: Did the poet of the *Cid* hit upon the device of *lèse-majesté* by accident? The odds are decidely in favor of a negative answer, in view of the following – admittedly circum-

---

for this is the fact that, of all the epics analyzed, only the *Cid* matches this special variation: a blow aimed at a "private" individual obliquely touches the king's interest, comes to be judged as an attack on the king's sovereignty, and is punished for that reason.

8. See chap. 8, n. 24 (Falk).

9. Falk, *Etude sociale sur les chansons de geste*, p. 16: "La *Chanson de Roland* nous offre un exemple de cette situation qui témoigne de la faiblesse du pouvoir suprême et de l'imperfection de la justice féodale."

stantial – evidence. The substructural pattern of narremes in the *Roland* and the *Cid* continue to parallel each other in exactly the same manner throughout. The family quarrel, which is subtly suggested in the *Roland*, expands sufficiently in the *Cid* to acquire a prologue (9/3–9/5). The apparent "fear" displayed by Ganelon in a moment of emotional stress (6/3–6/4) is transmuted into a clear case of undiluted cowardice at the bottom of every act of the Infantes. The insult, administered almost imperceptibly in the *Roland* through an excitingly clever thrust and riposte of a verbal duel, shows itself in the *Cid* in the form of several blunt episodes which leave no doubt of their purpose. And who can read the constantly reiterated remarks of the Cid to Alfonso, reminding him again and again of the royal responsibility for the marriages, without feeling the weight of emphasis attached to this point? The poet is establishing beyond the least doubt that the crime, like Ganelon's, is willy-nilly aimed at the king's authority.

Isembart also challenges the king's authority, but he does so directly and in his presence; landing in France with enemy troops, he is engaged in battle and killed. There is no question here of private warfare turning unintentionally into *lèse-majesté*. In the *Infantes de Lara*, there is also an act of treachery, but no attack on the king's authority is involved. Ruy Velásquez avenges an insult to his wife. The Infantes de Lara take vengeance for an insult directed against themselves. Years later, the youth Mudarra comes along to take his place in the family quarrel and avenge his father and brothers. All these individuals are acting within an acceptable frame of personal conduct in private warfare; in the end, the best man wins. In the *Roland* and the *Cid*, on the other hand, the substructural pattern takes a new turn: the narreme of punishment is expanded into an epilogue, in which the next step is to set in motion the king's justice.

13/8

THE INITIAL PUNISHMENT:
REACTION TO THE CRIME IN THE *ROLAND*

Is a public trial necessary to establish Ganelon's guilt? Charlemagne, it will be recalled, had several dreams which revealed to him that his brother-in-law would bring grave harm on France. These portents were sufficiently realistic and convincing for the emperor to disclose his worries to his counselor, Naimon, although there were no facts to give substance to his suspicions. The moment, however, that Ganelon tried to prevent Charlemagne from going to Roland's aid when the sound of the horn was heard over a distance of thirty leagues, any possible doubt as to the nature of the crime was eliminated. The emperor gave public demonstration of his belief that Ganelon was a criminal by handing him over to the kitchen boys. It is evident that a man of Ganelon's stature could not be treated in this fashion unless his guilt was certain. But if he was so obviously guilty, why did Charlemagne not attempt to take immediate vengeance for his beloved nephew Roland?

Perhaps, it might be said, Charlemagne did not yet know the full amount of harm accomplished by Ganelon. It did not take long, however, for the main army to reach Roncevaux. The sight that greated them there was one of desolation and disaster. The grief of Charlemagne and of the entire army at the discovery of Roland's corpse, the bodies of the Twelve Peers, and the twenty thousand troops of the rearguard, is pictured in minute detail. Surely, the impact of the scene might have suggested this as the proper time to dispose of the traitor. There was no one there who doubted his responsibility; the initial punishment of the beating delivered by kitchen boys and the humiliating chain around his neck as he rode along on mule-back reflected the acceptance of his guilt.

There must surely have been present there at the scene of carnage partisans of Roland's interests fully capable of dispatching Ganelon without further ado. But the poet does not even hint at this possibility. He has declared long in advance (8/2) that Ganelon would pay for his crime – but only after a public trial at Aix. Private vengeance, even in so well-deserved a case as this, would have rendered the avenger indistinguishable from the criminal in this respect, by justifying the latter's view of the conflict as a private war. It is the poet's explicitly stated intention to see to it that the Law takes its proper course.

13/9

PUNISHMENT IN THE *GORMONT* AND THE *INFANTES DE LARA*

The reaction to the act of treachery in *Gormont et Isembart* and in the *Infantes de Lara* underscores the difference in underlying purpose between those poems and the *Roland*. There is a wide range of similarity in the superstructural details of the betrayal in the three poems. In the *Gormont* and the *Roland*, a highly placed Frank, related to the king, is responsible for a Saracen attack on the Frankish forces; in the *Infantes de Lara* and the *Roland*, it is the treacherous in-law who conceives a deadly ambush and conspires with the Saracens to carry it through. The basic difference is that, unlike the *Roland*, the dispute in the *Gormont* and the *Infantes de Lara* is a mutual war of private vengeance, with both sides in each conflict acting solely on their own responsibility.

It is true that in the three poems the traitor is punished. In the *Gormont*, however, the traitor eventually sees the light and is restored to his faith before his death. In the *Infantes de Lara*, the avenger is a *deus ex machina*, a youth conceived in prison after the crime, the son of Gonzalo Gustioz and a Saracen maid; vengeance must wait until young Mudarra attains to manhood and fighting strength. Revealing how distant from the mind of the poet is the conception of justice as an organized force, the punishment of Doña Lambra has to be deferred until her protector, the Count of Castile, is dead and no longer able to defend her (she was certainly not less guilty while the count was alive). There is no comparison possible between these types of punishment (except as variants of the same narreme), and the public trial in which Ganelon has full opportunity to defend himself, like the Infantes de Carrión, before the bar of public judgment.

13/10

THE INITIAL PUNISHMENT: REACTION TO THE CRIME IN THE *CID*

The difference between superstructural story details and substructural narremic content is most clearly evident in the punishment narreme of the four poems. Superstructurally, the collaboration with the Saracen enemy in the wars and ambushes of *Gormont et Isembart* and the *Infantes de Lara* would seem to link these poems closely to the *Roland*; much more closely than the *Cid*, in which the *details* of the crime of treachery differ so radically from the others. Substructurally, however, there can be no doubt that it is rather the *Cid*, which is closer to the *Roland* since, in the first two, the punishment is direct and terminal, whereas in the latter two, there is an initial punishment, followed by an identical expansion.

The examples above indicate that the author of the *Cid* might have selected either private vengeance on a reciprocal basis or public justice through the royal authority as the means of punishing the traitor. Is it possible to determine that the author has made a deliberate choice in this respect? Américo Castro[10] has no doubt of this at all: "En 1929 llamaba la atención sobre le estructura curiosa del *Poema del Cid*: 'El juglar se deja impregnar de las sustancias ideales de su tiempo, en la misma forma que al versificar las hazañas de su héroe se incluye en la atmósfera internacional de la expresión épica. Las instituciones jurídicas no son en esa obra elementos que, por decír así, pudieron desglosarse, sino que están trabados con su misma razón de ser. ...' " Surely Castro is right; the juridical elements are not marginal[11] but interwoven in the structural fabric of the poem, its very *raison d'être*: "Cuando el Cid es informado de la afrenta de Corpes, un lector moderno esperaría alguna explosión de cólera. El Cid quiere vengarse, sin duda alguna, mas toda la rabia que brama en su alma va a verterse por cauces jurídicos. El Cid gana la partida, señero y espléndido, aunque procediendo según las normas rigurosas del gran juego medieval."

Several factors are made clear in these paragraphs: 1/ the Cid is definitely determined to have his vengeance; 2/ his passionate desire for vengeance is deliberately channeled into juridical paths; 3/ the result is a "curious structure" of a poem, although it breathes, at the same time, in the atmosphere of contemporary epic expression. In none of the other epics examined, however, except for the *Roland*, is there a parallel for the *estructura curiosa*, particularly for the scene which the poet invented:[12] a king's council acting as a court of law, whose judges are assembled from all parts of the realm and whose purpose is to administer justice in an affair of alleged private vengeance which turns out to be *lèse-majesté*. It remains to be seen if the parallel continues in the expansion of the last scenes.

13/11

EPILOGUE: THE KING'S COUNCIL

In the trials of Ganelon and the Infantes, the judges give the traitors full opportunity to state their case. The claim of the defendants, in both instances, is that they have acted within their

10. "Poesía y realidad," pp. 11–12.

11. This would be a formal view, however, not a functional one. The juridical elements are fundamental to the *form* which the punishment takes in this poem (and in the *Roland*), as a response to the act of unintentional *lèse-majesté*; it is the punishment which is functionally obligatory (whatever form it may take) in the structure of those poems centering around acts of treachery (whatever forms they may take).

12. See chap. 12, n. 8.

rights. At first, it seems likely that Ganelon will escape, since no one feels strong enough to challenge his champion Pinabel. A similar initial impression is created in the *Cid* when the Infantes return the Cid's swords as requested; the case appears to be over. The suspense is increased in the *Roland* by the physical appearance of Roland's champion Thierry, who outwardly seems no match for Pinabel; the suspense is similarly increased in the *Cid* by allowing the hero to make a second and then a third complaint, contrary to legal precept and expectation.

There is a superstructural difference to be noted in the fact that in the *Roland* the challenges are delivered by the weaker side (physically, not morally), whereas the champions of the *Cid* are both physically and morally stronger than the defendants. The two poets are consistent in their delineation of character. Ganelon and Pinabel cannot be accused of being cowards; therefore, their very strength can be used as a device to create suspense. The Infantes, on the contrary, are notoriously timid; for this reason, the suspense must be provided in some other fashion. The method selected by the author, a complaint unexpectedly split into three parts, furnishes the same result and deserves commendation for its originality. Both poems end this scene on a similar note: the judges confirm the *desfiance* and the acceptance of the gage of battle, decreeing that judgment will depend on the outcome of a judicial duel.

13/12
THE JUDICIAL DUEL

Despite his obvious physical superiority, and certainly not through fear, Pinabel tries at first to halt the duel by offering Thierry all his possessions in return for the latter's promise to reconcile Charlemagne and Ganelon. Thierry, on the other hand, is willing to speak to the emperor only on Pinabel's behalf, if he gives over his defence of the traitor, and the duel goes through. Righteousness, even against superior might, is triumphant. The traitor is adjudged guilty and is remanded for punishment. The sentence of hanging is changed to dismemberment.

The Infantes also try to halt the judicial duel. They declare that their return of the Cid's possessions has removed all basis for the quarrel. Just as their initial punishment consisted in part in their not being able to suppress the trial altogether, so now is this defense denied; the duels must be fought. In combat, the Infantes and their brother are decisively defeated. Contrasting with Pinabel's heroic death, they surrender in typical cowardly fashion, almost without striking a blow. The judges condemn them legally and brand them with indelible shame.

The three principal superstructural differences in the combat scene are: 1/ the *Roland* has a single duel, the *Cid* three; 2/ Roland's champion has the odds against him at the outset, the Cid's champions have the odds in their favor; 3/ Pinabel fights to the death, the fighters of Carrión surrender abjectly. The contrast of Pinabel's strength and the weakness of the Infantes has just been discussed above. The problem of Pinabel's death, as compared with the surrender of the Infantes, can best be considered in the matter of final punishment.

13/13

THE FINAL PUNISHMENT

Why does the author of the *Roland* select Pinabel to fight in Ganelon's place? One of the reasons may be that the latter, a man of unquestioned courage, would be expected in the circumstances to fight to the death, thus depriving the audience of a spectacular scene of legal punishment owed to a traitor who has committed so enormous a crime. But there are numerous other advantages. Pinabel has an unsurpassed reputation for skill in combat and is far superior to the others in size and strength. Above all, as a member of Ganelon's family, he is in this way assuming his share of the responsibility for Ganelon's crime. As a result of Ganelon's act, the flower of Frankish chivalry, Roland, the Twelve Peers, and twenty thousand brave troops have died. The final punishment for the traitor must be death as well. His relatives, who share in his guilt by supporting him, are hanged. It is proper that Pinabel, a brave and loyal man, should share in the punishment, but in the more heroic form of death in combat, the victim of an untenable defense.

The crime of the Infantes was an attempt to disgrace the Cid and his family. Since their victims are alive, however, there is no justification for the death penalty. To fit the crime, the final punishment must bring shame and disgrace upon the criminals and their family. For this reason, their brother is made to fight on their side, supporting and sharing in the crime; although his guilt is not active like theirs, he shares in the family responsibility. Like Ganelon, however, the Infantes, as the active criminals, are punished more severely than their supporters; they must now serve their former wives with the respect due to queens.

13/14

THE SUBSTRUCTURAL PATTERN OF THE
ROLAND AND THE *CID*

The functional analysis of the epic narremes, as described above, makes it possible to construct a schematic outline of the expanded core system which, with one exception – the prologue – is identical for both the *Roland* and the *Cid*.

I Expansion: The Prologue
   a/ The quest: the exiled Cid seeks vindication and glory.
   b/ The test: the Cid worthily achieves wealth and fame.
   c/ The initial reward: the Cid reconciles himself with the king, and his daughters are married to princes.
II The Autonomous Core System: The Main Plot
   1/ The family quarrel
      a/ between Roland and Ganelon.
      b/ between the Cid and the Infantes.
   2/ The insult
      a/ Roland mocks and laughs at Ganelon.
      b/ The Cid's court mocks and derides the Infantes.
   3/ The act of treachery
      a/ Ganelon plots with the Saracens to ambush Roland; this is an unintentional attack against Charlemagne.
      b/ The Infantes mistreat and desert their wives; this is an unintentional attack against Alfonso.
   4/ The initial punishment
      a/ Ganelon is beaten by the cooks and kitchen boys, chained like a bear, transported on mule-back, and held for trial.
      b/ The Infantes lose the support of Alfonso and are threatened with exile unless they appear for the trial.
III Expansion: the Epilogue
   i/ The king's council
      1/ Charlemagne summons his vassals from every part of the realm to assemble and act as judges in a royal council.
      2/ At the Cid's request, Alfonso does likewise.
   ii/ The judicial duel
      1/ Thierry, as proxy, defends Roland's cause against Pinabel, who is supporting the traitor Ganelon.
      2/ Pero Vermúdez, Martín Antolínez, and Muño Gustioz, as proxies, defend the Cid's cause against the Infantes and their brother Asur González, who is supporting them.

iii/ The final punishment

    1/ His doom sealed with the death of his champion Pinabel, Ganelon is dismembered; the thirty hostages, members of his family, are hanged.

    2/ The Infantes are forced to relinquish their illicit gains, are legally branded infamous cowards and traitors by their peers, and are now compelled to serve their former wives who have become queens and their superiors in rank.

13/15

THE REALITY OF THE NARREME

The *Roland* and the *Cid*, like the other epics and romances analyzed above, are long, narrative poems. The narrative has been defined (1/1) as "an unfolding account of events or experiences, ... [whose] structure ... depends on the arrangement of the incidents making up the story; each incident is a structural unit, with its own specific function to perform." Concerning the structure of the *Roland*, Knudson[13] has justly said: "Dans le scénario tout se tient. Aucun épisode majeur n'a de raison d'être qu'en vertu de la place qu'il occupe dans la structure et de la fonction qu'il remplit dans le développement de l'action."

No one who reads the *Roland* with this in mind can fail to admire the structural integrity of the poem, the balanced harmony of the parts, and the functional effectiveness of the major episodes which, according to Knudson, were invented[14] by a gifted poet: "... chaque épisode imaginé semble bien forgé en vue d'une fonction essentielle à l'économie du poème. Mais invention de toutes pièces, par la grâce souveraine du génie? Oui, certes, car le bon sens nous interdit d'attribuer aux hasards d'un travail légendaire l'invention de données fictives qu'on comprend le mieux et qu'on ne comprend vraiment que comme les éléments d'une construction savante, forte, et belle." The inventive genius of the poet cannot be denied, nor the skill with which he endowed the episodes of the *Roland* with life. The core of these episodes, however, seems to fall, equally undeniably, into a structural pattern which, as a narremic substructure, shares a great deal in common with the epic narratives of the period.

Although the *Cid* is more solidly based on historical facts,[15] the

13. "Etudes sur la composition de la *Chanson de Roland*," p. 54.
14. P. 65.
15. Menéndez Pidal, *Poema de Mio Cid*, p. 18: "... el Cantar concuerda en hechos fundamentales con la historia averiguada del Cid. ..."

poet did not hesitate[16] to select and even to invent episodes according to his needs. It is fair to assume that the poet had to have a basic theme and a structural pattern for his poem. Essentially, the theme of the *Roland* is the conflict of private vengeance and the royal authority, a conflict which develops as unintentional *lèse-majesté*. The author of the *Cid* was no less inventive and original than the author of the *Roland* in the superstructural details which breathe life into his episodes and characters. But it would seem equally undeniable that, except for the prologue which has its own *raison d'être*, the narremes of the *Cid* show too close a similarity to those of the *Roland*, and too much in common with contemporary narrative technique (in the possibilities of narremic opposition), to be the result of coincidence.

16. *Ibid.*, p. 32: "... el poeta tuvo acierto para entresacar de las múltiples noticias que corrían sobre la compleja vida del Cid acquellos rasgos que más armónicamente podían componer su figura heroica." See also p. 33: "Para esta elaboración poética de los elementos históricos o tradicionales el juglar echó mano también, como era natural, de episodios puramente ficticios."

14 Conclusion

The epics and romances of the twelfth century in France and Spain seem to be composed according to a substructural pattern which varies with relative freedom. In the *Pèlerinage de Charlemagne*, the conventional nature of the pattern is proved by the fact that the story is enclosed within a mere shell of a frame. The other poems are more complex, but all reveal the necessary presence of a frame which meshes in with the fundamental story, giving it meaning and direction; this frame is the substructure, an integrated series of narremes embodying the inner form of the narratives. The *Roland* and the *Cid* are no exceptions to this rule. On the contrary, their substructural patterns coincide to a much greater degree than any of the others.

All the poems analyzed begin with a quarrel. The first narreme of the epics is usually a family quarrel; the sole exception, the *Fernán González*, begins with a dynastic quarrel which develops into a family quarrel. The first narreme of the romances, clearly related to the epics, is a lovers' quarrel or a lovers'-triangle quarrel. This difference separates the romances from the French and Spanish epics by types of quarrel. Among the epics, the family quarrel may be based on a number of factors; for example, in the *Infantes de Lara*, it involves murder and retaliation as well as insult. Only in the *Roland* and the *Cid* does it serve as the prelude to a subtly described insult which drives the aggrieved parties to an act of treachery, to the surprise of the victims who are unaware of the overwhelming antagonism which they are arousing.

The quarrel leads everywhere to a motive supplying the driving force for continuing the action. In the Spanish epics, this second narreme may vary freely, involving killing in action, a fight for the inheritance, a disruption of the marriage, or an insult. At this point, the Spanish epics separate from the French epics and the romances, where the second narreme is always the insult. The insult, where it occurs, does not always lead to unexpected assaults, however. In the *Pèlerinage*, the *Guillaume*, and the *Couronnement*, as well as in the Arthurian romances, it serves to spur its victims on to greater glory. But jealousy and arrogance, in the *Roland* and the *Cid*, cause the smile of a Roland or a Cid to act as a sword-thrust into the heart of Ganelon and the Infantes, demanding payment in full.

The effect of the motive is to induce a deed. This third narreme in the romances consists of acts of prowess; in the Spanish epics, an act of treachery; in the French epics, it may be either the one or the other. Among the French poems, the *Pèlerinage*, the *Guillaume*, and the *Couronnement* exemplify the type using the acts of prowess; *Roland* and *Gormont*, the act of treachery. Among the Spanish poems, the *Fernán González* makes the act of treachery the result of the death in battle of a relative. The *Infantes de Lara* involves a pattern of reciprocal insults, motivated also by the death of a relative in a dispute. In *Sancho II de Castilla*, the treachery is caused by territorial greed; in the *Condesa traidora*, by illicit passion and dynastic greed. Here again, and differing from the nearest analogy, the *Gormont*, the *Roland*, and the *Cid* coincide by making the aggrieved parties hatch an act of personal vengeance which unintentionally becomes *lèse-majesté*.

The framework of all the poems requires the satisfactory resolution of the problem arising from the initial motivation. The fourth narreme of the romances, following the acts of prowess, is a happy reward. This is true for many of the epics also. After many adventures, Charlemagne forgives his queen. Guillaume is able at last to drive out the Saracens, justifying his wife's confidence. Fernán González lives happily with his wife in an independent Castile. Except for *Fernán González*, however, the poems which center around an act of treachery resolve their problem through some dramatic punishment of the traitor. In the *Infantes de Lara*, this is achieved by private vengeance; in a sense, an act similar to the original crime, since each new incident invites further retaliation as long as there are antagonists to continue the quarrel. In this respect, the *Roland* and the *Cid* depart from all the other examples by revealing a common intention and a common method.

Because of the nature of the act of treachery, the *Roland* and the *Cid* handle the narreme of punishment differently from all the other epics analyzed. They make the crime an attack on the king's authority. This calls for an initial punishment, to be followed by an expansion, involving the judgment of the traitors in open trial (a king's council), submission to the will of God, as expressed in a judicial duel, and the final punishment, as a lesson to the traitors. Except for an initial prologue in the *Cid*, the identity in narremic sequence seems too close to be the result of chance.

Equally difficult to ascribe to chance – whatever new information may be provided by the analysis of additional texts – are the following summarized findings.

1/ All five French and five Spanish epics contain as initial narreme a variant of the family/dynastic quarrel; all four romances a variant of the lovers'/lovers'-triangle quarrel.

2/ All five French epics and four French romances contain as second narreme a variant of the insult.

3/ All the French and Spanish epics divide into two basic types, containing as third narreme a variant of either the act of treachery or the acts of prowess; all the romances a variant of the acts of prowess.

4/ All the epics and romances contain as fourth narreme the appropriate cluster arrangement, punishment following treachery and reward following prowess.

5/ The principal structural difference between the French and the Spanish epics is the uniform preference of the former for a single motive, an insult within the family group, whichever type of action may follow; and a uniform preference of the latter for a single type of action, the act of treachery, whatever the preceding motive may be.

6/ The poet of the *Pèlerinage de Charlemagne*, according to the evidence, formally acknowledges an implicit convention of four narremes, by surrounding the acts of prowess with a bare minimum of accessory detail needed to provide the family quarrel, the insult, and the happy reward.

These findings lead to the conclusion that narremes are the constituent units in the narrative structures which have been analyzed; they furnish a working method for the functional analysis of the remaining medieval epics, and may provide a new basis for their ultimate reclassification. In the meantime, narremes reveal an inner functional and structural economy,[1] often disguised by the extensive variety of superstructural details, an economy which enriches the understanding of the literary work in question. They help also to unveil some of the continuing mysteries in the medieval technique of story-telling.

1. See Martinet, *Economie des changements phonétiques,* pp. 42–44, 94–152; *Elements of General Linguistics,* pp. 167–71; *A Functional View of Language,* pp. 2, 135–60. See also, Dorfman, "Economy in Verb Morphology," pp. 59–61; Zipf, *Human Behavior and the Principle of Least Effort,* pp. 19–22; Vinay and Darbelnet, *Stylistique Comparée,* pp. 184–88; Pei, *Glossary of Linguistic Terminology,* pp. 79, 98; Romeo, *Economy of Diphthongization in Early Romance,* pp. 23, 111–12.

Bibliography

TEXT EDITIONS: THE *ROLAND*

BÉDIER, JOSEPH. *La Chanson de Roland*, publiée d'après le manuscrit d'Oxford et traduite. Paris: H. Piazza, 1928.
BERTONI, GIULIO. *La "Chanson de Roland."* Firenze: Olschki, 1936.
GAUTIER, LÉON. *La Chanson de Roland*, texte critique, traduction et commentaire, grammaire et glossaire. Tours: Alfred Mame et fils, 1920.
HILKA, ALFONS. *Das altfranzösische Rolandslied nach der Oxforder Handschrift*, Rolandsliedmaterialien I. Halle: Max Niemeyer, 1926.
JENKINS, T. ATKINSON. *La Chanson de Roland*, Oxford Version, revised ed. Boston: Heath, 1929.
MICHEL, FRANCISQUE. *La Chanson de Roland ou de Roncesvaux du XIIe siècle*. Paris: Silvestre, 1837.
MORTIER, RAOUL. *La Chanson de Roland*, d'après le manuscrit d'Oxford, avec une transcription assonancée. Paris: Maloine, 1940.
———— *La Version d'Oxford*, Les Textes de la Chanson de Roland, vol. I. Paris: La Geste Francor, 1940. (*Roland* citations in this study are from this ed.)
PARIS, GASTON *Extraits de la Chanson de Roland*, publiés avec une introduction littéraire, des observations grammaticales, des notes et un glossaire complet. 11th ed. Paris: Hachette, 1911.

TEXT EDITIONS: THE *CID*

BATTAGLIA, SALVATORE. *Poema de Mio Cid*. Roma, 1943.
BERTONI, GIULIO. *Il Cantare del Cid*. Bari, 1912.
HUNTINGTON, ARCHER M. *Poem of the Cid*, reprinted from the unique manuscript at Madrid. The Hipsanic Society of America, Text, vol. I; Transl., vol. II, 1942.
MENÉNDEZ PIDAL, JIMENA. *Poema del Cid y otras gestas heroicas*, Biblioteca del Estudiante, dirigida por Ramón Menéndez Pidal, XXX. Madrid, 1923.
MENÉNDEZ PIDAL, RAMÓN. *Cantar de Mio Cid*, Obras de R. Menéndez

Pidal, III–V. 3rd ed., 3 vols. Madrid: Espasa-Calpe, 1954–56. (*Cid* citations in this study are from this ed.)

——— *Poema de Mio Cid*, Clásicos Castellanos. Madrid: Espasa-Calpe, 1913.

ROSE, R. SHELDON and BACON, LEONARD. *The Lay of the Cid*, transl. into English verse. Semicentennial Publications of the University of California, 1868–1918. Berkeley: University of California Press, 1919.

SÁNCHEZ, THOMÁS ANTONIO. *Colección de poesías castellanas anteriores al siglo XV*. Madrid, 1779.

SUPPLEMENTARY FRENCH EPIC TEXT EDITIONS

AEBISCHER, PAUL. *Le Voyage de Charlemagne à Jérusalem et à Constantinople*. Genève: Droz; Paris: Minard, 1965.

BAYOT, ALPHONSE. *Gormont et Isembart*, fragment de chanson de geste du XIIe siècle. Paris: Champion, 1914.

KOSCHWITZ, EDUARD. *Karls des Grossen Reisse nach Jerusalem*, Altfranzösische Bibliothek, hrsg. von Wendelin Foerster, II. Band. Leipzig: Reisland, 1923.

LANGLOIS, ERNEST. *Le Couronnement de Louis*, Les Classiques Français du Moyen Age. 2nd ed. Paris: Champion, 1925.

MCMILLAN, DUNCAN. *La Chanson de Guillaume*, Société des Anciens Textes Français. 2 vols. Paris: Picard, 1949–50.

SUCHIER, HERMANN. *La Chançun de Guillelme*. Halle: Max Niemeyer, 1911.

TYLER, ELIZABETH STEARNS. *La Chançun de Willame*. New York: Oxford University Press, 1919.

SUPPLEMENTARY SPANISH EPIC TEXT EDITIONS

MARDEN, C. CARROLL. *Poema de Fernán González*, Texto crítico. Baltimore: Johns Hopkins Press, 1904.

MENÉNDEZ PIDAL, RAMÓN. *La Leyenda de los Infantes de Lara*, Obras, I. Madrid: Espasa-Calpe, 1934.

PUYOL Y ALONSO, JULIO. *Cantar de gesta de Don Sancho II de Castilla*. Madrid, 1911.

ZAMORA VICENTE, ALONSO. *Poema de Fernán González*, Clásicos Castellanos. Madrid: Espasa-Calpe, 1954.

(For the story of the *Condesa traidora*, see *infra*: Blasi, *Epopea spagnuola*, and Menéndez Pidal, *Historia y epopeya*.)

ARTHURIAN ROMANCE TEXT EDITIONS:
CHRÉTIEN DE TROYES

Cligés. ed. W. Foerster. Halle: Niemeyer, 1921; ed. A. Micha. Classiques Français du Moyen Age. Paris: Champion, 1957; transl. into modern French, by A. Micha. Paris: Champion [1957].

Erec et Enide. ed. W. Foerster. Halle: Niemeyer, 1934; ed. Mario Roques, CFMA, Paris: Champion, 1952; transl. into modern French, by Myrrha Lot-Borodine. Paris: Boccard, 1924.

Lancelot (Der Karrenritter). ed. W. Foerster. Halle: Niemeyer, 1899 (Le Chevalier de la Charrete), ed. Mario Roques. CFMA. Paris: Champion, 1958.

Yvain. ed. W. Foerster. Halle: Niemeyer, 1912; transl. into modern French, by André Mary (*Le Chevalier au Lion, précédé de Erec et Enide*), Nouvelle Revue Française, 6th ed. Gallimard, 1944.

Arthurian Romances (Erec et Enide, Cligés, Yvain, Lancelot). W. W. Comfort (ed.), Everyman's Library, no. 698. London: Dent; New York: Dutton [1951].

CHRÉTIEN DE TROYES. *Wörterbuch zu seinen sämtlichen Werken.* ed. W. Foerster. Halle: Niemeyer, 1914.

GENERAL REFERENCE

ADAMS, HENRY. *Mont-Saint-Michel and Chartres.* Boston, and New York: Houghton Mifflin, 1936.

ADLER, ALFRED. "Sovereignty as the Principle of Unity in Chrétien's *Erec,*" *Publications of the Modern Language Association of America,* 60 (1945).

ALLEN, HAROLD B. *Readings in Applied English Linguistics.* 2nd ed. New York: Appleton-Century Crofts, 1964.

ALLEN, LOUISE H. "A Structural Analysis of the Epic Style of the *Cid,*" in Kahane and Pietrangeli, *Structural Studies on Spanish Themes,* pp. 341–414.

ALONSO, DÁMASO. *Ensayos sobre poesía española.* Buenos Aires: Revista de Occidente Argentina, 1946.

ANDERSON, JAMES M. "A Study of Syncope in Vulgar Latin," *Word,* 21 (1965), pp. 70–85.

ANDREAS CAPELLANUS. *The Art of Courtly Love,* ed. John Jay Parry. New York: Columbia University Press, 1941.

ANSHEN, RUTH NANDA (ed.). *Language: An Inquiry into Its Meaning and Function.* New York: Harper, 1957.

AUBRUN, CHARLES V. "La Métrique du 'Mio Cid' est régulière," *Bulletin Hispanique,* 44 (1947), 332–72. (See Navarro, Tomás; below.)

AUERBACH, ERICH. *Introduction to Romance Languages and Literature,* transl. by Guy Daniels. New York: Capricorn, 1961.

BARAHONA, LUIS. *Al margen de Mio Cid.* San Jose de Costa Rica: Publicaciones de la Universidad de Costa Rica, 1942.

BAYOT, ALPHONSE. "Sur Gormond et Isembart," *Romania,* 51 (1925), 273–90.

BEARD, MARY R. *Woman as Force in History: A Study in Traditions and Realities.* New York: Macmillan, 1946.

BECKER, PHILIPP AUGUST. Review of Theodor Fluri, *Isembard et Gormund;* and Rudolf Zenker, *Das Epos von Isembard und Gormund,* in *Zeitschrift für romanische Philologie,* 20 (1896), 549–54.

BÉDIER, JOSEPH. *La Chanson de Roland,* commentée. Paris: H. Piazza, 1927.

———— "La Légende des 'Enfances' de Charlemagne et l'histoire de Charles Martel," in *Studies in Honor of A. Marshall Elliott.* Baltimore: Johns Hopkins Press [1911?].

———— *Les Légendes épiques,* 4 vols., 3rd ed. Paris: Champion, 1926–29.

BELL, AUBREY. *Castilian Literature.* Oxford: Clarendon Press, 1938.

BELLO, ANDRES. *Bello;* Prólogo del doctor Gabriel Méndez Plancarte. México: Secretaría de Educación Pública, 1943.

BERTONI, GIULIO. "Il 'Cid' e la 'Chanson de Roland,'" *Cultura Neolatina,* 1 (1941), 131–32.

BLOOMFIELD, LEONARD. *Language.* New York: Holt, 1950.

BLASI, FERRUCCIO. *Epopea spagnuola.* Instituto di Filologia Romanza della R. Università di Roma, Modena, 1938.

BOAS, FRANZ. *Race, Language and Culture.* New York: Macmillan, 1949.

BORODINE, MYRRHA. *La Femme et l'amour au XIIe siècle: d'après les poèmes de Chrétien de Troyes.* Paris: Picard, 1909. (See also Lot-Borodine, Myrrha.)

BRUEL, ANDRÉE. *Romans français du moyen âge.* Paris: Droz, 1934.

BURKE, KENNETH. *A Grammar of Motives.* New York: Prentice-Hall, 1945.

CABAL, JUAN. *Los héroes universales de la literatura española.* Barcelona: Editorial Juventud, 1942.

CABANÈS, DOCTEUR AUGUSTE. *Mœurs intimes du passé: La Vie aux bains*, 6th ed., II, Paris: Michel, 1922–24.

CARROL, JOHN B. *The Study of Language: A Survey of Linguistics and Related Disciplines in America.* Cambridge, Mass.: Harvard University Press, 1953.

CASSIRER, ERNST. *An Essay on Man: An Introduction to a Philosophy of Human Culture.* New Haven: Yale University Press, 1948.

CASTRO, AMÉRICO. "Poesía y realidad en el *Poema del Cid*," *Tierra Firme*, 1 (1935), 7–30.

COHEN, GUSTAVE. *Chrétien de Troyes et son Œuvre: Un Grand Romancier d'amour et d'aventure au XIIe siècle.* Paris: Boivin, 1931.

———— *La Grande Clarté du Moyen-Age.* New York: Editions de la Maison Française, 1943.

———— *Le Roman courtois au XIIe siècle.* Les Cours de Sorbonne, Fascicule I, Centre de Documentation Universitaire. Paris: Tournier et Constans, 1934.

CORBATÓ, HERMENEGILDO. "La Sinonímia y la unidad del *Poema del Cid*," *Hispanic Review*, 9 (1941), 327–47.

CORREA, GUSTAVO. "El tema de la honra en el *Poema del Cid*," *Hispanic Review*, 20 (1952), 185–99.

CROCE, BENEDETTO. *La Poésie: Introduction à la critique et à l'histoire de la poésie et de la littérature*, transl. by D. Dreyfus. Paris: Presses Universitaires de France, 1951.

CROSS, TOM PEETE and NITZE, WILLIAM ALBERT. *Lancelot and Guenevere: A Study on the Origins of Courtly Love.* Chicago: University of Chicago Press, 1930.

CURTIUS, ERNEST ROBERT. "Antike Rhetorik und vergleichende Literaturwissenschaft," *Comparative Literature*, 1 (1949), 24–43.

———— *European Literature and the Latin Middle Ages*, transl. by Willard R. Trask. Bollingen Series 36. New York: Pantheon, 1953.

DE CHASCA, EDMUND. *Estructura y forma en "El Poema de Mio Cid."* Iowa City: State University of Iowa Press; Mexico: Patria, 1955.

———— "The King-Vassal Relationship in *El Poema de Mio Cid*," *Hispanic Review*, 21 (1953), 183–92.

DE KOK, BERTHA LOUISE. *Guibourc et quelques autres figures de femmes dans les plus anciennes chansons de geste.* Paris: Presses Universitaires de France, 1926.

DEL RÍO, ANGEL. *Historia de la literatura española*. 2 vols. New York: Dryden, 1948.

DEMBOWSKI, PETER F. "Autour de Jourdain de Blaye, Aspects Structuraux et Problèmes Connexes," *Neophilologus*, 51 (1967), 238–45.

DENOMY, ALBERT J. *The Heresy of Courtly Love*. New York: McMullen, 1947.

DIAZ-PLAJA, GUILLERMO. *El estudio de la literatura: los métodos históricos*. Barcelona: Ediciones Sayma, 1963.

DORFMAN, EUGENE. "Economy in Verb Morphology," *Proceedings of the Eighth Pacific Northwest Conference of Foreign Language Teachers*. Vancouver: University of British Columbia, 1957.

———— "El narrema en la epopeya y el romance medievales," *Comentario*, 11 (1964), 18–20, 40; transl. by J. Ricci.

———— "The Narreme in the Medieval Epic and Romance," *Proceedings of the Fourteenth Annual Meeting of the Pacific Northwest Conference on Foreign Languages*. Banff: University of Alberta, 1963, pp. 206–11.

———— *The Roland and the Cid: A Comparative Structural Analysis*. Ann Arbor, Mich.: University Microfilms, Publication no. 1843, 1950.

———— "The Structure of the Narrative: A Linguistic Approach," *History of Ideas News Letter*, 2 (1956), 63–67.

———— "Women in the Epic and Romance of the Twelfth Century." Columbia University Master's essay, 1947.

———— and LAMPACH, STANLEY. "Chronological Bibliography of the Works of André Martinet," in *Estructuralismo e historia: Miscelánea homenaje a André Martinet*, ed. Diego Catalán. I. Canarias: Universidad de La Laguna, 1957.

DUNDES, ALAN. "Structural Typology in North American Indian Folktales," *Southwestern Journal of Anthropology*, 19 (1963), 121–30. Reprinted in Dundes, *The Study of Folklore*.

———— *The Study of Folklore*. Englewood Cliffs, N.J.: Prentice-Hall, 1965.

DUNN, F. N. "Theme and Myth in the *Poema de Mio Cid*," *Romania*, 83 (1962), 348–69.

DYHERRN, ISABEL FREIIN VON. *Stilkritische Untersuchung und Versuch einer Rekonstruktion des "Poema de Fernán Gonçáles."* Leipzig, 1937.

ELLIS, J. M., MOWATT, D. G., and ROBERTSON, H. S. Review of ed. James Thorpe, *The Aims and Methods of Scholarship in Modern*

Languages and Literatures, New York: Modern Language Association of America, 1963, in *Modern Language Journal,* 5 (1966), 281–85.

ELSON, BENJAMIN and PICKETT, VELMA B. *Beginning Morphology-Syntax.* Santa Ana, Calif.: Summer Institute of Linguistics, 1960.

⸺ *An Introduction to Morphology and Syntax.* Santa Ana, Calif.: Summer Institute of Linguistics, 1962.

ENTWISTLE, WILLIAM J. "Remarks Concerning the Order of the Spanish Cantares de Gesta," *Romance Philology,* 1 (1947/48), 113–23.

FALK, JOSEF. *Etude sociale sur les chansons de geste.* Nyköpning: Impr. de la Société du Södermanands läns tidning, 1899.

FARAL, EDMOND. *La Chanson de Roland: Etude et analyse.* Paris: Mellottée, 1923.

⸺ "Gormond et Isembart," *Romania,* 51 (1925), 481–510.

FARNSWORTH, W. O. *Uncle and Nephew in the Chansons de Geste.* New York: Columbia University Press, 1913.

FAUCHET, CLAUDE. *Recueil de l'origine de la langue et poesie françoise, ryme et romans,* ed. Janet G. Espiner-Scott. Paris: Droz, 1938.

FIRTH, J. R. *The Tongues of Men and Speech.* London: Oxford University Press, 1964.

FITZMAURICE-KELLY, JAMES. *Chapters on Spanish Literature.* London: Archibald, Constable, 1908.

FLAKE, OTTO. *Der französische Roman und die Novelle: Ihre Geschichte von den Anfängen bis zur Gegenwart.* Leipzig: Teubner, 1912.

FLURI, THEODOR. *Isembard et Gormund.* Zürich dissertation, Basel: E. Birkhäuser, 1895.

FODOR, JERRY A. and KATZ, JERROLD J. *The Structure of Language: Readings in the Philosophy of Language.* Englewood Cliffs, N.J.: Prentice-Hall, 1965.

FORD, J. D. M. *Main Currents of Spanish Literature.* New York: Holt, 1919.

FRAPPIER, JEAN. *Chrétien de Troyes: L'Homme et l'œuvre.* Paris: Hatier-Boivin, 1957.

FRIEDMAN, LIONEL J. "Occulta Cordis," *Romance Philology,* 11 (1957), 103–19.

FUNDENBURG, GEORGE BAER. *Feudal France in the French Epic: A Study of French Feudal Institutions in History and Poetry.* Princeton, N.J.: University of Princeton Press, 1918.

Gesta Francorum et Aliorum Hierosolimitanorum: The Deeds of the Franks and the Other Pilgrims to Jerusalem, ed. Rosalind Hill. London, Edinburgh, Paris, etc.: Nelson, 1962.

GLEASON, H. A., JR. *An Introduction to Descriptive Linguistics*, rev. ed. New York: Holt, Rinehart and Winston, 1966.

GOUGENHEIM, GEORGES. *Système grammatical de la langue française*. Paris: D'Artrey, 1938.

GRÄF, HERMANN. *Der Parallelismus im Rolandslied*. Wertheim a. M., 1931.

GREEN, OTIS H. Review of Pedro Salinas, *Reality and the Poet in Spanish Poetry*, Baltimore: Johns Hopkins Press, 1940, in *Hispanic Review*, 9 (1941), 227–28.

GREIMAS, A.-J. *Sémantique structurale: recherche de méthode*. Paris: Larousse, 1966.

GRIMES, JOSEPH E. "The Thread of Discourse," Prepublication draft, 1968.

GUIRAUD, PIERRE. "Le Champ morpho-sémantique des composés tautologiques," *Zeitschrift für Romanische Philologie*, 77 (1961), 444–69.

———— "L'expression du virtuel dans le *Roland* d'Oxford," *Romania*, 83 (1962), 289–302.

———— *La Grammaire*. Paris: Presses Universitaires de France, 1961.

———— "Pour une sémiologie de l'expression poétique," *Langue et Littérature*, 21 (1961), 119–34.

———— *La Stylistique*. Paris: Presses Universitaires de France, 1954.

GUYER, FOSTER E. *The Main Stream of French Literature*. Boston: Heath, 1932.

———— *The Influence of Ovid on Chrétien de Troyes*. Reprinted from *Romanic Review*, 12 (1921). Chicago: University of Chicago Libraries, private ed.

———— *Romance in the Making: Chrétien de Troyes and the Earliest French Romances*. New York: Vanni, 1954.

HAASE, BERTHOLD. *Über die Gesandten in den altfranzösischen Chansons de geste*. Halle, 1891.

HALL, ROBERT A., JR. *Introductory Linguistics*. Philadelphia: Chilton, 1964.

HALLIDAY, MICHAEL A. K. "The Linguistic Study of Literary Texts," *Proceedings of the Ninth International Congress of Linguists*. The Hague, London, Paris: Mouton, 1964, pp. 302–7.

HARKINS, WILLIAM E. "Slavic Formalist Theories in Literary Scholarship," *Word* 7 (1951), 177–85.

HATZFELD, HELMUT A. "Esthetic Criticism Applied to Medieval Romance Literature," *Romance Philology*, 1 (1947/48), 305–27.

HAUDRICOURT, A. G., and JUILLAND, A. G. *Essai pour une histoire structurale du phonétisme français*. Paris: Klincksieck, 1949.

HELLER, LOUIS G. and MACRIS, JAMES. *Parametric Linguistics*. The Hague, Paris: Mouton, 1967.

HILL, ARCHIBALD A. *Essays in Literary Analysis*. Austin, Texas, 1965.

—— "Principles Governing Semantic Parallels," *Texas Studies in Literature and Language*, 1 (1959), 356–65. Reprinted in Hill, *Essays in Literary Analysis*, pp. 75–75; and in Allen, *Readings in Applied English Linguistics*, pp. 506–14.

—— (ed.). *Report of the Fourth Annual Round Table Meeting on Linguistics and Language Teaching*. Washington, D.C.: Georgetown University Press, 1953.

HINOJOSA, EDUARDO DE. "El Derecho en el *Poema del Cid*," *Homenaje a Menéndez y Pelayo*, 1. Madrid: Suarez, 1899.

HJELMSLEV, LOUIS. "Note sur les oppositions supprimables," *Travaux du Cercle Linguistique de Prague*, 8 (1939), 51–57.

—— *Prolegomena to a Theory of Language*, transl. by Francis J. Whitfield. Memoir 7. Supplement to *International Journal of American Linguistics*, 19, no. 1 (Jan. 1953).

HOCKETT, CHARLES F. *A Course in Modern Linguistics*. New York: Macmillan, 1962.

HOEPFFNER, E. "La Chanson de geste et les débuts du roman courtois," in *Mélanges de linguistique et de littérature offerts à M. Alfred Jeanroy* Paris: Droz, 1928.

HOIJER, HARRY (ed.). *Language in Culture: Conference on the Interrelations of Language and Other Aspects of Culture*. Chicago: University of Chicago Press, 1954.

HOLMES, URBAN TIGNER, JR. *A History of Old French Literature: From the Origins to 1300*. New York: Crofts, 1948.

HOPKINS, ANNETTE BROWN. *The Influence of Wace on the Arthurian Romances of Chrestien de Troies*. Wenasha, Wisconsin: Collegiate Press, Banton, 1913.

HORRENT, JULES. "Chanson de geste et roman courtois," *Romance Philology*, 20 (1966), 192–203.

—— *Le Pèlerinage de Charlemagne: Essai d'explication littéraire avec des notes de critique textuelle*. Paris: Les Belles Lettres, 1961.

—— "Tradition poétique du *Cantar de Mio Cid* au XIIe siècle," *Cahiers de Civilisation Médiévale*, 7 (1964), 451–77.

HUERTA, ELEAZAR. *Poética del Mio Cid*. Santiago de Chile: Ediciones Nuevo Extremo [*ca.* 1948].

HUGHES, JOHN P. *The Science of Language: An Introduction to Linguistics*. New York: Random House, 1962.

HUIZINGA, J. *The Waning of the Middle Ages*. London: Arnold, 1924.

HURTADO Y JIMÉNEZ DE LA SERNA, JUAN and GONZÁLEZ-PALENCIA, ANGEL. *Historia de la literatura española*. 5th ed. Madrid: [Sociedad Anónima Española de Traductores y Autores], 1943.

HYMAN, STANLEY EDGAR. *The Armed Vision: A Study in the Methods of Modern Literary Criticism*, rev. ed., abridged by the author. New York: Vintage Books, 1955.

HYMES, DELL (ed.). *Language in Culture and Society: A Reader in Linguistics and Anthropology*. New York: Harper and Row, 1964.

JAKOBSON, ROMAN. *A Bibliography of the Publications of Roman Jakobson on Language, Literature and Culture*. Publ. by friends and students of Roman Jakobson. Cambridge, 1951.

——— and HALLE, MORRIS. *Fundamentals of Language*. 's-Gravenhage: Mouton, 1956.

JENKINS, T. ATKINSON. "Why Did Ganelon Hate Roland?" *PMLA*, 36 (1921), 119–33.

JONES, LOUISA E. "The Position of the King in *Le Cid*," *French Review*, 40 (1967), 643–46.

JUILLAND, ALPHONSE G. Review of Charles Bruneau, *L'époque réaliste; première partie; Fin du romantisme et Parnasse*, Paris: Colin, 1953, in *Language*, 30 (1954), 313–38.

——— *Outline of a General Theory of Structural Relations*. 's-Gravenhage: Mouton, 1961.

KAHANE, HENRY R. and PIETRANGELI, ANGELINA. *Structural Studies on Spanish Themes*. Urbana: University of Illinois Press, 1959.

KELLER, JOHN ESTEN. *Motif-Index of Mediaeval Spanish Exempla*. Knoxville: University of Tennessee Press, 1949.

KELLER, J. P. "The Structure of the *Poema de Fernán González*," *Hispanic Review*, 25 (1957), 235–46.

KER, W. P. *Epic and Romance: Essays on Medieval Literature*. London: MacMillan, 1931.

KILGOUR, RAYMOND LINCOLN. *The Decline of Chivalry as Shown in the French Literature of the Late Middle Ages*. Cambridge, Mass.: Harvard University Press, 1937.

KNUDSON, CHARLES A. "Etudes sur la composition de la *Chanson de Roland*," *Romania*, 63 (1937), 48–92.

KÖNIGER, HERTHA. *Die Darstellung der Personen bei Chrétien de Troyes*. München: Voglrieder, 1936.

KRABBES, THEODOR. "Die Frau im altfranzösischen Karlsepos," in *Ausgaben und Abhandlungen aus dem Gebiete der romanischen Philologie,* ed. E. Stengel. Marburg: Elwert, 1884.

KRAPPE, ALEXANDER HAGGERTY. "The Dreams of Charlemagne in the Chanson de Roland," *PMLA,* 36 (1921), 134–41.

KRAUSS, WERNER. *Das tätige Leben und die Literatur im mittelalterlichen Spanien.* Stuttgart: Kohlhammer, 1929.

LADO, ROBERT. *Linguistics across Cultures.* Ann Arbor: University of Michigan Press, 1957.

LANGER, SUZANNE K. *Philosophy in a New Key: A Study in the Symbolism of Reason, Rite and Art.* Cambridge, Mass.: Harvard University Press, 1942.

LA RUE, GUILLAUME DE. *Recherches sur les bardes armoricains.* Caen, 1815.

LAZAR, MOSHÉ. *Amour courtois et "fin'amors" dans la littérature du XIIe siècle.* Paris: Klincksieck, 1964.

LE BRAS, GABRIEL. "Canon Law," in *Legacy of the Middle Ages,* ed. G. C. Crump and E. F. Jacob. Oxford: Clarendon Press, [1926, repr. 1962].

LEE, IRVING J. *The Language of Wisdom and Folly: Background Readings in Semantics.* New York: Harper, 1949.

LE GENTIL, P. *La Chanson de Roland.* Paris: Hatier-Boivin, 1955.

LEO, ULRICH. "La 'Afrenta de Corpes,' Novela psicológica," *Nueva Revista de Filología Hispánica,* 13 (1959), 219–304.

LOT-BORODINE, MYRRHA. *Trois essais sur le roman de Lancelot du Lac et la quête du saint graal.* Paris: Champion 1921.

LUCHAIRE, ACHILLE. *Social France at the Time of Philip Augustus,* authorized transl. from the 2nd ed. by Edward Benjamin Krehbiel. New York: Peter Smith, 1929.

LYNCH, JAMES J. "The Tonality of Lyric Poetry: An Experiment in Method," *Word,* 9 (1953), 211–24.

MCGUIRE, THOMAS A. *The Conception of the Knight in the Old French Epics of the Southern Cycle, with Parallels from Contemporary Historical Sources.* Michigan: Campus Press, 1939.

MAROUZEAU, J. *Lexique de la terminologie linguistique: français, allemand, anglais, italien,* 3rd ed. Paris: Geuthner, 1951.

MARTIN, JUNE HALL. "The Divisions of the *Chanson de Roland,*" *Romance Notes,* 6 (1964–65), 182–95.

MARTINET, ANDRÉ. *Economie des changements phonétiques: traité de phonologie diachronique.* Berne: Francke, 1955.

——— *Elements of General Linguistics,* transl. by Elisabeth Palmer. Chicago: University of Chicago Press, 1964.

——— *A Functional View of Language.* Oxford: Clarendon Press, 1962.

———— *Phonology as Functional Phonetics.* London: Oxford University Press, 1950.

MASSIEU, GUILLAUME. *Histoire de la poësie françoise; avec une défense de la poësie.* Paris: Prault fils, 1739.

MENÉNDEZ PIDAL, RAMÓN. *Castilla: la tradición, el idioma.* 3rd ed. Madrid: Espasa-Calpe, 1955.

———— *La Chanson de Roland y el neotradicionalismo: Orígenes de la épica románica.* Madrid: Espasa-Calpe, 1959.

———— *El Cid campeador.* 3rd ed. Madrid: Espasa-Calpe, 1955.

———— *El Cid en la historia.* Madrid: Espasa-Calpe, 1921.

———— *De Cervantes y Lope de Vega,* 5th ed. Madrid: Espasa-Calpe, 1958.

———— "Dos poetas en el *Cantar de Mio Cid,*" *Romania,* 82 (1961), 145–200. Reprinted in Menéndez Pidal, *En torno al Poema del Cid,* pp. 107–62.

———— *La epopeya castellana a través de la literatura española.* Buenos Aires: Espasa-Calpe, 1945.

———— *España, eslabón entre la Cristiandad y el Islam.* Madrid: Espasa-Calpe, 1956.

———— *Los españoles en la literatura.* Buenos Aires: Espasa-Calpe, 1960.

———— *Estudios literarios,* 8th ed. Madrid: Espasa-Calpe, 1957.

———— *Los godos y la epopeya española: "chansons de geste" y baladas nórdicas.* Madrid: Espasa-Calpe, 1956.

———— *Historia y epopeya,* Obras, vol. II, Madrid: Impr. de Librería y casa editorial Hernando, 1934.

———— *Miscelánea histórico-literaria.* Buenos Aires: Espasa-Calpe, 1952.

———— *Poesía árabe y poesía europea: con otros estudios de literatura medieval,* 4th ed. Madrid: Espasa-Calpe, 1955.

———— *Poesía juglaresca y juglares: Aspectos de la historia literaria y cultural de España,* 4th ed. Madrid: Espasa-Calpe, 1956.

———— *De primitiva lírica española y antigua épica.* Buenos Aires: Espasa-Calpe, 1951.

———— *Problemas de la poesía épica.* Roma: Instituto de Lengua y Literatura, 1951.

———— *Los romances de América y otros estudios,* 6th ed. Madrid: Espasa-Calpe, 1958.

———— " 'Roncesvalles:' Un nuevo cantar de gesta español del siglo XIII," *Revista de Filología Española,* 4 (1917), 105–204.

———— *En torno al Poema del Cid.* Barcelona, Buenos Aires: E.D.H.A.S.A., 1963.

———— *Tres poetas primitivos.* Buenos Aires; México: Espasa-Calpe, 1948.

MENÉNDEZ Y PELAYO, MARCELINO. *História de la poesía castellana en la edad media*, I. Madrid: Surez, 1911–13.

———— *Tratado de los romances viejos.* Antología de poetas líricos castellanos, vol. XI, Biblioteca Clásica CCXIII. Madrid, 1903.

MERTENS, PAUL. *Die kulturhistorischen Momente in den Romanen des Chrestien de Troyes.* Berlin: Chasté, 1900.

MESSING, GORDON M. "Structuralism and Literary Tradition," *Language*, 27 (1951), 1–12.

MICHEL, FRANCISQUE. *Examen critique de la dissertation de M. Henri Monin sur le Roman de Roncevaux.* Paris: Silvestre, 1832.

MILÁ Y FONTANALS, MANUEL. *De la poesía heroico- popular castellana*, ed. Martín de Riquer and Joaquín Molas. Obras, I. Barcelona, 1959.

———— *Tratados doctrinales de literatura*, Obras Completas, I. Barcelona: A. Verdaguer, 1888.

MIREAUX, EMILE. *La Chanson de Roland et l'Histoire de France.* Paris: Michel, 1943.

MOLDENHAUER, GERHARD. *Herzog Naimes im altfranzösischen Epos.* Halle: Max Niemeyer, 1922.

MONGE, LÉON DE. *Etudes morales et littéraires: épopées et romans chevaleresques*, I. Paris, Bruxelles, 1887.

MONIN, H. *Dissertation sur le Roman de Roncevaux.* Paris: Impr. royale, 1832.

MONTEVERDI, ANGELO. "Alda la Bella," *Studi Medievali*, Nuova Serie, 1 (1928), 362–79.

NAVARRO, TOMÁS. Review of Charles V. Aubrun, "La Métrique du 'Mio Cid' est régulière," *Bulletin Hispanique*, 44 (1947), reviewed in *Romanic Review*, 40 (1949), 135–36.

NICHOLS, STEPHEN G. "Roland's Echoing Horn," *Romance Notes*, 5 (1963/64), 79–84.

———— "Style and Structure in *Gormont et Isembart*," *Romania*, 84 (1963), 500–35.

NITZE, WILLIAM ALBERT. "Sans et matière" dans les œuvres de Chrétien de Troyes," *Romania*, 44 (1915/17), 14–36.

———— "Two Roland Passages: Verses 147 and 1723," *Romance Philology*, 2 (1948/49), 233–37.

———— and DARGAN, E. PRESTON. *A History of French Literature: From the Earliest Times to the Present.* 3rd ed. New York: Holt, 1938.

NORTHUP, GEORGE TYLER. *An Introduction to Spanish Literature.* 3rd ed. Chicago: University of Chicago Press, 1938; Rev. Nicholson B. Adams, 1962.

OWEN, D. D. R. "The Secular Inspiration of the *Chanson de Roland*," *Speculum*, 37 (1962), 390–400.

PAINTER, SIDNEY. *French Chivalry: Chivalric Ideas and Practices in Mediaeval France*. Baltimore: Johns Hopkins Press, 1940.

PARIS, GASTON. *La Légende des Infants de Lara*. Extrait du *Journal des Savants* (mai et juin 1898). Paris: Imprimerie Nationale, 1898.

———— *La littérature française au moyen âge*. Paris: Hachette, 1913.

———— *Mélanges de littérature française du moyen âge*, ed. Mario Roques. Paris: Champion, 1912.

PAUPHILET, ALBERT. *Poètes et romanciers du moyen âge*. Paris: Bibliothèque de la Pléiade, 1939.

———— "Sur la Chanson de Roland," *Romania*, 59 (1933), 161–98.

PEI, MARIO A. *French Precursors of the Chanson de Roland*. New York: Columbia University Press, 1948.

———— *Glossary of Linguistic Terminology*. Garden City, New York: Doubleday (Anchor Books), 1966.

———— "An Immortal Character in French Literature," *French Review*, 18 (1945), 189–95.

———— Review of Italo Siciliano, *Le Origini delle canzoni di gesta: teorie e discussioni*, Padova: Milani, 1940, in *Romanic Review*, 31 (1940), 285–92.

———— and GAYNOR, FRANK. *A Dictionary of Linguistics*. New York: Philosophical Library, 1954.

PELLEGRINI, SILVIO. "Epica francese e Cantare del Cid," *Cultura Neolatina*, 3 (1943), 231–38.

———— "Intorno al vassallaggio d'amore nei primi trovatori," *Cultura Neolatina*, 4–5 (1944/45), 21–36.

———— "L'ira di Gano," *Cultura Neolatina*, 3 (1943), 157–58.

PATRICONI, HELLMUTH. "Das Rolandslied und das Lied vom Cid," *Romanistisches Jahrbuch*, 1(1947/48), 215–32.

PLATH, KARL. *Der Typ des Verräters in den älteren Chansons de Geste*. Halle, Saale, 1934.

PROPP, V. *Morphology of the Folktale*, ed. Svatava Pirkova-Jakobson, transl. Laurence Scott. Publication 10, Indiana University Research Center in Anthropology, Folklore and Linguistics, *International Journal of American Linguistics*. Bloomington, 1958.

QUINN, JAMES A. "The Development of Domestic Institutions," in *An Introduction to Western Civilization*, ed. George A. Hedger. New York: Doubleday Doran, 1933.

QUINTANA, M. J. *Vidas de españoles célebres*. 3rd ed. Madrid: Espasa-Calpe, 1959.

RENOIR, ALAIN. "Roland's Lament: Its Meaning and Function in the *Chanson de Roland*," *Speculum*, 35 (1960), 572–83.

RICHTHOFEN, ERICH FRHR. VON. *Studien zur romanischen Heldensage des Mittelalters.* Halle, Saale: Niemeyer, 1944.

RIEDEL, FREDERICK CARL. *Crime and Punishment in the Old French Romances.* New York: Columbia University Press, 1938.

RIFFATERRE, MICHAEL. "Criteria for Style Analysis," *Word*, 15 (1959), 154–74.

——— "Stylistic Context," *Word*, 16 (1960), 207–18.

——— "The Stylistic Function," *Proceedings of the Ninth International Congress of Linguists.* The Hague, London, Paris: Mouton, 1964, pp. 316–23.

——— "Vers la définition linguistique du style," Review article in *Word*, 17 (1961), 318–44.

RIQUER, MARTÍN DE. *Los cantares de gesta franceses: (sus problemas, su relación con España).* Madrid: Editorial Gredos, 1952.

ROBERTSON, HOWARD S. *La Chanson de Willame: A Critical Study.* Chapel Hill: University of North Carolina Press, 1966.

ROMEO, LUIGI. *The Economy of Diphthongization in Early Romance.* The Hague, Paris: Mouton, 1968.

ROQUEFORT-FLAMÉRICOURT, JEAN-BAPTISTE-BONAVENTURE DE. *De l'état de la poésie françoise dans les xiie et xiiie siècles.* Paris: Fournier, 1815.

ROQUES, MARIO. *Etudes de littérature françaises.* Société de Publications Romanes et Françaises, 28. Lille, Genève, 1949.

ROUGEMONT, DENIS DE. *Love in the Western World*, transl. by Montgomery Belgion. Rev. and augmented ed. New York: Pantheon, 1956. (First publ. in French as *L'Amour et l'occident.*)

RUGGIERI, RUGGERO M. "A proposito dell'ira di Gano," *Cultura Neolatina*, 4–5 (1944/45), 163–65.

——— Review of Salvatore Battaglia, *Poema de Mio Cid*, in *Cultura Neolatina*, 4–5 (1944–45), 171.

RYCHNER, JEAN. *La Chanson de geste: Essai sur l'art épique des jongleurs.* Genève: Droz; Lille: Giard, 1955.

SAPIR, EDWARD. *Language: An Introduction to the Study of Speech.* New York: Harcourt, Brace, 1921.

——— *Selected Writings of Edward Sapir in Language, Culture and Personality*, ed. David G. Mandelbaum. Berkeley and Los Angeles: University of California Press, 1951.

SAPORTA, SOL and SEBEOK, THOMAS A. "Linguistics and Content Analysis," *Trends in Content Analysis.* Urbana: University of Illinois Press, 1959.

SAPORTA, SOL. (ed.). *Psycholinguistics: A Book of Readings.* New York: Holt, Rinehart and Winston, 1961.

SCHÜRR, Friedrich. *Das altfranzösische Epos: Zur Stilgeschichte und inneren Form der Gotik.* München: Huber, 1926.

SEBEOK, THOMAS A. "The Structure and Content of Cheremis Charms," in Hymes, *Language in Culture and Society*, pp. 356–70. New York: Harper and Row, 1964.

———— (ed.). *Style in Language.* Published jointly, Technology Press of Massachusetts Institute of Technology, and New York: Wiley, 1960.

SÉMICHON, ERNEST. *La Paix et la Trêve de Dieu.* Paris: Didier, 1857.

SHELDON, E. S. "Why Does Erec Treat Enide So Harshly?" *Romanic Review*, 5 (1914), 115–26.

SMITH, HUGH ALLISON. "A Theory for a New History of the French Epic," *Wisconsin Studies in Language and Literature*, 20 (1924).

SPENCER, JOHN (ed.). *Linguistics and Style.* London: Oxford University Press, 1965.

SPITZER, LEO. *Lingüística e historia literaria*, 2nd ed. Madrid: Editorial Gredos, 1961.

STENDER-PETERSON, AD. "Esquisse d'une théorie structurale de la littérature," *Travaux du Cercle Linguistique de Copenhague*, 5 (1949), 277–87.

STERNBERG, ELSE. *Das Tragische in den Chansons de Geste.* Berlin: Mayer und Miller, 1915.

SWADESH, MAURICIO. *El lenguaje y la vida humana.* México: Fondo de Cultura Económica, 1966.

TAYLOR, HENRY OSBORN. *The Medieval Mind.* 2 vols. Cambridge, Mass.: Harvard University Press, 1962.

THEODOR, HUGO. "Die komischen Elemente der altfranzösischen Chansons de Geste," *Beihefte zur Zeitschrift für romanische Philologie*, XLVIII. Heft. Halle: Max Niemeyer, 1913.

THOMPSON, STITH. *Narrative Motif-Analysis as a Folklore Method.* FF Communications, no. 161. Helsinki: Academia Scientiarum Fennica, 1955.

THORPE, JAMES (ed.). *The Aims and Methods of Scholarship in Modern Languages and Literatures.* New York: Modern Language Association of America, 1963.

TYRWHITT, THOMAS. *Canterbury Tales of Chaucer.* Oxford: Clarendon Press, 1798.

ULLMANN, STEPHEN. *The Principles of Semantics*, 2nd ed. New York: Philosophical Library, 1957.

VEHVILAINEN, PAUL VEIKKO. *The Swedish Folktale: A Structural Analysis.* Ann Arbor, Mich.: University Microfilms, 65–5472, 1964 (xeroxed copy).

VINAVER, EUGÈNE. "La Mort de Roland," *Cahiers de Civilisation Médiévale*, 7 (1964), 133–43.

VINAY, J-P. and DARBELNET, J. *Stylistique comparée du français et de l'anglais: Méthode de traduction*. Bibliothèque de Stylistique Comparée. Paris: Didier, 1958.

VORETZSCH, KARL. *Einführung in das Studium der Altfranzösischen Literatur*. Halle: Max Niemeyer, 1925.

WALTZ, MATTHIAS. *Rolandslied, Wilhelmslied, Alexiuslied: Zur Struktur und geschichtlichen Bedeutung*. Heidelberg: Carl Winter, 1965.

WELLEK, RENÉ. Review of *A Prague School Reader on Esthetics, Literary Structure, and Style*, selected and transl. ... by Paul L. Garvin. With an appendix: A critical bibliography of Prague School writing on esthetics, literary structure, and style. Publications of the Washington Linguistic Club, no. 1, mimeographed. Washington: Washington Linguistic Club, 1955, in *Language*, 31 (1955), 584–87.

—— and WARREN, AUSTIN. *Theory of Literature*. New York: Harcourt, Brace, 1956.

WHATMOUGH, JOSHUA. *Language: A Modern Synthesis*. New York: St. Martin's Press, 1956.

WHITEHALL, HAROLD and HILL, ARCHIBALD A. "A Report on the Language-Literature Seminar," in ed. Harold B. Allen *Readings in Applied English Linguistics*, 2nd ed. New York: Appleton-Century-Crofts, 1964, pp. 488–92.

WHITEHALL, HAROLD et al. "English Verse and What It Sounds Like," *Kenyon Review*, 18 (1956), 411–77.

WHORF, BENJAMIN LEE. *Language, Thought, and Reality: Selected Writings*, ed. John B. Carroll. Published jointly, Technology Press of Massachusetts Institute of Technology, and New York: Wiley, 1956.

WIENER, NORBERT. *The Human Use of Human Beings: Cybernetics and Society*. Boston: Houghton, Mifflin, 1950.

WILMOTTE, MAURICE. *L'Epopée française: Origine et élaboration*. Paris: Boivin, 1939.

WOLF, FERDINAND. *Über die neuesten Leistungen der Franzosen für die Herausgabe ihrer National-Heldengedichte; Ein Beitrag zur Geschichte der romanischen Poesie*. Wien: Beck, 1833.

ZENKER, RUDOLF. *Das Epos von Isembard und Gormund: Sein Inhalt und seine historische Grundlage*. Halle: Max Niemeyer, 1896.

ZIPF, GEORGE K. *Human Behavior and the Principle of Least Effort*. Cambridge, Mass.: Addison-Wesley, 1949.

Index

daughters, 171; invention of materials (Menéndez Pidal), 218–19;
motive of Infantes, 158; new marriages of Cid's daughters, 189;
plot against Abengalbón, 159
—*Roland*: deferral of Ganelon's punishment, 117–18; description of
technique – Bédier, 129 n. 3 – applied by author to *Cid*, 129 – Knudson,
15 n. 24; purpose of Ganelon's trial, 212
—*Roland* and *Cid* compared, 151, 210, 212, 215
in romances: criticism of Chrétien de Troyes (Comfort), 74
Porteros, 177
Private vengeance, 119 n. 22, 120 n. 23, 121 n. 24, 211, 213
Prologue (*see also* Core system, expanded), 49–50, 56–58, 64, 68, 75, 197,
217, 221–23; dependent core, and minor narremes, 50, 57–58
Public justice, 118, 212–13
Public trials (*see also* Trial), 10
Punishment (*see also* Reward)
  comparison, 39–40, 213–14
  double (*see also* Double), 33
  final, 122–27, 194–96, 198, 211, 216, 218, 221–23
  function in the structure, 26
  inconclusive, 65
  initial, 117–18, 178–94, 211–13, 217, 221–23
  interrupted, 34
  as marginal narreme, 25, 56
  minimal features, 73
  as narremic cluster unit, 70
  in narremic oppositions, 70–71
  placement, 221–23
  reward, compared to, 21
  summary, French epic, 26; Spanish epic, 36–37
  in epics, French: *Couronnement*, 25; *Gormont*, 18–19, 21, 212–13;
    Roland, 107–27, 211–12, 221–23
  in epics, Spanish: *Cid*, 169–98, 221–23; *Condesa*, 35–36; *Fernán González*,
    31; *Infantes de Lara*, 33, 212–13; *Sancho II*, 34
  in *romances*: *Cligés*, 56, 58; *Lancelot*, 65
Puyol y Alonso, Julio, 17 n. 2, 33

Queja (*see also Rencura*) 174
Quest, as minor narreme, in prologue, 48, 50, 68, 217
Quarrel; *see* Family, Judicial, Lovers', Lovers'-Triangle quarrel
Querella, judicial; *see* Judicial quarrel
Quinn, James A. 131 n. 7

Raoul de Houdenc, 44
Reconstruction of epic subject matter, 17–18, 31, 33–34, 202
Renaud de Beaujeu, 44
Rencura (*see also Queja*) 174, 181, 190; *grand rencura*, 174 n. 7
Renoir, Alain, 6 n. 1, 112 n. 10
Reward (*see also* Punishment)
  classification, according to treachery-punishment; prowess-reward, 21
  comparison, in epics and romances, 221–23; in French and Spanish
    epics, 39–40

UNIVERSITY OF TORONTO ROMANCE SERIES

This book

was designed by

ALLAN FLEMING

with the assistance of

ELLEN HUTCHISON

University of

Toronto

Press